ALSO BY ELIZABETH McCAUSLAND

American Processional, The Story of Our Country

Careers in the Arts, Fine and Applied

Art Professions in the United States   EDITOR

A. H. Maurer   CATALOGUE FOR AN EXHIBITION

Charles W. Hawthorne, An American Figure Painter

Work for Artists, A Symposium

George Inness, An American Landscape Painter

The Life and Work of Edward Lamson Henry, N. A.

Picasso: 1934–1944

Käthe Kollwitz: Ten Lithographs

Changing New York   TEXT FOR 97 PHOTOGRAPHS BY BERENICE ABBOTT

PHOTO EDITOR   Poems of the Midwest   BY CARL SANDBURG

SELF-PORTRAIT WITH HAT, *ca.* 1927. OIL ON GESSO PANEL, 39X23⅞ IN.
COLLECTION: WALKER ART CENTER

A. H. MAURER

BY ELIZABETH McCAUSLAND

PUBLISHED FOR THE WALKER ART CENTER

BY A. A. WYN, INC · NEW YORK · 1951

Mirth is the mail of anguish

EMILY DICKINSON

Contents

New York

8. ILLNESS AND DEATH: 1932

A contrast in lives. Louis Maurer feted at 100. Alfy's last work. His operation and slow recovery. The father dies. Two weeks later Maurer hangs himself, aged 64.

EPILOGUE: 1932–1950

Events since Maurer's death. A graph of continuing neglect. Studying one more of America's forgotten men of art. Value of such projects for the American tradition.

Reference Appendix

Illustrations

ILLUSTRATIONS

Foreword

ALFRED MAURER is an artist whose riddle time has not read. Almost a score of years have passed since his death, yet he remains to be discovered. Maurer was a pioneer of modern art who experimented tirelessly for thirty years and left work of enduring merit. His research was carried on in isolation so complete, however, that little report of it survives except his paintings. Maurer had many friends but no disciples; he created a personal expression but no school. He explored new aesthetic territory; but he blazed only a lonely road to suicide. At the end the "immortal residue" of his life's work was carted to the warehouse and forgotten.

Maurer was the first of the Americans in Paris to break with naturalism, and with John Marin he was the first of the American artists whom Stieglitz exhibited at 291 Fifth Avenue in 1909. Earlier than most Maurer aroused hostility with his new manner. Longer than most he endured neglect. Till his death in 1932, he suffered from abuse and misunderstanding. During these decades others conquered frontiers he had surveyed first. They achieved recognition and reputation; he did not.

By the turn of the century Maurer was an arrived artist. In 1901 he had won the Carnegie first prize and medal; and in the next four years he won four more medals. He could have repeated conventional triumphs. Then material recognition, worldly acclaim and a felicitous old age would have been his history instead of an unhappy tale of silence.

Maurer refused to travel the safely charted road of success. He turned away from salons, medals and prizes, to repudiate the sterile facility of academies and their audiences. A new philosophy of art was enticing the young men of Paris away from the familiar and the accepted. Underlying their revolt was passionate criticism of that cold milieu against which the earlier generation of Cézanne, Gauguin, and van Gogh had protested. With his generation Maurer rejected a narrow aesthetic view. He was seeking, by implication, a broad, humane world outlook in life and in art.

Success stamps the first half of the Maurer plot, failure the second. From 1897 to 1904, Maurer faced a future which might well be full of rewards. In contrast, the years from 1904 to 1932 spelled defeat. In 1914 the outbreak of World War I forced him to flee to the United States, and he was never able to return to Paris. Till his death he lived in his aged father's New York dwelling. About 1925 the contents of his Paris studio were sold, and he lost almost all the work he had done from 1897 to 1914. His missing paintings may well be casualties of two world wars for the most part, though in 1950 over a score were "discovered" in Paris.

Maurer did not find support until ten years after his return to America. He was then fifty-six years old. Early in 1924 E. Weyhe purchased the contents of his studio and immediately exhibited a group of the paintings. Thenceforth Maurer exhibited at Weyhe's almost every year till his death. He did not, however, win popular attention. He had friends but no home of his own. He was steadfastly encouraged by Arthur Dove, who had first known Maurer in Paris and who introduced his work to Sherwood Anderson. He painted, and he visited old Paris friends in New York and its vicinity. He made an *ersatz* home for himself at Shady Brook, Marlboro, N. Y. Such was his existence.

He had neither wide acclaim to support his morale nor sales to make him financially independent. A graver lack, he had no close emotional bonds to feed his spirit: casual loves do not ease loneliness or quench anger. The comfort he had was what he might find, as an aging man, compelled to live with a father almost a hundred years old and with a younger married sister. Maurer lived and worked in such a scene of frustration and failure. Unrest and resentment twined and twisted in him and thrust up bitterly profane invective. Seething forces found outlet in his painting and finally in his life's desperate conclusion.

On August 4, 1932, Maurer hanged himself in the family residence at 404 West Forty-third Street. His last years were marked by illness, surgery, slow recovery, and unfounded fear of cancer. In the late 1920s his father (a Currier and Ives artist before the Civil War) rejoiced in a rising reputation as the rediscovery of America by American intellectuals brought Americana into favor. On February 21, 1932, Louis Maurer celebrated his one-hundredth birthday for two days, the second being the two-hundredth anniversary of George Washington's birth. In April Alfred Maurer went to the hospital. He returned to his father's house shortly before his father's death on July 19. On the eighteenth anniversary of the outbreak of the war which drove him home from Paris in 1914, he committed suicide. A tragic life had come to its tragic end.

That Maurer's life was a tragedy, some deny. He was always happy and gay, jesting and joking, they say, always perfectly contented in the bosom of his family, surrounded by friends, leading a normal life. Maurer's friends loved him dearly, as scores of them witness, and Maurer is honored in their continuing love. Nonetheless his life was tragic, unless death by one's own hand is a comedy. Maurer bore deep scars on his soul. His anger at his fate was often reiterated. Finally, the manner of his dying is incontrovertible: suicide cannot be glossed into proof of a happy life.

A delicate realm of pretense surrounds biography, and the biographer must walk warily therein. The author was told many times that Maurer suffered from cancer and that fear of a lingering and painful death drove him to suicide. This is one of those fabrications which are supposed to make truth endurable. For several years before his death Maurer had been afflicted with benign prostatic hypertrophy; but the condition responded to surgical treatment. There was no physiological reason why he should not have lived for years, in good health and able to work as he had done. His riddle needs a different reading.

Maurer was torn by irreconcilable conflicts. His energy for creative revolt was dual. He was engined by jest and oath, laughter and anger. Mirth was the mail of his anguish. Yet he wore his armor in vain. He grew older, his mail was rent asunder, naked agony shone forth.

Louis Maurer died. Alfred Maurer was free from economic and emotional dependence; but he was fixed in a rigid way of life. He inherited a modest financial competence as his share of his father's estate; yet he had no will to live. He had raged too long and lived on anger; he had suffered too long and fed on pain. It was too late: he could not rebuild all he had seen destroyed, he could not regain all he had lost. Only self-annihilation and the nothingness of non-existence (he must have argued) could resolve his life's dilemma.

Aesthetic reaction, however, cannot be allowed to take comfort from the case of Alfred Maurer. Wretched his life was at its close, and tragedy was the final content of his art. Yet he evoked noble emotions, as he learned to elevate painting from self-catharsis to universal statement. So he conquered personal anguish to present human experience as affirmative albeit tragic. In his last years his inner suffering grew intolerable. Then despair and grief increasingly illuminated his vision, till his tortured faces utter "a cry from the heart"—as Gerhart Hauptmann wrote of Käthe Kollwitz —"such a cry of pain as was never heard in ancient times." By his agonized cry of pain, Maurer is sealed as a modern man.

For contemporary civilization confronts man with the spectacle of events and experiences for which the art languages of the age have no terms. The creative spirit is forced to make individual confession of terror and pity. Thus the art of our period has oscillated between polarities: artist who seeks to move outward to general human experience and artist who ever moves inward to purge a tortured soul.

The supreme type of artist who would move outward is the superbly gifted Picasso. Plumbing the soul, he came to the reality of Guernica. Vicariously enduring the deaths others died, he cried out against the barbarity of the age. He had, alas, no public lan-

guage for history's stupendous burden. He has confessed his pity
and terror, therefore, in a private language, a language powerful,
plastic, and compelling, but not a language intelligible to all, or
to many. Wanting that democratic iconography which artists in
modern times have lacked, Picasso has been heard, even in his
most urgently passionate entreaties, only by the few. Nonetheless,
his has been a public theme: mankind's life and death.

At the opposite pole, Maurer, within the range of his ability and
conviction, also used a private language. His theme, however, was
private: over and over he repeated his allegory of the life and
death of one man's hope. For years he hoarded pain and frustration until his dammed-up torment burst finally into the fable
whose agonized faces mask one gigantic self-portrait. Not narcis-
sism created the recurring heads of Maurer's personal portrait
gallery, not their creator's need to impose a destroying will on self-
invented images, but his soul's hunger for knowledge. In those
heads Maurer sought to understand the meaning of life—his own
life, life as he saw it in others' faces. At the end he found his answer only in endurance. To that degree he transcends his private
language and speaks for all who suffer yet endure.

THIS BIOGRAPHY and the Maurer exhibition (held in 1949 by the
Walker Art Center in Minneapolis and the Whitney Museum of
American Art in New York and circulated to museums throughout the United States in 1950 and 1951) were undertaken in the
profound faith that the American tradition is enriched by every
serious study of its cultural figures. We have no standard to es-
timate what we have contributed to world culture because we have
no complete survey of what has been done by our painters, sculptors, writers, musicians, scientists, scholars in social studies, and
the like. We have been accustomed to believe that the American
arts and sciences are derivative of European civilization, as if all
creative energy flowed westward even as air masses customarily
move eastward. The validity of this assumption is open to question. When all the documents are in, we shall be better able to see
what the panorama of our aspiration has been and to evaluate our
achievement.

The face of Alfred Maurer's art has been restored to the American public. The biography, we trust, will give the man to that public he did not have in life. For undertaking and underwriting this project, the Walker Art Center deserves the gratitude of all who believe that our tradition is richer and deeper-rooted than we used to believe. Individual thanks have been made in the Reference Appendix. No acknowledgment can repay the kindness of all those who cooperated in the study which underlies both biography and exhibition, a generosity the more notable in that often documents were sparse and had to be augmented by friendly remembrance.

So we leave Alfred Maurer to the world. He must survive on his own merits. We, at least, have rescued him from the warehouses, where it does no good to hide our artists, living or dead. Perhaps this endeavor will restore a worthy American to America. Then Alfred Maurer will have been added to the heritage of our native tradition, which is the soil in which each generation's continuing creative expression is rooted.

A. H. MAURER

Prologue

IT WAS 1868. The Civil War had ended three years before, and the United States was launched on a vast industrial expansion in which national wealth accumulated and the custom of the country changed. In New York, homes pushed northward up Manhattan Island to invade the farms which in 1860 had stood at the corner of Broadway and Sixtieth Street. Brownstone front houses already lined Forty-third Street west of Ninth Avenue, and the new "El" would soon shower live coals and ashes on pedestrians below. On April 21 of this year Alfred Henry Maurer was born, the second child of Karl Ludwig and Louisa (Stein) Maurer. The drama of his life was to be played out within the family home at 404 West Forty-third Street; but Alfred was born at 512 West Fifty-seventh Street, near Tenth Avenue. For, though his father (Lewis or Louis Maurer in the city directories then, now known as Louis) had recorded his purchase of the West Forty-third Street house on April 1, the family did not take up residence there until later.

The Maurer house was a typical four-story single family dwelling of the time, a few doors west of Ninth Avenue on the south side of the street. It stood on Lot 36-B, a characteristically narrow and long building plot eighteen feet seven inches wide by one

hundred feet five inches long. It seems probable that the house
had been built the year before by William Affleck, a hay dealer
whose business was located at the foot of West Thirty-third Street;
for a mortgage of $6,000 was recorded on June 1, 1867. The elder
Maurer purchased the house from William and Emma Affleck
for the sum of $13,500 and assumed the mortgage. Thus had Louis
Maurer, the German immigrant boy, achieved worldly success at
thirty-six. In contrast with the authentic brownstone front of
"404" was the plain brick front of Senator James A. O'Gorman's
house at 408. The Maurer facade was adorned with an iron balcony outside the parlor floor, seen at the extreme right in Louis
Maurer's *Forty-third Street West of Ninth Avenue, New York*
(page 27), painted in 1883 when the father had retired from the
printing business to return to his first love, art. By 1932, while the
Maurers, father and son, were still alive, the house had been
"modernized" and the balcony removed. After their deaths, the
house was sold and remodeled into a rooming house, the steps
being taken off and the facade covered with rough stucco. When
his father painted this well-known subject, fifteen-year-old Alfred
was beginning to think of art as a career. Even in early life he
viewed painting differently than his father, as is evident in student
work in the Inness manner.

"404" was not only the stage of Maurer's drama, but the villain.
To the eye, and to memory, it wears an innocent look, however.
Thousands of houses like it filled New York then, and fill New
York today, with almost identical floor-plans and dimensions. A
stoop led up from the street to the parlor floor, while the basement
was reached by descending a few steps. Facing the dark areaway was
the dining room, and at the back looking out over the garden
was the kitchen, where the family cat and a German cook presided
over copper pots and pans. The hot water boiler was of copper,
too, and a big range was recessed at one side of the kitchen. Neighbors recall the sauerkraut dinners to which Mrs. Maurer invited
them every winter, continuing long after they had moved away
from Forty-third Street. Alfy (as young Alfred was known from
boyhood) liked German cooking, though he rejected the house-
hold's German mores, refusing to learn to speak and write German well but speaking French fluently and grammatically. Long

LOUIS MAURER AND ALFRED MAURER IN THE FORMER'S STUDIO
AT 404 WEST FORTY-THIRD STREET, NEW YORK, ABOUT 1931

FORTY-THIRD STREET WEST OF NINTH AVENUE, NEW YORK, 1883
A GENRE PAINTING BY LOUIS MAURER. OIL ON CANVAS, 18x24 IN.
COLLECTION: MACBETH GALLERY

COVERED BRIDGE, 1890
WATERCOLOR ON PAPER, 5X7 IN. COLLECTION: MISS ROSELLE FITZPATRICK

EUGENIA MAURER, 1896–1897
PASTEL ON PAPER, 25X18 IN.
COLLECTION: MR. AND MRS.
HUDSON D. WALKER

FIGURE STUDY, 1896
WATER COLOR ON PAPER, 26x14 IN.
COLLECTION: ALFRED L. MAURER

LANDSCAPE, *ca.* 1897
OIL ON CANVAS, MOUNTED ON BOARD, 9½×13⅜ IN.
COLLECTION: ALFRED L. MAURER

after, in the 1920s, when friends cooked sauerbraten and dumplings for him on his visits to them in the Bronx, he would dance around the kitchen, urging the dumplings to hurry up and come to the top of the kettle.

The parlor floor was furnished in Victorian style. Here stood the grand piano which Louis Maurer gave to Eugenia (page 28), youngest of the three Maurer children, and on which she later accompanied his flute solos. Here, too, stood the ornately inlaid bookcase, cabinet and desk made by grandfather John Maurer, a German cabinetmaker who had brought his family to the United States in 1851. Here, in the central position above the fireplace, hung Alfred's prize-winning painting at the 1901 Carnegie International, an arrangement in the Whistlerian manner, and near by hung the gold medal awarded with $1,500 in cash as the first prize. In the back parlor stood a large glass-front cabinet containing Louis Maurer's collection of two thousand shells, valued at $5,000. On its top lay a kaleidoscope and a big foghorn. On Christmas Eve, tree decorated and candles lit, Louis Maurer would blow the foghorn as loud as he could, pumping it up by hand, and so summon his family to celebrate the feast day.

Later Louis Maurer's paintings hung here, including Buffalo Bill, riding, hunting and shooting scenes, Indians, Snow White and the Seven Dwarfs, and the New York Riding Club. When the family moved into their new home in 1868, the father did not, however, hang his now well-known Currier and Ives lithographs in the parlor. At that time these examples of American popular art were considered of no importance and they sold for a quarter. At the end of his life, the father did not even own any of his prints, by that time collector's items bringing in hundreds of dollars each. Rather, the naturalistic art to which he returned at the age of fifty was that which he later displayed in his home. "Western scenes most of them were, with horses galloping through," wrote a latter-day enthusiast, continuing, "Buffalo Bill . . . rode in some of them. One of them showed the fine old scout guiding a line of white-topped prairie wagons across the plains. Indians in yellow and vermillion [sic] of their beloved paint skimming the plains on the wing-like hoofs of their ponies. A study of a Norse legend. Foxes quarreling over a mangled mare."

All this was later. Later, too, were the "striking contrasts" noted by the *Post's* roving reporter, Louis Sherwin, who visited the Maurer residence in 1930. There he saw "canvases with a brilliant, incongruous French touch." Whose were they, he asked. "Deprecatingly," Louis Maurer replied that they were his son's, and he added, "He doesn't paint as I taught him. He is modern, post-impressionist." The reporter had his own point of view: he commented that Alfred Maurer was an admirable painter "even if he did get the Carnegie medal." The next year the same writer reported that if the old gentleman lived to be 198, he would never cease shaking his head at his son's work, and yet "a competent French critic declared . . . one of Alfred's canvases . . . was the first real painting seen from an American brush."

The second floor of "404" was divided into the typical front sitting room (or library) and master's bedroom. Late in life Louis Maurer had the front room for his bedroom, while his daughter and her husband occupied the back bedroom. After his return to the United States in 1914, Alfred had the third floor back bedroom, while the large third floor front room facing north was used as a studio by his father. Many news photographs show Louis Maurer's studio in 1930 and 1931 (page 27), when Mr. Currier and Mr. Ives' sole surviving artist had been rediscovered. Alfred's narrow living and working quarters were not recorded photographically. His walnut bed took up considerable space, and his paintings were stacked against the walls. Old friends who went to see his work had to sit on the bed to make room for themselves and the canvases. A family account contests the "third floor hall bedroom" description of his quarters. The room was, this account says, "a full-sized bedroom with two full-sized windows, a large closet for storage and a connecting bathroom, furnished with a three-quarter bed, a bureau, two work benches and a small mahogany table and three chairs"—a quantity of furniture for one room in a house built on a lot eighteen feet seven inches wide. The account adds that "the reason visitors 'sat on the bed' (which is too trivial a matter to be stressed) is that it was a better vantage point from which to view the paintings, the chairs being used to support them." This is ahead of our story, a question of the es-

sence of truth which could only arise when Alfred Maurer's tragedy was deeply probed.

Such was the setting of Alfred Maurer's drama.

II

FAMILY LIFE behind that facade was as typical as the brownstone front. The Maurers' was a characteristic American success
story of immigration, hard work and thrift, with material comfort
as the reward of industry and sobriety. Karl Ludwig—as Louis
Maurer was christened and as he gave his name for Alfred Henry's
birth certificate—was born on February 21, 1832, in Bieberich,
a small town on the Rhine near Wiesbaden, the son of Johannes
and Catherine (Marx) Maurer. His father was a master cabinetmaker. How many brothers and sisters he had neither family accounts nor New York public records show. One sister, Margaret
(Maurer) Marx came to the United States with her husband and
died here; and a privately printed brochure of her poems, in German, survives in the family's possession.

Young Louis began to draw at five and to play the flute at nine.
He was educated in public and private schools near Bieberich, had
studied Latin by the time he was fourteen, and was taught mechanical, perspective, and architectural drawing at Mainz. He mastered a meticulous rendering style by drawing wooden tableaux
of animals in the natural history classes; and he sketched horses in
the stables of Adolph of Nassau and red deer in the ducal pre-
serves. At the Frankfurt-am-Main academy, he took up painting
and ivory carving, having already become proficient at wood carving in his father's workshop. At this point accounts are contradictory. He wanted to paint in oils; but as one of a large family,
he had to contribute to the family income. At sixteen he was apprenticed, it seems, to a lithographer Kramp. Then he studied at
Düsseldorf with his uncle Marx, "who was a painter of reputation," and he was also associated with "a tool and scale maker and
learned the art of working in steel and other metals." While with
this master, it is said he made his first gun, which he brought with
him to America.

Among Louis Maurer's papers there is a letter dated March 16, 1851, from Elberfeld, and addressed to an unidentified "beloved and dearest Edward," which apparently was never finished and never sent. In thin, spidery script the nineteen-year-old Louis tells of quarreling violently with his uncle, of abandoning "wretched art," and of apprenticing himself to a new master, the mechanic Strathmann. It is a tale of adolescent outrage and shock, of a life-long trauma whose effects would be felt in others' lives. Where his parents were, or what voyage he wanted money for, are questions which remain unanswered. Come to the new world Karl Ludwig did, and come Johannes Maurer did. Louis Maurer, according to the most reliable of several contradictory accounts, came to America in July, 1851, with his whole family, including his cousins. They traveled on the packet *Seine* from Le Havre, the voyage taking thirty-nine days.

New York city directories of the early 1850s list John Maurer "cabinet maker," first at 194 Seventh Street and then at 166 Sixth Street, though not till the 1858–1859 issue is there an entry for "Louis Maurer, lithographer, h. 166 Sixth." Like many newly arrived Americans in that period, the Maurers made their home on the East Side, east and south of Cooper Square, where Peter Cooper opened the Cooper Union for the Advancement of Science and Art in 1859. This location was convenient for Louis when he later worked for N. Currier with his "shop" at 192 Nassau Street and his "factory" at 33 Spruce. At this time the artist-lithographer was a young hopeful with long, full, waving dark hair and close-cropped chin whiskers.

Like an Alger hero, Louis Maurer had borrowed tools from an acquaintance and gone to work for a wood carver within a week of landing. After about three months he found employment with T. W. Strong, lithographers, 98 Nassau Street, and worked there about six months. He met Charles Currier who suggested he apply to brother N. Currier for a better position. For the next eight years Louis Maurer worked continuously and exclusively for the firms of N. Currier and (after 1857) of Currier and Ives. At first one of four workmen, twenty-year-old Louis Maurer soon (according to his own later account) headed a department of twelve artists.

Long before he had the opportunity to travel in the West, Louis Maurer drew Indian and big game subjects from composite sources. At his best he drew scenes of daily life which he observed about him—the elder Vanderbilt driving in Central Park, firemen turning out in brilliant regalia, hunting and shooting and riding. When he had been in the United States about three years he drew his best known prints—*The Life of A Fireman* series: 1. *The Night Alarm—"Start Her Lively Boys"*; 2. *The Race—"Jump Her, Boys, Jump Her!"*; 3. *The Fire—"Now Then With A Will." "Shake Her Up, Boys!"*; and 4. *The Ruins—"Take Up."—"Man Your Rope."* Young Maurer had quickly trained eye and hand to record the American scene as later he recorded the view along West Forty-third Street. From 1852 to 1860 he drew many famous trotting horses, Flora Temple and Highland Maid, Lancet and Flora Temple, Pocahontas, Lantern and Whalebone, Ethan Allen and Mate, and others. *The Celebrated Horse Lexington,* published by N. Currier in 1855, is the epitome of academic draughtsmanship, a living replica of the wooden tableaux of school days. In the same year he drew the stone for *Deer Shooting in the Shattagee,* one of the *American Winter Sports* series, possibly after a design by A. Tait. The favorite *Preparing for Market* is a scene of rural life sketched at a farmhouse near Paterson, New Jersey, where the artist-lithographer was recovering from illness. An unlisted print, dated 1857 and called *Young America,* shows a young child with exploding firecrackers in each hand, a bit of jovial Americana in the days when fireworks were not lethal. In 1852 he had drawn a portrait of George Washington for N. Currier.

Louis Maurer made good use of manual skills mastered in Germany when he drew on the lithographic stone. Later he turned to the varied activities of marksmanship (he taught a rifle and revolver club at Weehawken Heights during the Civil War), of horsemanship (he won a blue ribbon with Rock at the first New York Horse Show in 1883), and of music (at seventy-nine he mastered the intricate Böhm-system flute). Educated in the tight rendering style of naturalism, which is well adapted to the representation of genre subjects, Louis Maurer at his best drew the visual image of a part of the life of his time, with due fidelity to natural appearances. Those "prints for the people" did not require a

searching philosophy of life or profound aesthetic penetration. At
the most they called for familiar subjects, action, humor, and senti-
ment akin to the frontier spirit of Bingham and the early Mark
Twain, plus a touch of filial piety.

Such equipment for art Louis Maurer had, and he might have
followed a well defined path for many years had he not fallen in
love and felt a new ambition. Did the experiences of his adoles-
cence—as well as the need to support a wife—imbue him with his
drive toward material success? At home in Germany there was
cousin Ludwig's villa as a symbol of achievement to spur on Karl
Ludwig in the land of opportunity. He had his memories, too, of
unhappy master-apprentice relationships with early teachers and
the enforced abandonment of "wretched art" in favor of a paying
craft. Was the complex of these motivations the engining power
of Louis Maurer's life?

By 1860 he was earning $15 a week with Currier and Ives. He
fell in love with a young American-born girl of German descent,
Louise Stein. Louise Maurer's first name (like Louis Maurer's) is
spelled variously. On her marriage certificate it is Louise; but in
her will and her obituary, Louisa. Jacob Stein is listed in the 1852–
1853 directory as a milkman at 207 Mott Street; and Alfred told
friends his maternal grandmother kept a milk shop on Hester
Street. The 1853–1854 directory lists Jacob Stein as living at 20
Mott Street, with a milk business at 207 Mott. At her death Louisa
Stein Maurer left New York real estate which she had inherited
from Jacob Stein, so that the Steins also seemed to have prospered.

How the young people met is not recorded; but meet and marry
they did, and Louis had to find a better paying job. This he did at
$25 a week with Major and Knapp, who had recently bought out
the lithographic business of Napoleon Sarony. The young people
were married at the farm of Anna Fox at the corner of Broadway
and Sixtieth Street; and afterwards there was erected on this site
the Miller building, otherwise the Lincoln Square Arcade, where
Alfred Maurer had a studio the last years of his life. There is no
entry in the directories (except for 1862–1863, when Louis Maurer,
lithographer, is listed at 237 Seventh Street) until 1866–1867 when
"Lewis [sic] Maurer, lithographer" is listed as living on "W. 57th
n. Tenth Av." The next year Louis Maurer, "Artist," is listed at

312 West Fifty-seventh Street, an error for 512, which the 1868–1869 directory gives correctly, as does Alfred Henry's birth certificate. By 1869–1870 Louis Maurer, "mer.," (probably, merchant) was living at 404 West Forty-third Street. He had been naturalized in 1861, and his first child, Charles L. Maurer, had been born in 1862.

The Civil War intervened. Louis Maurer, a tiny man (as was Alfred), was probably not eligible for military service; nor was he naturalized at the outbreak of hostilities although he had lived in the United States nine years. Coaching the Weehawken Heights rifle and revolver club was his contribution to the Union cause. Meanwhile years of war brought prosperity not alone to large-scale dealers in defective arms and shoddy uniforms. Trade in general boomed, and the printing trades with it. By the end of the Civil War Louis Maurer was earning $100 weekly and thus could buy the West Forty-third Street house. In contrast with the dramatic revival of his Currier and Ives prints, curiously little is known of his work for Major and Knapp. His designs for commercial art in the family's keeping are of a later date and do not tell much of his artistic evolution.

In 1872, or 1874, Louis Maurer went into business for himself, with F. Heppenheimer forming the firm of Heppenheimer and Maurer. After the senior partner's death in 1876, Louis Maurer continued in business with the Heppenheimer heirs till 1884. Relations must have been cordial; for Louisa Maurer bequeathed to her son Charles "the silverware that I received from Mr. Heppenheimer [a son] as a silver wedding present [in 1885] and the golden cup which I received [in 1910] as a golden wedding present." The Heppenheimer and Maurer premises at 22-24 North William Street had advertisements on the windows for cigar and liquor labels, probably the bulk of an undoubtedly profitable printing business. Louis Maurer did not esteem the art worth of this work any more than he had that of the Currier and Ives lithographs; and few examples of his designs survive. Yet this genre is notable in the period's popular art.

Louis Maurer retired from business in 1884 when he was fifty-two. Alfred was then sixteen, the age at which Karl Ludwig had left school and been apprenticed to a lithographer in Germany.

The father had enough to feel comfortable, an admirer wrote, and he wanted to "study his first love . . . painting." The account continued: "From that time to this [1931] he has been a retired gentleman of leisure, leading the most ideal kind of life, collecting sea shells, playing the flute in concerts, shooting at his rifle club, and painting very delightful pictures of American life, and especially of his friend Buffalo Bill." Louis Maurer was also an ardent horseman. He rode, he later said, every day for seventeen years in Central Park, where he used to meet Edward Stieglitz, father of Alfred Stieglitz who gave Alfred Maurer his first one-man show in 1909. From 1875 to 1895 Louis Maurer spent almost $16,000 for the purchase of horses, veterinarian's care, boarding, saddles, riding habits and the like; in the same twenty years he spent a total of $460 for the riding expenses of his wife plus two or three dollars for "rides for the boys"—all this according to a pocket diary he kept, now preserved in the family records.

Louis Maurer returned to the study of his first love, painting, at the Gotham Art School and with the then leading teacher, William M. Chase. At some time he turned the desirably northlit third floor front bedroom into a studio for himself. Perhaps this was at the time when his elder son, Charles, married and left home. About 1885 Louis Maurer traveled west and met Buffalo Bill, with whom and with whose family he proudly kept up a correspondence for years. He sketched Rocky Mountain elk, antelope, big-horned sheep, and bears, to use this material in the early 1900s for big game illustrations in *Field and Stream*. In 1875 he had painted his wife and two of the children watching the swans in Central Park, and in 1883 he produced the 18x24-inch canvas of West Forty-third Street (page 27) which is his genre masterpiece. Postmen, garbage cans, boys playing in the street, and the now demolished Ninth-Avenue "El" figure in this bit of reportage. During these years he painted in the tight naturalistic technic of his youth. This manner has an archaistic appeal in mid-nineteenth century American naive popular prints, whether those of Louis Maurer or others. But art was changing, as the world was changing. The Hudson River School had yielded place to Inness' personal impressionism, and the lonely masters Homer and Eakins sought to look beneath the skin of nature and of life. Alfred Maurer would take part in this continuing search; his father did not.

III

ALFRED MAURER's childhood and youth are shadowy. No baby photographs, baby shoes or baby socks seem to have survived—nor facts of greater immediacy. What school did he attend? When did he graduate? Where did he receive his art training? How was it he went to business in Jersey for the family firm if the father had sold out in 1884? No answers have been had from his sister, Eugenia (*Eugenie* in their mother's will) nor from Alfy's boyhood friend, the girl across the street, Roselle Fitzpatrick, whom he called "Riz" till late in life. What is the mystery of his life? Merely that he did not conform to conventional success but rather rebelled and broke with naturalistic art and assured material rewards. For his heresy he became an outcast, perhaps tolerated but never appreciated, surely at times persecuted. About the time Alfred was forced to leave school and go to work, another tragic artist, Paul Gauguin, was writing of himself in 1885 that he was "a monster not to be earning money in an age when only the successful are respected." So say all the lonely artists of modern times who have taken the road to self-fulfillment at the price of loneliness and loss of success.

Alfred's mother was the core of his life. Kindly, warm and loving, she was essential cushioning for home and family. When the aesthetic paths of father and son separated, after Alfred's break with naturalism in 1904, she sought to reconcile their opposing points of view. Louise-Louisa Maurer was eight years younger than her husband; and when she died on December 16, 1917, they had been married for fifty-seven years. As befits a *hausfrau,* she was quiet and devoted to her children. Later Alfy made several trips back from Paris to visit his mother; and he wrote her oftener than any other members of his family—or perhaps only his mother saved his brief notes. In later years Mrs. Maurer held "At Homes" on the first Friday of the month, and daughter "Gene" played the piano. As she grew older, she grew plump and comfortable in ap-

pearance, wearing a braided, fitted shirtwaist with a watch pinned
to her shoulder. She loved modish clothes, apparently, and some of
hers have been immortalized in her son's paintings—a shawl
bought in Italy, a full striped satin skirt, and the like. This love she
passed on to Alfy who was to be much sought after as a companion
for his woman friends on shopping trips.

Outside the home Alfred Maurer was formed by his early
schooling and his apprenticeship to a lithographic printer. His
formal training for art was not great, and he had little academic
education. Charles and Alfred attended Public School No. 58 at
317 West Fifty-second Street, whose principal was a Mr. Robin-
son. Teachers included P. D. Goodrich and Samuel Ayres, and
classmates Zabriskie, Carl, Stewart, Munster and Briggs, none of
them identified. Alfy was a sturdy, dark-haired, studious, well-
mannered lad, greatly admired by a classmate, Charles S. Oakley,
with whom he sometimes walked home after school. Young Oakley was the son of the Rev. John G. Oakley, pastor of the Forty-
fourth Street Methodist Episcopal Church, and the Oakleys lived
at 463 West Forty-fourth Street. Alfy usually came and went to
and from school along Ninth Avenue which was closer to his
home, as the school lay between Eighth and Seventh Avenues, and
Charles used Tenth Avenue which was nearer to his home. The
two boys (this was from 1882 to 1884, just before Alfred ended his
formal schooling) never visited each other at home.

Some years ago examples of the Maurer brothers' early art
work were hanging in the auditorium of P. S. 58. No Maurers,
either by Alfred or by Charles, hang there now; and there is no
record of them. Perhaps they were like the early water colors of
Alfy's *Covered Bridge,* dated 1890, which is his earliest known
painting (page 28). Maurer spoke and wrote ungrammatically,
though with an authentic American rhythm. He regretted his lack
of formal education and often berated the fate which had taken
him from school at sixteen. When people said, years later, that
they didn't understand his paintings, he would reply rather rue-
fully: "I don't see why you should understand my pictures. *I* don't
understand grammar."

Brother Charlie was six years older than Alfy. He married in
1885 and by 1892 had bought his own home at 657 West 187th

Street. On the sharply pitched hillside of the heights on which Washington took a last stand for the defense of New York against the British troops, narrow, high-gabled houses still stand, one of which his was. In the summer of 1948, it was sold by his only child, Alfred Louis Maurer. Till then it sheltered family heirlooms, the inlaid furniture made by grandfather John Maurer, naturalistic and abstractionist paintings by A. H. Maurer, examples of the commercial art of Charles L. Maurer, and memorabilia of Louis Maurer and his family, including medals won by Alfred in the early 1900s and the gaily painted and gilded "casting plugs" he carved.

Charles had no conflict of aesthetic allegiances. He was a printer and a commercial artist who accepted the conditions of his life. He was trained in the family printing business, and at one time he was a member of the firm of Maurer and Bachmann, lithographers, at 132-134 Mulberry Street. He was also in business with Charles Stahl. In his spare time he painted naturalistic, sentimental landscapes and figure studies, not unlike the "pretty picture," "candy-box" style of Alfred's *Figure Study* which Alfy painted in 1896 for his sister-in-law, Belle Maurer. This work (page 29) is signed "A. Maurer," the only known instance of such a form for his signature, though his name was so inscribed on the medal from the 1905 Liège Exposition. In the early 1920s Louis Maurer and Charles L. Maurer vied with Alfred Maurer in the annual exhibitions of the Society of Independent Artists, though their representational style did not win them much attention.

Alfy went to work at sixteen, going to business in New Jersey every day. At first he went to work for Heppenheimer and Maurer, which had moved to Union City. There he mastered the practical craft of drawing on the lithographic stone, a manual skill which served him well all his life, witness the drawing and modeling of his paintings. About 1894 Maurer got work as an artist with the firm of A. Lenhard, at the corner of Elm and Reade Streets in New York. He earned $25 or $30 a week then as a commercial artist, making water colors and drawings for the lithographic trade. The painter Carle M. Boog was then working for the Lenhard firm as a studio boy, making $2 a week. He stretched paper for the artists, ran errands, and was learning the trade from the ground floor up. Alfy designed calendars, show cards, booklets, and the like. Young Boog stretched the elephant folio of Whatman paper for Alfy to make the water color design for "Grandpa's Wonder Soap." In this, bewhiskered grandpa broke through the paper, enhaloed in a fine lather of soapsuds. The Hoffman House Bouquet cigar was advertised with a design showing a bouquet of roses, in the center of each of which was the face of a well-known actress. Another soap advertisement—this was before the days of "soap operas"—flaunted a girl holding a cat in her arms.

Maurer's art education was as scanty as the known facts about his youth. He did not study with J. Q. A. Ward at the National Academy of Design, but with Edgar Ward. When work was slack at the Lenhard shop, Alfy would go up to the National Academy, then at the corner of Twenty-third Street and Fourth Avenue, to work in Ward's class. If a rush job came into the lithographic shop, the foreman would send studio boy Boog flying up to the Academy, to call Alfy back to work. "Oh, hell," he'd say. He also attended Ward's Sunday morning class at the Tenth Street Studio Building. In the nearly sixty years since, souvenirs of Alfy's atelier life have vanished. He was probably encased in the tight, high-lapeled jacket of the period and luxuriantly bearded, as he was when he escorted his mother, sister and Riz to the Chicago World's Fair in 1893. The aura of Bohemia which still hovered over art and artist-life must have been Alfy's consolation for the business he had not chosen and for the lack of a higher education.

Did Alfred Maurer study with William Merritt Chase, or did he not? From the weight of evidence, he did not. In 1901, when Maurer won the first prize at the Carnegie, critics said that he did; and this statement was repeated for years after. Old friends from New York and Paris days, among them Alice Woods and the late Fra Dinwiddie Dana, both of whom studied with Chase, the former about 1902, have stated that he did not. According to his own account, the father did study with Chase. Perhaps this explains the confusion. Chase knew Maurer and even visited him in his Paris studio and bought some of his work. He did not sell his Maurers immediately when Alfy took up with modernism; on the contrary two of Maurer's paintings went on sale in the Chase auction in 1912, a number of years after his break with naturalism. One of these is *The Rendezvous, ca.* 1904. Yet Maurer could no more escape the overtones of his age than can any young, talented, sensitive soul, groping for his way in life, searching for his own tongue, but ineluctably hearing the echoes of those who preceded him. Chase bravura has touched his early work, notably in the *Self-Portrait,* 1897 (page 55) and even in the pastel portrait of his sister Eugenia, dashed off with spirit in the years 1896–1897 (page 28). Such was the imprint of aesthetic trends of the time, which no one can avoid completely.

Maurer's early work does not suggest the career of aesthetic rebellion which was to be his. Like a schoolgirl, Alfy flowed on a thin wash of water color to paint *Covered Bridge* (page 28)—a subject which intimates of his youth cannot identify. He was twenty-two when he painted this small 5x7-inch item, which the Fitzpatrick sisters bought for a bazaar at the Church of the Holy Cross on West Forty-second Street and which they liked so much they bought it in for themselves before the bazaar opened. There is no unmistakable stroke which would sign the picture *Maurer.* Even the signature is composite of the time's vague ornamentation in calligraphy and typography. *Head,* signed with a similar signature (in capitals) and dated 1894, is a student work of sufficient competence. With careful, neat strokes, such as he needed to draw on the lithographic stone, Alfred modeled the face and bust in conventional dark-and-light values to create the illusion of roundness. Perhaps the pastel has more merit than this description would imply; it seems a young learner's sincere attempt to grapple with a problem. Not as much can be said for *Figure Study,* 1896, in which late nineteenth century advertising art is all too clear. Perhaps Alfred worked from composite sources, as Louis Maurer had done for some of his first N. Currier prints.

The portrait, in pastel, of his sister Gene goes beyond student work (page 28). It was one of the last of Maurer's works before, at twenty-nine, he left the family shelter. Eugenia was five years younger than Alfy and, like her father and younger brother, small. Youngest of the children and the only girl, she was the family pet. No divided loyalty between father and brother had then arisen. She posed for her brother willingly, albeit pridefully. Was the uplifted chin a pose assumed to minimize the Maurers' characteristic heavy jawbone? With skill and feeling Alfy drew with ineradicable strokes of his pastels, to portray not only the heavy blond hair piled on top of Eugenia's head, the evening cloak and the Empire chair, but also the spirit of the last of the Maurers who continued after her father's and her brother's deaths to seek just and deserved renown for both. He saw his little sister affectionately and sentimentally, with a glow of tenderness, as he saw himself the young artist in a romantic half-light. Later, in 1901, on one of his brief visits to the United States, he lacked models and pressed Roselle Fitzpatrick into service to pose for him, as perhaps he had his sister. His portraits of Riz have tenderness, also; but there was an especial feeling for Eugenia.

At the last of his youth and young manhood he began to move away from his teachers, his tradition, and perhaps even his family ties. About 1897 he painted the small *Landscape* (page 30) in which the romantic mood of Inness is more evident than the representational delights of naturalism or the surface dexterity of Chase's school. A yellow moon lights the ground, and hoarfrost lies on the foreground marshes. Light and air envelop the simple theme. Maurer was on his way to aesthetic revolt.

The custom of the time may have inspired him to break not only with the prevailing fashions in art but with the standards of middle class society. The Maurer house was typical of post-Civil War architecture. Family life was typical, with the father dominant in the domestic hierarchy. Typical were other values. In 1893 Louisa Maurer, Eugenia, Roselle Fitzpatrick, and Alfy visited the World's Columbian Exposition in Chicago. Gene wore a little cadet's cap and the other women the then fashionable fedora hats, styled and blocked like men's. Alfy wore a black, curly, close-cut beard, later modified to long, curled mustachios and goatee, and finally to waxed mustaches alone. The party reached the Fine Arts Building and wandered through, reveling in the wonders offered them. They came to a gallery given over to paintings of the nude, a classic subject for art throughout the ages, from the Venus of Dordogne to Ingres' *La Source*. "I see no excuse for this," said Mama Maurer, not warmly, and the party swept out.

Perhaps in Paris Alfy got his hand in painting the nude. No

example survives, except a canvas which cannot definitely be attributed to him. When he painted the nude, as he did for a brief year about 1928, he destroyed the greatest part of this work, painting tortured heads over the free and flowing figures which are another proof of his essential bent toward human sympathy and tenderness. Had the social and moral attitudes of his young manhood returned as a Freudian censor? Eakins at the Pennsylvania Academy of the Fine Arts had encountered a similar taboo; and only in 1890 had Manet's *Olympia* been admitted to the Louvre, after a public subscription initiated by Claude Monet.

Alfred Maurer was almost thirty years old. He had lived in the shadow of that symbolic "404" through childhood, youth, and young manhood. He had left school and gone to work. He had worked hard and studied. He had saved his earnings to make his future free. He had not married young, as his brother had. As a commercial artist he was not following his chosen career. He had reached a turning point in his life. He must make a break. He must get away. He must be an artist. He must go to Paris, to study and to paint freely. So he thought. So he decided. At this point in his history, less than nothing is known of his interior life. We can say what Alfred Maurer looked like and what he wore, where he worked and what he did. What dreams and hopes inspired him we can but imagine. As his hermetic tale proceeds may we learn more.

PARIS

1. *Young Artist*

ALFRED MAURER was almost thirty. He had worked for fourteen years as a lithographic printer and designer. In his spare time, he had studied painting. The years were passing. If he was ever to be an artist, he must act, he could not wait longer. On November 13, 1897, he sailed from New York on the *Rotterdam*, bound for Paris and the attainment of his ambition. How he yearned to be free from the cold, unfriendly climate of his native land, how he aspired to that warm hospitable milieu toward which he was journeying, lies unspoken in the silence which even then surrounded his private life. For the generation of American artists of his time, as for the generations which preceded and followed him, happiness was there where one was not.

At twenty-nine Alfy was a romantic. He saw himself in the luminous, glamorous chiaroscuro of fashionable portrait painting (page 55). He was short, only five feet two or three; but he made the most of his young man's charm. His wide, upward-curling mustache was groomed with careless care, while his features wore a serious, sober look. At heart Alfy was always serious and sober in his devotion to painting, as sculptors, painters and photographers portrayed him from 1902 to 1931. His eyes were "coal-black" an old friend said, but they were really very dark brown, though he later painted them almost pure black with white high-lights. He had worked through water color washes and Inness crepuscules, through smoothly drawn pastels and the facile com-mercial art of the moment, to that theatrical palette and lighting system compounded of Chase, Duveneck and Hals which Ameri-can painters like Robert Henri and George Luks followed with success. Sunlight streamed through the windows behind his head, and he set the heavy mass of his big-boned face against a tan wall. With awakening aesthetic independence, he mingled deep rich reds, blues and purples—hair and mustache purple-black, skin Indian red with purple overtones, vermilion lips contrasted with white folded-down collar and dark red ascot, and for a base on which weight might rest the mass of his coat, dark blue with purple shadows. Alfred Maurer had escaped the horrors of bitumen, to paint with a personal color sense. Romantic he was but sensitive also, and possessed of skill and conviction. His self-portrait was, indeed, his life. How far he traveled from the vision of 1897 to that of 1927!

Maurer sailed for Paris, not to return to the United States till the fall of 1901. He came home then to spend Christmas with his family and he returned to Paris in May, 1902. This trip (during which he painted his Carnegie prize-winning picture) has caused confusion about the date of his first departure for France which earlier publications stated was about 1900. Maurer was in Paris in January, 1899, when he wrote to his father about his work and affairs in general, a rare letter happily preserved in the family's hands. In the seventeen years during which he made Paris his home, he traveled to New York several times to visit his mother. In turn his parents and sister, his brother, sister-in-law and young nephew, and more distant family connections visited him in Paris up to 1911 or so.

Alfred Maurer's early years in Paris were the happiest years of his life. For the first time he was free. Free from the shadow of the brownstone front. Free from middle-class chaperonage. Free from the compulsion to go to business in Jersey. Free to paint, and for the remainder of his days his life was painting. He was free to live, to work, to love, free to have what friends he chose, to eat what food he wished, to drink what wine he liked, to cherish whom he

would. He was free to be himself, to be that Alfy still treasured in
the memory of old friends. How long does freedom last? How free
is the human soul? Time gave Alfred Maurer desperate answers.
For an interval, nonetheless, he believed that the world can be
wide and the self untrammeled.

After his arrival in Paris, Maurer studied at the Academie
Julian for a week or so. He quickly deserted that mecca of American students and turned to himself as his own best teacher: French
academic instruction found no greater favor in his eyes than
American. In the new world of art he looked for vast horizons and
illimitable prospects. Copying nature by rule was not that creative
vista he sought, nor was it to be found by sweltering in an atelier
where sixty or seventy young hopefuls sweated in overheated, ill-
ventilated studios. Thirty-year-old Alfy may even have felt like an
old man among the youths with brunette and blonde hair parted
in the middle and brushed tightly down to swirl in ringlets at
either side. So they posed then for photographs, groups of earnest
young men in the classrooms and in their own high-ceiled, shawl-
draped studios. They would be in shirt sleeves, but wearing vests
with high lapels, an ensemble topped by "handle-bar" mustaches
of surprising curliness and luxuriance. Contrariwise, what could
Maurer learn from tottering graybeards like Bougereau and the
rest, who came into the classes infrequently, peered around, and
vanished without a trace? Alfy went off to sketch in the Louvre.
He would learn from the masters, he assured himself. Perhaps
this education was as disappointing as the atelier's; for he poked
fun at others who did the same. In an early canvas, now dark and
crackled, he painted two young women, whose long, flowing skirts
almost hide the high stools on which they are perched. Why did
Alfy, champion of women and friend of Fra Dinwiddie Dana,
Alice Woods and Grace Leighton, all art students in Paris, caricature women artists? Perhaps he ridiculed the method of study, and
not the sex. Finally, in desperation, he fell back on painting, painting, painting, as the best means of mastering his chosen work.

In the life of every creative spirit, one inescapable question
recurs: *What did he live on?* By the sale of his work, by the grace
of a patron, by subsidies from universities and foundations, or by
more personal stratagems? Alfy did not have a rich wife—a pre-

scription often recommended for artists. Did he receive an allowance regularly from his father? Later, did he have the income of a
small legacy from his mother? Such data are no concern of the
historian, some say, arguing that only an artist's art may be discussed. This is history in a vacuum, considering the havoc wrought
in creative souls, and indeed in all souls, by the lack of economic
security. At this time in Alfy's life the antagonism between father
and son had not developed overtly, and Louis Maurer did give his
younger son financial gifts, as he gave Eugenia a grand piano.
This was not a regular allowance within which he could budget
expenses. Early in 1899 Alfy wrote his father acknowledging the
receipt of a letter of credit for £100, drawn on the Credit Lyon-
nais. He added "Thank you for the Christmas present."

Maurer had been in France about a year and was making slow
progress with French, a language without end, he thought. He
had sent a painting to the Salon the year before and was planning
to send a larger picture this year. He had made some money on
"robes for the Newburgh people"—evidently a commercial job—
and would spend this for a frame and colors. He had two paintings
on exhibition at the American Club; and about them he wrote
one of the rare fragmentary self-revelations of his history. One he
had painted the year before and given up in disgust; paradoxi-
cally all the students liked it. The other was the head of an old
man which he painted on the last day for submitting work to the
Salon. He thought it quite good, but it was hanging in a bad
light and he could not be sure if the pigments had changed in
drying. He was eager to see the painting in a better light. He sent
love to all and signed himself "Alf."

During his first years in Paris, Alfy seems to have been almost a
forgotten man. Old Paris friends, like Eugene Paul Ullman and
his first wife, Alice Woods, George Ullman, Mahonri Young,
Charles Bittinger, Edward Steichen, the late Arthur G. Dove, Mrs.
J. H. Phillips *née* Grace H. Leighton, and Mrs. E. L. (Fra Dinwiddie) Dana, knew him a little later, as did Max Weber, Bernard
Karfiol, Jo Davidson, the Edward W. Sawyers and Phillip Sawyer,
May and James Preston, the Glackens and the George Luks. In
1900 Louis Maurer, Louisa Maurer, and Eugenia went to Europe
and visited Alfred. Roselle Fitzpatrick had planned to accompany

them but was refused permission at the last moment by her mother. What must the Maurers (fresh from their brownstone front) have thought of Alf's studio at 19 rue Daguerre. Fra Dinwiddie, who had married a wealthy Montana ranchman in 1896, thought little enough of it years later. It was on the ground floor and too damp for comfort, really an old barn, she remembered; nobody except the very poor ever hired a ground floor studio. After his return to Paris in 1902, with his $1,500 prize money in hand, Maurer moved to a more elegant studio at 9 rue Falguière.

To Alfy, freed from the constraints of his New York life, even a dark ground-floor studio in which he could paint his first dark pictures seemed paradise. Perhaps his greatest human happiness he found in creameries like that on rue Delambre opposite the Café du Dome and with the simple families who ran them and the girls who frequented the Bal Bullier and other cafes patronized by the American colony. He liked the girls, and they liked him. They were human, and they were friendly, they were warm. Early in life Alfy became the defender of women, especially if he believed them to be badly treated. He was also a charmer, a gay man about town. But particularly he responded to the mark of living in their faces. That imprint of experience was not only saddening and sometimes coarsening, but also expressive of their own hard-won tolerance and sympathy. When Maurer painted the girls in cafes, sitting at tables, dancing with Zouaves or with each other, standing in twos and threes conversing, he did so with tenderness for the worldly airs they affected, but also with understanding for the fatigue and ennui in the lines about their eyes and mouths, with a gallant nod toward the pathetic finery in which they displayed their charms.

Maurer was not a profound critic of social manners, as Lautrec was, but he was not poor in humanity. One or another of these girls was his sweetheart at different times, but whether Gabrielle and Jeanne were among his casual loves, friends do not verify. Even in that halcyon refuge for rebels against the bourgeois standards of "home," lines of etiquette and morality were drawn. Maurer did not, for example, take his sweetheart when he went to dinner with the Doves or other married couples. Often the young artists of that period found their girls a domestic convenience: they kept house, marketed, cooked, washed out shirts, sewed on buttons, and were companions for hours of leisure.

Paris before World War I was indeed a dream world such as the rebels could not find at home in America. Not only its attitudes toward sexual behavior and its urbane appreciation of the arts made it heaven, but the kindliness and friendliness of the small people among whom the American students and artists lived. No student ever had to starve; Parisians were full of trust. One would not be in Paris long before the baker would be leaving rolls and milk at the door every morning. No passports were needed. The franc had not been devalued. In the 1900s painter, sculptor, writer, composer, could live in luxury on five francs a day; he could live on much less. A meal at Diot's on rue de la Grande Chaumière cost sixty-five centimes. A studio in a new building, with modern plumbing, rented for $20 a month, and poor artists often paid no more than $20 rent a year for less lavish quarters. There was a market for art, too. Many South Americans in Paris bought paintings and sculptures by North American artists, as a generation earlier North America's new rich had been buying European works; and wealthy tourists from Middle-Western cities also patronized their compatriots. Narrow though that universe might prove to be in the light of the succeeding half century, it was then seen as an expanding universe with an horizon of hope.

II

WHEN MAURER went to Paris in 1897, Whistler still cast his long, long shadow over painting. The figure study represented emancipation from naturalistic genre, military memoirs, sentimental literary painting and the like. In the early 1900s Matisse would turn to oriental art for inspiration; earlier, Whistler had found a pattern in the long flowing line of Japanese prints. He began his vogue in rebellion from painting stereotypes; but that very vogue had become almost a stereotype by the turn of the century, a fashion which found favor with artists as different as Alfred Maurer and Charles Hawthorne. To the critical eyes

SELF-PORTRAIT, 1897
OIL ON CANVAS, 28¾x21 IN.
COLLECTION: MR. AND MRS. HUDSON D. WALKER

AN ARRANGEMENT, 1901
OIL ON CARDBOARD, ON STRETCHER, 35X31⅞ IN.
COLLECTION: WHITNEY MUSEUM OF AMERICAN ART

AT THE SHORE, 1901
OIL ON CARDBOARD, ON STRETCHER, 22½x19¼ IN.
COLLECTION: CURT VALENTIN

EVENING AT THE CLUB, *ca.* 1904. OIL ON CANVAS, 29x36 IN.
COLLECTION: ADDISON GALLERY OF AMERICAN ART

CARROUSEL, *ca.* 1904. OIL ON CARDBOARD, 28⅞x35⅞ IN.

COLLECTION: BROOKLYN MUSEUM

AU CAFÉ, *ca.* 1904
OIL ON CARDBOARD, $35\frac{7}{8} \times 31\frac{1}{2}$ IN.
COLLECTION: STATE HERMITAGE, LENINGRAD, U.S.S.R.

GABRIELLE WITH PARASOL, *ca.* 1904
OIL ON CANVAS, 36x29 IN.
COLLECTION: MRS. HUDSON D. WALKER

JEANNE, *ca.* 1904

OIL ON CANVAS, 74¾×39⅜ IN.

COLLECTION: MAURICE LEFEBVRE, PARIS

"ALFY / A. H. MAURER / PARIS 1904 /
MAHONRI"
A STATUETTE BY MAHONRI M. YOUNG
PATINED PLASTER, 14⅞ IN. HIGH
COLLECTION: MAHONRI M. YOUNG

"ALFY / A. H. MAURER / PARIS 1902"
A DRAWING BY MAHONRI M. YOUNG
SANGUINE CHALK ON PAPER,
9¼x5⅞ IN.
COLLECTION: MAHONRI M. YOUNG

of half a century later, the formula appears dated. Yet to the eyes of 1900 the "arrangement" was unorthodox.

In Paris Maurer began by painting two kinds of subject, a series of dark interiors, with figures posed in the story-telling genre manner, and figure studies in which his chief concern was with line, composition, and decorative color. He had not yet been won away from the half-light; but he was beginning to be enticed by newer styles. Perhaps the first work Maurer did in Paris is that scene of two women copying in the Louvre. Perched before a large virgin canvas, the students wear long black cloaks, veils and hats. Like many of Maurer's paintings this is in bad condition and hard to read. At the same time Alfy painted an interior showing a Victorian marble fireplace, stove set on the hearth, white china coffee-pot on its top, and over the fireplace a mirror to reflect the further wall. At the left a seated man can barely be seen, so darkened and discolored is the paint. Alfy wanted to paint like the old masters, some say, and therefore simulated crackle. This seems nonsense. He wrote that he was distressed by the darkening of his pigments. Time and neglect did the rest. Unfinished or deteriorated canvases show other scenes of daily life—women sitting at small marble-topped tables on a terrace, perhaps that of the Dome, though this darkling painting is almost impossible to read; or two men seated at a table inside a creamery with proprietress standing at one side, making out *l'addition*.

Alfy painted and painted. He painted a woman in a Japanese kimono seated on the floor, with Chinese pottery beside her, and he painted a standing woman in hat, muff and short winter jacket, posed against a door, as he later painted *The Peacock: Portrait of a Lady*, purchased in 1903 for the Wilstach Collection and now in the Philadelphia Museum of Art. Seated women inspired his brush, one at a tall dresser for dishes, body and head turned three-quarters away, another seated sidewise on a chair, with her back to the spectator, as she peers through parted curtains at the scene outside the window. Not till 1900 did Maurer give an unmistakable view of the goal toward which he was driving. Like his master, he painted a small figure study all in white, which he proudly signed and dated *Paris, 1900*. He must have felt that he had achieved his ambition when he would affix his hand and seal to a canvas. Neither then nor later did he sign many pictures, and he never dated more than a few. Fragile and nostalgic was the Whistlerian vogue; fragile and nostalgic in some respects was Maurer's world outlook. But his early figure study has a personal quality: it is wistful and sympathetic, well disposed and kindly. Then he painted a larger figure study, signed but not dated. Maurer worked hard to master his craft: the second study, with a standing woman holding a parasol and wearing a beribboned hat while a black velvet ribbon encircles her waist, is skilfully drawn and painted, brush stroke firm and sure, texture of paint on canvas pleasing. Alfy was making progress.

After calendars, cigar and liquor labels, soap advertisements, musical score covers and the like, the Whistlerian mode was a liberation. Maurer was enticed not alone by the novelty of Whistler's preferred tall, elongated format, which he employed later in his own 2x1-meter canvases like *Gabrielle* and *Jeanne* (page 61) but also by crepuscular delicacy of tone and value, as contrasted with the theatrical chiaroscuro he had brought to Paris or with the sentimental overtones of his early pastels. Maurer continued to paint figure studies, particularly *Woman in White* and *Man at the Door;* the latter won a bronze medal at the Pan-American Exposition in Buffalo in 1901, while the former was exhibited at the Art Institute of Chicago in the same year. Both have authentic appeal, despite darkening of paint and checking of their wood panel supports. In *Man at the Door,* also called *White Door,* Maurer painted one of his rare works using a male model.

Maurer was mastering the superficies of his art. At the same time he was seeking diligently to create a base for his career as an artist. He sent paintings to exhibitions in Europe and the United States, in Paris, Berlin and London, and in New York, Chicago, and Philadelphia. Most of these works were lost when hundreds of his paintings vanished in Paris about 1925. Among them perhaps were the *Fortune-Teller,* exhibited at the Pennsylvania Academy of the Fine Arts in 1900, and *Portrait, An Arrangement,* and *Cafe in Paris,* shown there in 1901. On winning the Carnegie prize in 1901, Alfy may have felt that he had solved a major problem of the artist, the economic. He had toiled liked Jacob for Rachel, putting in seven years plus seven years, and then he had worked intensively for four years in Paris. Yet almost as if by accident he made his brilliant coup at Pittsburgh.

One day in the fall of 1901 Maurer rushed into Maurice Sterne's studio. He was on a visit to the United States to see his family and had found a studio in the building where Sterne had his. With characteristic impetuosity, Alfy begged Sterne to let him have a canvas at once; he had someone upstairs in his studio he wanted to paint. In those days Sterne could not afford canvas, but he had a number of large gray cardboards about and gave one to Maurer. Alfy seized it and ran off tempestuously. Tempestuously he painted, as he talked, swore, danced tempestuously. A little earlier he had come into the possession of the full black ruffled skirt emphasized in *An Arrangement* (page 56). He posed his model and got to work. In rapid, furious strokes he painted the woman's face half-turned away, with a flush on the cheek, dark brown hair with stray wisps escaping on the nape of the neck, sparkling white shirtwaist, yellow-gold belt around a trim waistline, and the ruffled skirt in full flounces with gleaming highlights of dark blue-black against black. His arrangement used the typical apparatus of the time, an oriental screen in the background, blue-and-white ginger jars, blue and tan Chinese rug, and the flowered gray kimono which the young woman held in her hands, this last figured with red, gold, black, white, and blue motives. This was not so vivid a color scheme as that of the 1897 self-portrait; but it was good color used honestly and with a genuine feeling for the painter's materials. So Alfy painted in a frenzy, inspired to prove that his years abroad had not been wasted and that he was possessed of those qualities called for in the artist.

Maurer had only returned from Paris a short time before when he was seized by his painting fever. He was not abreast of current art news. Again it was Maurice Sterne who encouraged him. Sterne advised him to send his new painting to the sixth Carnegie International and gave him entry blanks, since Alfy had none. A few days later Sterne saw the "canvas." The heavy cardboard had been tacked on to a conventional stretcher and put into a heavy gold period frame. Sterne admired the work very much; but he could not help calling attention to a blemish, as he thought it. Reluctantly he pointed out a bristle which had stuck in the paint.

When Sterne tried to remove it, Alfy became frantic. "It ain't a pig's hair," he shouted, "it's one from my chest—and I put it there on purpose for good luck." Sterne then saw that the hair was black and curly, unlike the pig's bristles used for artists' brushes. Evidently the hair on Alfy's chest was a powerful talisman: he won the first prize. On the proceeds he later "treated" Sterne and another old friend, the late Ernest Fuhr, an illustrator, to dinner at Mouquin's on Sixth Avenue, a favorite artists' rendezvous.

The arrangement was sent off to Pittsburgh. The jury was composed of John Caldwell, president, John W. Alexander, Winslow Homer, Thomas Eakins, Aman Jean, Clarence M. Johns, Robert W. Allan, Frank W. Benson, Frederick W. Freer, and R. W. Vonnoh, as they signed Maurer's certificate of award. This mixed bag of artists unanimously voted to give the first prize to Maurer. The award was a money prize of $1,500 and a gold medal. Both medal and painting for years hung in places of honor in the Maurer West Forty-third Street residence. When Alfred Maurer's estate was settled, the medal was sold to Tiffany for its weight in gold, thirteen ounces, a quantity which today would realize about five hundred dollars. Photographs of obverse and reverse sides show the engraved name of the recipient and the medal's inscription, a quotation from Cicero. *Honos alit artes*, it read, literally, "honor nourishes the arts." Honor nourished Maurer a few years longer. He won a silver medal at the 1904 St. Louis Exposition. At Munich in 1905 he received a gold medal for *Jeanne*, probably the large canvas here reproduced (page 61). He was awarded a bronze medal at Liège the same year, perhaps for *Danseuse*. After he broke with naturalism in 1904, how long it would be before honor nourished Maurer's art.

III

THE CARNEGIE PRIZE launched Maurer on a private thirty years' war. He had won one of the American art world's major awards when he was only thirty-three years old, and after but a brief period of study and work. If he had not won academic honors early in his struggle, he might have abandoned his endeavor and gone back to business in Jersey, leaving the world the poorer for his paintings and for the example of his perseverance. Material recognition and critical encouragement were surely factors in his decision to go on with painting.

In 1901 Alfred Maurer's stock was rising. Never had there been such agreement among the judges, wrote one critic. Mr. Maurer, according to a fragment pasted into a little scrapbook, was one of New York's best painters, as well as distinctly modern. The *Sun* praised his efforts highly:

> The winner of the gold medal is Alfred H. Maurer, a young painter who returned from Paris about a year ago and made his first appearance at the Salmagundi Club exhibition, gaining on that occasion the George Inness, Jr., prize. It will be remembered that the subject of that picture was a lady in black silk skirt and white waist sitting at a tea-table, and the same model reappears in the present one, "An Arrangement," where she is sitting on a very low seat, sideways and a little turned from the front, gazing at a thin black shawl embroidered with rosebuds that trails from her knees to the floor. The latter, covered with a drab and blue rug, runs up in a rather exaggerated perspective—for it is painted from above and seen on the level—to a Japanese screen, at the back of which stand two blue jars. In fact, this picture recalls the earlier one in its fresh shrouded light, in the sobriety of its cool, clear coloring, in the skilful treatment of textures and the absence of any motive except a very refined and artistic rendering of all these qualities. It is a picture distinguished by style; painted with remarkable assurance, revealing a comprehension at once large and subtle in suggesting that, if Mr. Maurer can but develop motives as strong as his technique, he will be one of our foremost painters.

Mixed praise came from Charles H. Caffin, usually a discerning and sympathetic critic. In 1909 he would sponsor Alfy; in 1901 he rejected Maurer's experimentation. In the *International Studio* Caffin described the Carnegie prize-winning picture as "very clever but far from great." He modified his comment by calling *An Arrangement* "a painter's picture . . . entirely directed to securing beauty of tone"; and he added that it had "spontaneity and freedom of brushwork that are in themselves a very marvellous accomplishment." Other critics were more favorable. "Near by," wrote one, "is an admirable thing by Alfred H. Maurer . . . among the best things shown by Americans. . . . It is a low-tone picture . . . and like Whistler's 'Mother,' but is not an imitation, nor is it vague and artistically slouchy. Every touch is firm, yet refined; that combination of strength and tenderness which is the greatest thing in the world—after charity."

Another wrote that if Maurer continued to progress at his present rate he should soon receive the recognition he deserved. Maurer was, they said, quite young and yet he distinctly made his mark so that "the way in which the subject has been seen and felt and recorded . . . hails it as a true artist's work." Further, he had already demonstrated his ability to draw and to express the niceties of values. Finally, a more friendly critic than Caffin concluded that Maurer looked through his own eyes with a vision essentially artistic and ended with a handsome compliment to the effect that Maurer had "the true point of view and the technical skill" to go far. He prophesied that Maurer's "self-imposed task of unassisted study warrants the confidence that he must have the individuality and character which will soon produce more important work."

No wonder that the prize-winning painting and the gold medal hung in places of honor in the Maurer parlor where later Alfy's incongruous French touch would not be at home. Yet only eight years later Louis Maurer would stand in front of Alfy's modern paintings at "291" and weep with rage, quavering "Who will buy this stuff?"

Maurer did not return immediately to Paris, after his American triumph. For some time he had a studio at 318 West Forty-second Street, marked with a tacked-up card on which "Studio I" was printed and his name written in longhand script, no doubt like the signatures to his early canvases. There he worked at more figure studies, those of Mrs. Dana in a full black gown and those of his boyhood friend, Roselle Fitzpatrick, as well as some paintings for which he employed paid models. He also pressed his sister Eugenia into service, as in the large 30x29-inch oil, in which he used the striped satin skirt which belonged to his mother and which appeared in other figure paintings. Why did he not paint his father and mother? Whistler had done the famous portrait of his mother as a precedent, which another of Whistler's admirers, Charles Hawthorne, had patterned himself on in painting his mother. Perhaps Alfy's young women friends were more docile models, submitting to standing for long periods of time without complaint?

Uncomplaining was Roselle Fitzpatrick. There are several paintings of her in various poses, full length standing, in a rose silk skirt, with a black lace scarf which Mrs. Maurer brought from Italy, and in other costumes. Maurer was revealing the interest in women's clothes which made him an ideal companion on a shopping tour. Alfy took many photographs of Riz as notes for his paintings. A generation of American painters, from E. L. Henry to Thomas Eakins, had been interested in photography not as a medium of personal expression but as a tool for the painter. Alfy, while rejecting the wooden surface of his father's naturalistic manner, did not at this time reject the naturalistic representation of objects; and he was glad to have photographic aids in his work. There was an amateur photographic darkroom in the basement of "404" where he developed and printed negatives he took of poses for paintings. At least once he made a double portrait, opening the shutter and then dodging into the picture to make an ectoplastic montage of Riz and himself.

On this visit, Alfy probably painted one of his rare bits of Americana, *At The Shore* (page 57). The scene is a bathing beach close to New York, perhaps Far Rockaway. As in *An Arrangement* he used a deceptively quiet palette. To the casual eye the painting might be done in monotones. Yet in it he exploited the close values of cerulean blue sky, white clouds, the white of women's summer dresses, the black of men's suits, touches of bright red as in the costume of the performing monkey "spotted" in the center of the composition or the toy pail in the lower right-hand corner of the design. Accents of bright colors appear on the sailor collars of the women's bathing dresses and in the American flag flying from the flagpole in the background. Neutral-colored sand provides a backdrop against which shows to best advantage that luminosity which pervades Maurer's painting, both in its academic and in its modern phases. Truly Maurer never lost sight of light as one of the painter's materials.

In May, 1902, Alfy returned to his beloved Paris. He was an oldtimer in the Latin Quarter, and now he was a great man, decked with honors, medals, and cash. *Alfy is back,* the news spread through the studios of the Left Bank. The aspiring, hopeful artists of the colony had heard of his great success in America. They were happy for him, and perhaps a little envious. The rendezvous for young American painters was a creamery on rue Delambre just off the Boulevard Raspail. It had two rooms, the front room for the uninitiated (*les nouveaux*); the oldtimers (*les anciens*) frequented the back room, like a non-dues-paying club. Each room boasted a couple of marble-topped tables, and a glass partition with lace curtains made an effective barrier between them.

To this friendly meeting place, Alfy came home. With him that day were Edward W. (Jimmy) and Phil Sawyer, Leon Walden, Maxwell Miller, and Hans Schuler. Alfy called out his greetings to *maman* and to Jeanne and Kiki, the daughters, and kissed them all. This was Maurer's home-coming to Paris. So nebulous are the tiny bits of fact from which Maurer's life must be recreated that it is indeed fortunate Mahonri Young (then *un nouveau*) was in the front room and could report the gaiety and zest with which Maurer was greeted by his friends. The fall before, Young had come to Paris. He was ten years younger than Maurer. Now Young saw him for the first time.

With his prize-money, Maurer took a new studio at 9 rue Falguière. He was also earning money—as much as $100 a month—designing rugs for American manufacturers. For a little while longer he painted figure studies and academic-naturalistic works. He exhibited for some years longer at the Pennsylvania Academy and the Carnegie, sending subjects called *Girl in White; The Moth; Confection; La Trottine; A Garden near Robinson, France; Brushing Up; On The Stairway; Woman in Dressing Jacket; The Vrunhard;* and *A Parisian.* These have not been located and may have been lost. A few known works, such as *Le Bal Bullier, Mademoiselle Jeanne* and *Gabrielle,* were also exhibited in these years. Toward the end of this period, Maurer made his first sale to a museum, though indirectly. In 1903 the Wilstach Collection purchased *The Peacock,* and this early figure study is now in the permanent collections of the Philadelphia Museum of Art.

After his return to Paris Maurer reached out for new subject matter. Perhaps he had been prodded by critical comments on the monotony of his arrangements. In 1902 he began to paint small thumb box sketches of genre scenes like the canal at Charentes, women pulling each other's hair in the Moulin Rouge, and a blacksmith's workshop interior, which his friend Grace Leighton Phillips bought from him that year. He painted at night also, sketching street scenes. To do so he laid out a simple palette so that he would not be deceived by the illusions of night lighting. Then he sat in cafes and painted directly from nature. Whistler, on the contrary, painted his night scenes from memory. A few of Maurer's night sketches have survived. He often used to invite Fra Dana to accompany him on these expeditions. A little later he devoted his thumb box 8x10-inch panels to impressionist landscapes; and indeed the thumb box must have been a handy piece of equipment for Maurer, who was not a large man and who could thus save his energy to paint 2x1-meter canvases in the studio. Much later Maurer found other ways to save his physical strength; for on his return to the United States he made many outdoor sketches in oil on paper and he also painted directly on composition-board panels which are lighter than canvases on stretchers.

Maurer loved fun, jokes, dancing, drinking, women, parties. Genre was his natural direction. Complete dandy as he showed himself in cape, broad-brimmed felt hat, spats and cane, he was also a simple soul. He turned from the cafes to fishing at Chezy with equal zest. There and at Châlons in the Marne country and at Chateau-Thierry, he sketched, fished and relaxed with friends. At easel with paint brush in hand or standing nonchalantly with fishing rod, he wore the loose corduroy trousers of the French *oeuvrier* which American artists of that time made their own. This was the life, he seemed to say, carefree and gay. He loved those jaunts into the country. Typical, probably, was the outing with Young and another friend. The three went off to Chezy for the weekend and stayed at an inn where the only divertissement was a music box which played "La Paloma" interminably. It was gray and rainy. The fish were not biting. There was nothing to do except listen to "La Paloma." Even Alfy's dancing soul tired of that. The first meal the innkeeper put three bottles of *vin ordinaire* on the table. The three friends drank one bottle. The second meal he put three bottles of wine on the table. They drank two. The third meal he put three bottles of wine on the table. They drank all three. What is there to do on a rainy day except spend convivial hours with friends?

Like Luks and Glackens, whose acquaintance he made about this time, Maurer was responding to the pull of the human comedy which in the early 1900s weaned them and the others of "The Eight" away from the Academy's genteel refinements to report the daily life of New York streets and parks. Maurer and John Sloan were not intimates; yet years later the two so different American rebels were associated in the Society of Independent Artists, Sloan as the society's long-time president and Alfy as a director from 1919 to his death. Under happier skies might Maurer's abilities have made a robust reportage of the American scene? The sad girls whom he painted again and again in the early 1920s he knew from personal friendship and observation. How could he have transmuted their pathetic song into the less lonely and withdrawn image of life which he recorded in Paris cafes and streets? In 1902 Alfy found new interests in the circus, the cafes and the clubs where simple people found relaxation and diversion, gaiety and play. No doubt he rode the carrousel (page 58) with as much glee as any child. Much later he returned to the circus as a painting subject, in New York about 1927 and 1928; but his tone had grown less mirthful. So, too, in those last years when he painted dancers, there is an inner torsion as well as an outer, as much the mirror of the artist as of his theme.

That time to come was half a world and half a life away. In Paris, in 1902, Alfy enjoyed life and its broadening pleasures and opportunities. Though he was not always the carefree, smiling, happy-go-lucky Bohemian of fiction, as Mahonri Young's drawing of 1902 shows him (page 62), he was what he longed to be, an artist. He could paint, he had proved that; had he not won worldly success? He was young, and he had years in which to realize his dreams of art. Did he himself know precisely what those dreams were? Did he sense the slow twilight drawing down on the world

in which feuds of art and artists would be engulfed? Did he antic-
ipate if but dimly the private war his life would be? Alfy was now
thirty-four, but he looked older in Young's portrait. The cape, the
cane, the mustache, the broad-brimmed hat, could not hide the
face of a man who in his own way deliberated on the purpose of
his life and work. Was that look already changing?

2. *The Rebel*

AT THIRTY-SIX Maurer broke with artistic conservatism. Three years earlier he had been launched on a career of conventional success. If naturalism was not likely to bring him in a competence on which he could retire at fifty as his father had done, it would probably have provided him with an adequate livelihood and a respectable role in society. Abruptly he renounced medals and honors, put down his brushes, and went away to the country to ponder on art and the artist's duty. Maurer answered his self-posed questions with a total rejection of his aesthetic past. He adopted modern art as his new creative faith, while the sole responsibility he accepted as an artist was to be true to his deep inner need to be himself. For his choice he paid in personal loneliness and loss of material comfort. What motives inspired him? He was not a mere satellite of Leo and Gertrude Stein's circle, as has been said. Was not Maurer's revolt inherent in the spirit of the time? The period demanded creative revivification, and forward-looking individuals responded. Maurer's way was to prove the way of self-immolation. Doubtless he did not foresee the long and lonely years ahead. Could he have done so, would he have made another choice?

His rebellion did not take place immediately on his return from

America. In his new studio he worked away at figure studies and less academic genre subjects. He painted hundreds of these, but only a few survive. From May, 1902, to spring, 1904, he did not depart radically from the premises by which American art had operated for a century. In *The Peacock* he made use of the stock fixtures of the fashionable figure study—standing woman posed before oval mirror, Paisley shawl showing dull orange-reds and blacks against a rose-tan wall. In a Paris cafe he saw a fragment of real life which he reproduced in *The Rendezvous*. A woman sits in the foreground, waiting for the expected one to come. She is in black with black hat and veil, and her black poodle's head is topped with a bright red ribbon bow. White paneled walls, cream-colored ceiling, gray floor, dark red banquette, painted black wooden chairs with straw seats, two seltzer bottles blue with white highlights and silver-colored spigots, all fall within the conventional formula, as do the red hat of the woman sitting at the right and the yellow dress and hat of the one standing. The painting follows the rules of naturalism; but it is sensitive also, hinting at the emotions of the woman who sits waiting, and waiting perhaps in vain. The luminous lighting of the 1897 self-portrait is evident here, enveloping the canvas in a physical glow not unlike the artist's feeling toward his theme. William Merritt Chase bought the painting after it had been exhibited at the Pennsylvania Academy of the Fine Arts in 1905. Again the young artist won honor and encouragement.

Maurer was rapidly adding to his art equipment. He could draw according to the rulebooks, and now he was learning to depart from rule. He could handle the painting medium conscientiously and skillfully, in accordance with the day's technical tradition. Soon he would broaden his mastery of materials, also. He had an eye for color, though it was the color of a subdued naturalistic palette. To mid-twentieth-century eyes, the system seems dull, yet in reality Maurer's early works are amazingly fresh and clean in color. When he paints *Carrousel* (page 58) in a park, the canopy around the merry-go-round is a brilliant red, the bandstand gold, blue and red, the horses gray, black, bay, and roan, and the women wear pink dresses and one a gold-ocher hat. This is a gay and colorful world, lively and entertaining. This, indeed, is the Alfy

who loves fun and gaiety, dancing and red wine, parties and the
girls. So Maurer chronicled the world he had chosen for his own
with its simple pleasures and amusements. Or he painted an *Evening at the Club* (page 58) as an ordinary scene in which ordinary
people meet at the end of the day to relax in friendly conversa-
tion with old cronies over a glass of wine or beer. Again his
color scheme is conventional, based on observation of nature. Gas-
light throws bright yellow spots on the wall, and a yellow lattice is
picked out against green. The men standing chatting and idling
wear black suits, relieved with touches of white. A white cat poses
in the center of the composition, and white chalk lines for some
game or other are drawn on the floor to add another accent. The
problem may not be a profound aesthetic one, but Maurer suf-
fuses the painting with human sympathy and warmth.

So he worked away and painted, saw his friends and lived his
life. Young romantic in 1897, in 1899 long-haired with a flowing
black Windsor tie, in 1902 more sophisticated, by 1904 he was the
arrived artist. In this role Mahonri Young "sculpted" him in full
regalia of cape, blackthorn cane, black felt slouch hat, and curling
mustache (page 62). Alfy groomed his mustache with care then
and took great pains with his dress. Cape and cane became the costume in which he posed for a photograph in sculptor Rudulph
Evans' studio, sitting beneath a cast of a relief from the Parthenon
and flanked by Romanesque columns. At that time he held the
soft felt hat poked out of shape, not unlike the shapeless headgear
later made famous by another Alfred—Stieglitz. Other times he
posed in a broad-brimmed Stetson of the sort possibly introduced
to Paris by "Wild Bill" Noble. He would sit before a curtain of
fleur-de-lis pattern, holding Stetson and gloves in one hand, and
cross his knees to display neatly buttoned spats. His hair was cut
shorter now, and his mustache was somewhat less feline in the
wispy curliness of its ends. Or he stood in his own studio in front
of his easel on which rested a new work, a scene inside a shop—the
photograph is too dim to say exactly what the subject is, and no
such painting has been located. This time he wore a pepper-and-
salt suit, with bow tie and high white collar, contrasting well with
the oriental rug on the wall behind him. His hair had been
brushed into a neat curling scallop from part to ear. Thus the

camera recorded him in those years which otherwise left little record.

Alfy was now famous as an American colony Beau Brummel
and a great man of the Latin Quarter. With assurance and ease he
could walk the great boulevards and frequent the Left Bank cafes.
Max Weber, coming to Paris in 1905, found him almost a mythical
figure. "There goes Maurer!" cried a friend with whom young
Maxie was riding on an omnibus. There Alfy stood at the corner
of rue de Rennes and Boulevard Montparnasse, clad in knicker-
bockers and tweed jacket. Long afterwards, when fashion had
veered to plus-fours, he clung to his close-fitting knickers. Maurer
has been remembered by some old friends as Mephistophelian in
appearance; Weber, however, recalls him as always gentle, loving,
kindly, patient, and sweet. Alfy obviously reveled as much in the
simple camaraderie of his existence as in his new-found celebrity.
He worked and he played. With William Glackens and an unidentified woman model he sat on the floor at a party, all three
dressed in Japanese kimonos. Not only had the vogue for oriental
art spread; not long before, *The Mikado* had burst on the world
in a flurry of libretto and whistle-able tunes. Or, in the fashion of
the day, he decorated a hand-painted four-panel standing screen
in the studio of sculptor Edward W. (Jimmy) Sawyer, also located
at 9 rue Falguière. At a preview his handiwork was cheered by
the first Mrs. George Luks ("Babe" Luks), Luks, and Phil and
Jimmy Sawyer, while the artist sat cross-legged on the floor to
view his masterpiece. All admired the theme, a group of curates
passing a "little midinette who discreetly shows a pretty leg—
which the priests appreciate," as Phil Sawyer annotated a photograph for the author.

These brief years were productive for Maurer. He gained in
technical adroitness and mastery of his medium, and he grew also
in human understanding. At Le Bal Bullier and other popular
dancehalls he watched the crowds and painted them, permeating
his naturalistic color with friendliness and kindliness. In a *Cafe
Scene* the dull red-brown of the railing which separates the raised
dining section from the dance area and the gray-green floor are
brightened by the red uniform hats and trousers of the Zouaves
which set off their blue coats and black belts, while the women's

straw hats decorated with ribbon bows and stuffed birds are also notes of color and gaiety. The scheme of *Le Bal Bullier* is more elaborate. The color elements comprise spots of yellow light from the gas mantles, a neutral-toned floor, a woman's black skirt (in the center) relieved by a lavender blouse and red hat, or at the right a white ruffle on a black skirt, or a dull green hat and light green blouse on the blonde at the left facing left. From these he evolved one of the most successful of his genre works. Its merit lies, however, not in the fidelity with which he observed and represented nature, but in the understanding with which he projected his human material, the girls standing waiting for clients or dancing while they waited. Their traffic was not highly organized and certainly not highly lucrative; it was fatiguing and demoralizing. Maurer painted the girls' faces as miniature portraits. Highly rouged and painted, they look tired. For the most part they are not beautiful or even pretty; but their big noses, heavy lips, high cheekbones, are plastic and appealing. More than that, Alfy saw the girls as human beings on whose faces living had written its history. Within a small scope he said a great deal in regard to his own view of humanity. Beneath the surface gaiety of life he must have sensed deep currents of sadness and suffering which in his own life would deepen into anguish.

That time would come many years later. In the meantime he painted other scenes of daily life, among them *Au Café* (page 59) and *Au Jardin,* both of which are now in the State Hermitage in Leningrad. The art collections of the Hermitage and the Museum of Modern Western Art in Moscow were removed for safekeeping at the outbreak of World War II, and news of these Maurers could not be obtained until 1948, when the collections were brought back to these two Soviet museums. No doubt both are painted in palettes not unlike those described. The two have a new feature, however, in that they have been seen from a point of view above the picture plane, a device Maurer used later in *Nude* (page 196) and which he may have borrowed from Lautrec's *At The Moulin-Rouge.* Again these paintings have the documentary appeal, plus the human: ornamented women's hats, napkins tucked around the neck, oval platters of *hors d'oeuvres,* indoor-outdoor cafe architecture, garden setting, a woman's fitted gored

LANDSCAPE, 1907
OIL ON ACADEMY BOARD, 21½x18 IN.
PRIVATE COLLECTION, PARIS

ROAD, *ca.* 1908
OIL ON WOOD, 8¼x10¾ IN. PRIVATE COLLECTION, PARIS

HOUSE, *ca.* 1908
OIL ON WOOD, 8¼x10¾ IN. PRIVATE COLLECTION, PARIS

ARBOR (?), *ca.* 1908
OIL ON WOOD, 8¼×10¾ IN. PRIVATE COLLECTION, PARIS

GARDEN (?), *ca.* 1908
OIL ON WOOD, 8¼×10¾ IN. PRIVATE COLLECTION, PARIS

HEAD, *ca.* 1908
TEMPERA ON GESSO PANEL, 18¼x15 IN.
COLLECTION: MR. AND MRS. HUDSON D. WALKER

redingote and plumed hat, all show the *face* of a period. These
Maurers were first in the collection of I. A. Morozov, who, with
S. I. Shchukine, became friendly with the Steins about 1905 or
1906 and who then bought many contemporary western works of
art to take back to Russia. On their way back to Moscow after
buying expeditions in Paris, the two would stop off in Berlin and
exhibit their recent purchases at the Fritz Gurlit Gallery, which
may explain the invitations Maurer had to exhibit in Germany.
After 1918 the paintings were in the collections of the Museum of
Modern Western Art, and since 1948 they have been allocated to
the Hermitage.

At the same time Maurer was painting ambitious 2x1-meter
canvases. Only two have been located, *Jeanne* (page 61) and
Gabrielle (not shown); the former was exhibited in 1905 at the
Pennsylvania Academy. Jeanne has been identified by the Paris
firm of Lefebvre-Foinet (Maurer's oldtime dealers) as a model who
posed for Whistler, as she is said also to have posed for Jimmy
Sawyer. The painting was a favorite. It won a medal at Munich in
the 1905 Internationale Kunstausstellung, and it was shown at the
Berlin Secession in 1906 and in London and Bremen, as well as
at the Panama-Pacific Exposition in 1915. The canvas has with-
stood travel and time. Today the life-size Jeanne looks forth from
her black and gray background with a brilliant display of white
and color accents, as in black fringed sash, straw hat with bird,
brown hair, black eyes, white feather boa, and white cigarette.
From the time Southworth and Hawes photographed the famous
Lola Montez before the Civil War with cigarette in hand, to Maurer, perhaps no one had portrayed more engagingly a woman
smoking. Jeanne is what the Victorians could only have called a
minx, alluring as a kitten and as pettable. Surely Alfy did not
paint this canvas solely as a set piece.

Nor could he have painted the companion *Gabrielle* only as an
exercise in technic. Gabrielle posed for at least three paintings,
the one reproduced (page 60), the large work, and the small
panel of about 1905 owned by Mahonri Young. The 75x39½-inch
Gabrielle was formerly in the collection of the late Fra Dinwiddie
Dana. In the early 1900s the canvas used to stand on the floor in
the Maurer house on West Forty-third Street, being too large and

too heavy to hang. Mrs. Dana bought it, she recalled, for two reasons: she wanted it, and Alfy needed money. Gabrielle had posed in a mandarin coat which Maurer later gave Fra Dana and which she wore occasionally till her death in 1948. To judge from this, and other documents in the Maurer archive, Paris forty years ago must have been a veritable rainbow of oriental costume. In this painting the coat's dark blue, middle blue, light blue, and white contrast with the neutral black-gray background. Black hair and eyes, white gloves, and white evening frock with a short train and long sleeves, give accents. Perhaps less enticing than *Jeanne, Gabrielle* was well received by the American art press; for critical as well as popular demanded the grandiose and exotic. In 1906, *The Collector and Art Critic* called Gabrielle "a magnificent example of the work of this young artist" and added that "His work denotes an independent spirit, one that is not tied down to the conventional poses of handsome models, but that expresses itself first and last in harmonious colors and tones." Maurer, the review concluded, "is one of the strongest men of whom future American art history will speak."

More brilliant and less conventional is his *Gabrielle with Parasol* (page 60), painted about 1904. Gabrielle sits forward in the Empire walnut chair. Maurer has used a neutral background, black fading to a dull dark green at the right. She is in an "Alice blue" ribboned hat and dress and white lace guimpe and holds a black ruffled parasol. The brush stroke shows more dash and bravura than that of the 2x1-meter *Gabrielle;* but again the important merit of the painting lies in Maurer's human approach. Gabrielle, as he has seen her in this instance, is a woman of character and strength, less coquettish perhaps than Jeanne, but perhaps more dependable. The small oil which Maurer gave to Mahonri Young when the latter left Paris in 1905 is more hastily painted; but it also shows a woman of sense. Its quickly brushed-in strokes suggest that Maurer has already begun to break away from naturalism and adopt impressionist devices. A larger oil also seems to be painted from the same model; but the high lace collar and flowered hat conceal the face.

Among "exhibition" canvases, there is also a "lost" painting called *The Ballet Dancer,* said to be six feet high and painted between 1901 and 1904. Could this be the painting which won a bronze medal at the Exposition Internationale des Beaux-Arts at Liège in 1905? There was no catalogue for the exhibition; but the *Gazette des Beaux-Arts* referred to a *Danseuse* by Maurer as *"un morceau remarquable"* ("a remarkable piece"). The reproduction which survived in Fra Dana's keeping shows a woman in a classical ballet costume, holding a paper-wrapped bouquet of flowers. "Alfy found humor in this old face and figure of a dancer," recalled Mrs. Dana, "again bedecked in the costume of her youth and assuming the same precious pose she once had." Perhaps the humor was rather in the eye of this beholder: for the subject is in the line of Degas, whose work Maurer knew, at least by 1902, and the spirit of that tradition of hard-worked ballet dancers is hardly humorous. A final unlocated work, apparently also one of those 2x1-meter canvases, is *Mademoiselle Renée,* which shows a woman with fan, draped in a fringed dark shawl and posed against an oriental wall-hanging.

Maurer worked industriously and systematically, putting in long and sustained hours mornings and afternoons, as he did all his life. What the total quantity of his work at this time was, one can but surmise. The output of half his life was lost later; and only a few examples survive to enable us to reconstruct his creative direction. He was about to put a drastic period to this phase of his painting. He was approaching his thirty-sixth birthday. For twenty years he had worked in commercial art and fine art. Where was he going? What does art mean? What should he seek in life and art?

II

MAURER was at the crossroads. Only decisive action could resolve his dilemma. The hidden emotions which had increasingly brought a look of soberness to his own face, and perhaps to the faces in his paintings, reached the breaking point. An old friend soliloquized thus:

One night Alfy came into the creamery on the rue Delambre near the Boulevard Raspail where we all used to go—Jimmy and

Phil Sawyer, Leon Walden, Maxwell Miller, Hans Schuler, and the rest.

He called out, "Hello, maman! Hello, Jeanne! Hello, Kiki!" He kissed maman, and he kissed Jeanne and little Kiki. They all laughed. They were all glad to see him.

He wore his cape and black felt hat and carried his cane.

By that time I had been admitted to the back room, I was un ancien too. Alfy came in and began to dance a funny little jig he used to do. He would click his heels together and tap with his cane. Then he would jump up on one of the marble-topped tables and dance there.

Suddenly he stopped. Before our very eyes he changed to a middle-aged man. All the gaiety went out of his face.

His eyes glared. He was a frantic sight.

"Twenty years ago today," he said, "my father put me to work." It was his thirty-sixth birthday.

From that day on, he painted like a wild man. He was never the light-hearted, gay Alfy we had known.

Thus Mahonri Young saw the transformation take place under his own eyes on April 21, 1904, Alfy's thirty-sixth birthday. All through the years from 1884 to 1904, had resentment been seething under Alfy's outwardly gay bearing until now it burst forth? Could only rejection of everything connected with his past serve his psychological needs? Where could he find an art which, casting aside representation of nature, founded itself on modern principles?

Maurer had learned much in his seven years in Paris, and not only a more than competent control of naturalistic manners. He had become acquainted with the modern movement as well as the great tradition which he had studied in the Louvre and in Italy. With Leo Stein and Mahonri Young he had gone, late in 1902, to the home of Paul Durand-Ruel, the dealer who several times almost ruined himself financially in seeking to find support and understanding for the impressionists. There Maurer saw the Monets, Sisleys, late Degas pastels and other impressionist works which filled the house. He was fascinated by Degas. Other experiences also prepared him to cast off his academic heritage. He, Leo

Stein and Young dined together once a week for two years, in 1904 and 1905; and then, too, he was an early habitué of the Steins' circle. In 1903 the insurgent Salon d'Automne held its first exhibition. Maurer exhibited in the Autumn Salon; but he was opposed to the official Salon and resigned from the Société Nationale des Beaux-Arts of which earlier he had been a member. In 1905 the work of *"les fauves"* ("wild beasts") was shown at the Autumn Salon; and the Indépendants this year gave one large wall to van Gogh and another to Seurat. The revolution of Cézanne and Gauguin, of Seurat and van Gogh, was beginning to recruit a second generation, headed by Matisse and Picasso. The elder masters were dead, all except Cézanne, and he would die in 1906; but their work was becoming known, to Maurer among many others of that time.

The time was fertile for rebellion; the seed had been sown; now it germinated. Maurer gave up painting entirely. To rediscover himself, his purposes in life, his creative goals, he went to Chezy. There he fished, catching fish almost as long as he was tall. Perhaps he sat in the sun and dreamed. Surely he communed with himself; for somehow, sometime, he made his decision. He would break with naturalism, he would explore the strange new land the masters of postimpressionism had surveyed a generation before. Perhaps at the beginning the aesthetic war he plotted was to be a private war, undertaken for private motives. At the end Maurer found himself one of many, though the first in time, of the American pioneers of modern art, who warred on academicism in their search for meaningful expression.

To outward knowledge Maurer did not change immediately. He continued to live as he had done. His friendship with the Steins must have been encouragement to him, especially in the time when he did not paint. Gertrude Stein had gone to Paris from Johns Hopkins in 1904, and shortly afterwards she and her brother Leo bought their first Cézanne from Vollard, long friend and patron of the master of Aix. Alfy met them, it seems, soon after their arrival in Paris. Let Alice B. Toklas tell of him, as she did in her *Autobiography*, "ghosted" (one hastens to add) by Gertrude Stein. She is describing her own first visit to the Steins in 1907. It is clear from the context that Maurer was an intimate of long standing. The passage reads:

> Then there was a sharp tap at the atelier door. Gertrude Stein opened it and a little dark dapper man came in with hair, eyes, face, hands and feet all very much alive. Hullo Alfy, she said, this is Miss Toklas. How do you do Miss Toklas, he said very solemnly. This was Alfy Maurer, an old habitué of the house. He had been there before there were these pictures, when there were only japanese prints, and he was among those who used to light matches to light up a little piece of the Cézanne portrait. Of course you can tell it is a finished picture, he used to explain to the other american painters who came and looked dubiously, you can tell because it has a frame, now who ever heard of anybody framing a picture if the picture isn't finished.

The sparse information about the Maurer-Stein friendship constitutes another missing piece in the puzzle of Alfy's life. Apparently the Steins did not own any examples of his work. Later, when Gertrude Stein visited the United States on a lecture tour, the author sought to obtain information from her in a personal interview, the reference in the then recently published *Autobiography* implying that Gertrude Stein could tell much more if she wished. This was in 1934 when the Maurer memorial exhibition was current at the Uptown Gallery, an event which might have been expected to evoke reminiscence. No data were forthcoming. The passage continues:

> He had followed, followed, followed always humbly, always sincerely, it was he who selected the first lot of pictures for the famed Barnes collection some years later faithfully and enthusiastically. It was he who said when later Barnes came to the house and waved his checkbook, so help me God, I didn't bring him. . . . But to return to that first evening. A few minutes after Alfy came in there was a violent knock at the door and, dinner is ready, from Hélène.

So the party went in to dinner. Picasso and Fernande were present. "Alfy" adds Gertrude Stein "paid compliments to Fernande and she was soon calm and placid." Alfy always was a favorite with the women.

The letters from Maurer to Leo and Gertrude Stein in the papers bequeathed the Yale University Library do not fill in any holes in the puzzle. Probably Leo Stein did not take such a patronizing tone toward Alfy, as his sister did. On August 2, 1905, Maurer wrote from 9 rue Falguière to Stein, then in Italy. The two had planned to travel together, studying Italian painting particularly. Maurer was unable to travel due to illness. He wrote to Leo Stein, regretting that Stein had bought sheets for two and advising him to use them for "canvasses." Meanwhile Alfy was acting as cicerone for visiting Americans in Paris. He added:

> Am to meet your friends tomorrow night and have dinner with them. And will take them to see your pictures. Young and I shocked some Americans the other day with them. The lady wanted to know if I was in earnest.

So Alfy had inherited not only Whistler's crepuscule, but also his *épater le bourgeois*. He signed himself "Sin—Alfie," though customarily, in the few letters found, he spelled his nickname with a *y*. The "Sin" was a joke which he reserved for old friends, including Grace Leighton Phillips.

Two undated notes to Gertrude Stein may have been written earlier. Maurer began one "My dear Miss Stein" and signed it "Alf." Yes, indeed, he wrote, he would be glad to come to dinner, if the invitation had not been for the previous Friday. The other he addressed to "Dear Gertrud." Apparently the final *e* of her first name was added as an afterthought. Perhaps his rejection of all things German had not become conscious at that time. A later note, dated March 13, 1913, is also an acceptance of an invitation to dinner. A decade later, when World War I had intervened and his life had been radically changed, he wrote the last letter to her which has survived. This was on the occasion of his first exhibition at Weyhe's in 1924. Thus the friendship, whatever its depth and reach, continued long after Maurer's return to the United States.

Maurer's life went on uneventfully on the surface. Underneath currents of change and revolt were racing. It took courage in those days for a man to step out, away from the academic, Max Weber recalls today. No matter what the so-called "moderns" exhibited they were always accused of copying, of being imitators. Their opponents did not know the work of Cézanne and Picasso, but it was always of copying Cézanne and Picasso that the experimenters were accused. Maurer was also accused of copying Matisse; and the myth surrounding his life is mirrored in the often-repeated though groundless rumor that he studied with Matisse and that Maurer's first fauvist paintings were but echoes of Matisse. Weber has exploded that myth. Matisse's school was held two winters, in 1907–1908 and 1908–1909; and Maurer was not in the classes, with which Weber assisted. So much for the goddess Fama. It had always seemed unlikely that Maurer, a man nearing forty, would have felt it necessary to study with a man only a year or so his senior. Another rumor which has persisted is that Maurer derived his long-necked women from Modigliani. This also seems contrary to logic. Modigliani came to Paris in 1906. He was then a youth of twenty-two, and Maurer a mature man of thirty-eight. Modigliani lived in poverty and obscurity, befriended only by younger French painters and sculptors; and his work did not win recognition in the United States till after his death in 1920. By that time Maurer had been back in America a number of years. Let Maurer have the last word in the controversy. "Who is this man Modigliani?" he is often quoted as asking.

Botticelli, however, may have been a real influence in his aesthetic development. No doubt Leo Stein, fresh from years of contemplation of the Italian masters, had imbued Maurer with his passion for Renaissance painting. In 1906 Maurer took the trip to Italy which he had been unable to make the summer before. Postcards to his friends the Phillipses in New York give the only clue to this journey. His messages to them were of the "wish-you-were-here" variety, signed "Sin, A. H. M." In the pictures he selected, Alfy, however, revealed his taste. These were Botticelli's *Primavera* and *Calumnia* in the Uffizi, as well as details from the former and views of Il Duomo in Florence and the Doges' palace in Venice. He did not discuss art; but he mentioned the "fine" weather, the "fine" place he was in, the "fine" room he had overlooking the Arno, and the like. He would be back in Paris, he added, for the Fourteenth of July. Was it Bastille Day's historic significance he responded to, or the dancing in the streets? Family connections still remember such merrymaking with him in 1913.

Happy days were drawing to a close. Soon his private aesthetic war would begin. To look back on his life and work, it almost seems as if there were two Alfys, two Maurers, two lives, two bodies of work. If more of the paintings he had to leave behind him in Paris in 1914 had been found, his evolution might present a continuous graph of growth instead of the picture of a wide gulf separating two unjoinable halves.

III

MAURER began his aesthetic revolt by experimenting with impressionist and fauvist theories. The afterglow of these persisted into the 1920s when he was still concerned with theoretical abstractions like color wheels and Jay Hambidge's system of dynamic symmetry. In 1907 and 1908 he went sketching outdoors with his friend the late Arthur Dove. Dove, then a successful illustrator in the United States, had saved up enough money to come to Paris to work and paint. He, like Maurer, hated the existence of a commercial artist. A deep friendship grew up between the two which only death ended. Dove, more than anyone else, understood Maurer's interior life. Lamentably, in the years when the author knew and loved Dove, his health did not permit discussion of Maurer's tragedy. Only fragments suggest the Alfy of those years.

Seemingly Maurer continued a routine existence. In 1908 he exhibited a large canvas, *Mademoiselle Renée*. Critic Charles H. Caffin wrote of this more cordially than he had of the Carnegie prize-winner in 1901:

> Among the figure subjects I must particularly mention Alfred H. Maurer's *Mademoiselle Renée*. This American artist has of late been little represented in the exhibitions, but is remembered for the brilliant debut he made some years ago. . . . He showed himself to be an unusually clever painter, winning at his first appearance a prize for the woman in black, posed in whitish gray interior. Similarly low-toned schemes of colour had continued to occupy his attention; but his present salon picture marks a new departure. It is a

study in several tones of blue, relieved in accents of crimson; involving a certain audacity of colour, that, however, has been thoroughly controlled. It is, indeed, a very handsome canvas; charmingly painted, both in the vigorous treatment of the large masses and in the exquisite fineness with which the dainty arabesques of the damask patterns are rendered. Moreover, it exhales a strangely haunting witchery, a little weird but inevitably alluring.

So much for Caffin's change of heart. Early the next year he wrote an enthusiastic note for Maurer's first one-man show which was held at Stieglitz's Photo-Secession Gallery, 291 Fifth Avenue. Maurer's own opinion was less flattering. On December 18, 1908, he wrote a long letter from Paris to Louis Maurer. His mother had wanted to know how he had made $200. Well, he had painted *Mademoiselle Renée* as a potboiler, which he hoped to sell out of the Salon. Failing that, he had sold it to a man who was taking pictures to Brazil and got $60 for it. At the same time he sold another painting to this dealer for the same price, and he managed to pick up $20 at a time, selling some of his small sketches to Americans in Paris. The problem of finding a market for works of art confronted him, as it does artists today. The inescapable reality of economics could not help but influence Maurer. He could, he added, sell more paintings to the Brazilian dealer, at the same price; but it was giving things away. He hoped, rather, to be able to dispose of his works for better prices to Americans. Then as now, rich American tourists were apparently susceptible to a good sales talk.

He continued in a conversational tone:

> I wish I could make a little money to run home more often, I have been more busy trying to sell than trying to paint lately. Have been going out quite some. I have a great many pictures that I have painted and every thing that I paint don't succeed, very often I paint a canvas over. I just put up a rack to put pictures in so I can keep my place in order.

Like most artists, Maurer could not understand how other artists succeed in obtaining big commissions when he did not: he couldn't see where Fred got an order for $5,000. He went on:

> Living is so much cheaper here and especially rents that I don't
> see how I could get along in New York just at present, over ther
> one has to spend so much money amongst ones friends for drinks
> that, that alone keeps you poor.

At the same time he understood that his new work would not be
easy to sell, literally or symbolically:

> I am doing very impressionistic things, which are accepted here
> and in New York they would howl at them now, but I think later
> on they will be accepted over there too, I have to receive a great
> many visitors on account of my new work, they all want to see it
> and some like it and others are horrified.

And so he ended "with love to all and a Merry Christmas and
Happy New Year."

Almost immediately New York would be howling at his new
work, the "very impressionistic things," some of which Edward
Steichen had carried to America in the fall of 1908 and which
were soon to be exhibited at "291." Indeed it would be at least
twenty years before Maurer's work would be accepted in his native
land. When that time came, his role as pioneer had been over-
shadowed by men who took up modern art later. Meanwhile Maurer was leading a double life, aesthetically speaking. He painted
his potboiler, but he also painted his new work, impressionist
landscapes on 8x10-inch thumb box panels like the ones here reproduced (pages 80-81) which were recently found in Paris. He
had also aligned himself with secessionist American painters and
sculptors in "The New Society of American Artists in Paris." It
was a time of revolt in the arts. In Paris, Berlin, and New York,
"secession" was the slogan. In New York, secession took the di-
verging roads of the Stieglitz group and "The Eight." In Paris the
secessionists, wrote the *New York Times*, "frankly declared war
on the old society of the same name, which, as already cabled, has
long been a power in politics of international art." This "full-
fledged secessionist movement," continued the *Times'* special cable,
"promises to equal in importance similar movements which have
been in existence in Munich, Berlin, and Vienna." Note how manners change: today art news does not rate cables. In this instance,

the news was of such burning concern that the correspondent who sent the dispatch critical of the old regime lost his job.

The secessionists had met in Steichen's studio in February, 1908, and the governors elected were Steichen, Maurer, Weber, Brinley and MacLaughlan. Others in the group were Jo Davidson, Duffy, Kunz, Marin, Bruce, Sparks, and Fischer. The *Times* continued:

> Complaint has been made for some time against the old society, which has been a close corporation made up of men of international reputation. Outside artists say it has used its influence in Europe to monopolize honors and emoluments and to keep from recognition any persons not in its good graces. It has been called the "Decoration Trust."

> "It is a notorious fact," said one of the leaders in the new movement recently, "that while practically every member of the Society of American Painters in Paris is decorated with the Legion of Honor, not more than three or four members of that petrified body are doing anything for American art. In fact, very few of them continue to paint. In the course of years it has become a purely political organization, holding a monopoly of official recognition. The younger American artists have decided that this injustice must end."

Maurer took his stand with the rebels of the art world, as later he would be a director of the Society of Independent Artists. He had already established himself in Paris as an aesthetic radical. The *Times* deemed art news worthy of a column and a half. How an artist today would enjoy so detailed a criticism. The special correspondent wrote:

> Any lover of good pictures who pays a visit nowadays to the studio of Alfred Maurer will receive something of a shock when he discovers that that eminent young New York painter had gone over to impressionism of the most advanced kind. There are a score of impressionist pictures in his studio at present, landscapes, interiors, portraits, still life, all of them fairly singing with light and color, beautiful always in design and composition. Better impressionist pictures probably do not exist in Paris, although Maurer himself says that he is not yet quite sure what he wants to do.

But they inspire almost as much regret as they do admiration. They are not the Maurers known in America, or by his friends here of a year or so ago. The admirable technique, the originality of vision, and inevitable touch of humor which won him success in the old field are not always here apparent. Besides, many of Maurer's admirers found him, at his best sufficiently impressionistic before he became a convert to impressionism.

Any one who has seen his vibrant and stirring view of the Bal Bullier will appreciate the truth of this. The whirl of skirts, the quick movement of feet, the unconsciously grotesque contortions of awkward dancers, the shimmer of artificial light on tawdry decorations are rendered with a brilliancy which could not have been translated otherwise. Such pictures are essentially impressionistic, although in no instance do the color transitions shriek nor the draughtsmanship falter and grope.

These earlier works of Maurer can hold their own with any of the artist's recent pictures, although many of the latter, it must be admitted, are as full of real sunshine as "all out of doors" on a June afternoon. Especially happy are his visions of bare fields and wooded hills just as the first color of Spring is creeping into them. The tender greens of the meadow, the purple haze of the tree tops, and the fathomless blue of a pure sky are treated in such a way that they are absolutely limitless. The same abundant atmosphere, in slightly lower key, envelops his interiors and studies of still life.

What did Maurer himself think his new direction was? His answer to the *Times* correspondent is one of his rare pronouncements on aesthetic matters. He is quoted as follows:

"I admit," said Maurer, "that for the moment I am all in doubt. I believe that I saw right before, but I am equally sure that I see right now. I can't explain the difference. Such pictures as I am painting now I would not dare to exhibit in the United States. Impressionism grows on one the more he studies it. I am painting pictures now which I could never have dared imagine even a year or so ago. See, here is one of the first impressionist pictures I painted and when I did I thought I was doing something terribly bold."

He brought out a delicate little Spring landscape all in pale violets, greens and yellows.

"But now, as I compare this to some of my later work, it appears absolutely tame. The transition from the old school to the new is not an easy one, but it is exciting to a degree. When I decided to make the change I had to lay my brushes aside for almost a month and think nothing but impressionism. Then I went at it slowly and timidly, feeling my way. I am still in transition I know. I can't tell what tomorrow will bring about."

The unassertive quality of his statement is characteristic. His gentleness, until it wore out, would never allow him to present himself, his ideas or his work dogmatically or aggressively. No matter how long he stayed in Chezy and fished, or meditated on art, he would not have come forth with an imposing and articulate body of theory for interviewers. His theories of art he put into practice by painting.

The *Times,* however, ended with a prophecy as to Maurer's future development.

Maurer's case is but one of many in Paris at present, for impressionism is making strides as yet unimagined in America. There is not an exhibition held in Paris to-day but what one or two disciples of the new school are strongly in evidence. In many instances pictures are being painted so widely different from their predecessors that no one could guess their common origin. In Maurer's case, however, there is a strong relationship between much of what he is doing nowadays and his best work of a year or so ago. Many of his friends believe that the result of the transition he speaks about will result in a new impressionism peculiar to himself. He is keeping all the vim and verity of his old-time draughtsmanship. His temperament remains unchanged. The present movement will serve to put him in the foremost ranks as a colorist.

So much for prophecies. After years of search and struggle Maurer did arrive at a personal expression, and in his last mature works he utilized all his resources, among them draughtsmanship and impressionist color. But the road from his first tentative impressionist landscapes to his final masterpiece, *George Washing-*

ton, 1932 (page 239) was a long and arduous one. Traveling it, Maurer formulated goals for himself, human and plastic, far removed from the mechanical formulas of complementary colors. Thus do the aesthetic revolutions of an earlier day dwindle in retrospect.

Maurer was growing older. In 1907 Jo Davidson "sculpted" a bust of which all record has vanished save for a yellowed photograph, fortunately preserved in the sculptor's Paris studio. The bust was sent to the Pennsylvania Academy in 1908 and exhibited there. What happened to it after that its maker does not know; it never came back to him. The genial Davidson saw Maurer in a sober light, as Mahonri Young had earlier. The mustache is still there, and it still curls at the ends. But the neatly scalloped waves of hair at the brow are less stylized, and the forelock has begun to wear a slightly frantic air. The face is serious and contemplative, and the forms of the bones beneath the skin are prominent. More than half his life is behind him, and Alfy is still in doubt. Like Gauguin, he might have asked *Whence come we, what are we, where are we going?* Indeed, was not his whole life's endeavor to find answers for these questions? Meanwhile more practical questions were soon to face Maurer. He was about to make his New York debut at "291."

3. The Exile

IN NEW YORK they would howl at his new "impressionistic things," Alfy had written in December, 1908. Howl they soon did, and with fury. "What is it? A bursted tomato? A fireman's hat? A red rock? A couple of people under an umbrella? Nobody can make it out." Thus the critical storm raged; and Louis Maurer stood in front of his son's new work and wept. What was Maurer after, asked the *Sun's* James Huneker—"a Catharine wheel at full tilt on a Fourth of July night or an ordinary apoplectic aura." The *Globe's* critic, Arthur Hoeber, recently elected a member of the National Academy, fulminated against the "bacilla [*sic*] of the Matisse craze" which had entered into Maurer's soul and "what is worse, into his paintings." Maurer had "capitulated, horse, foot, and dragoons," Academician Hoeber wrote, and ended courteously that "of all the pure forms of imbecility that have overtaken youth time out of mind, these are the limit." The sketches, stated the *Herald*, "suggest a yellow hornet escaping from purple fly paper." Thus the old aesthetic order slowly yielded to the new.

The exhibition at the Photo-Secession Gallery, 291 Fifth Avenue, was Maurer's first one-man show—in America or abroad. At the same time Stieglitz exhibited John Marin's European water colors. Maurer's display comprised fifteen items, the first listed as

ILL LIFE, *ca.* 1908
L ON BOARD, 18¼x21¾ IN. COLLECTION: BERTHA SCHAEFER GALLERY

PORTRAIT, *ca.* 1908
OIL ON CANVAS,
21¾x18 IN.
COLLECTION: BERTHA
SCHAEFER GALLERY

TEAHOUSE, CHÂLONS, 1911
OIL ON CARDBOARD, ON STRETCHER, 24x20 IN.
COLLECTION: MR. AND MRS. A. W. VENINO

IN THE VINEYARD, *ca.* 1912
OIL ON CARDBOARD, ON STRETCHER, 30⅞x25⅜ IN.
COLLECTION: E. WEYHE

FLOWERS, *ca.* 1912
OIL ON CARDBOARD, ON STRETCHER, 21¼x18 IN.
COLLECTION: WHITNEY MUSEUM OF AMERICAN ART

Sketch in Oil, followed by ditto marks repeated fourteen times. The exhibition's catalogue was a small four-page folder, headed " I I PHOTO-SECESSION GALLERIES I I / EXHIBITION OF SKETCHES IN OIL BY / ALFRED MAURER, OF PARIS AND / NEW YORK: AND WATER-COLORS / BY JOHN MARIN, OF PARIS AND / NEW YORK: MARCH THIRTIETH TO APRIL / SEVENTEENTH, MDCCCIX I I I I I I I I . " The Maurer check list appears on the left-hand page, and Marin's twenty-five water colors are listed on the right-hand page. Unlike Maurer's uninformative listings, Marin used complete descriptive titles such as *Café du Commerce, Meaux.* For the exhibition Charles H. Caffin wrote brief essays, printed on a single-leaf flier, one side of which was given over to Maurer and the other to Marin. It would seem that Maurer had the preferred position. His side is headed with his name in small capitals and signed by Caffin at the bottom, at the right, in small capitals. The reverse side is similarly headed with Marin's full name and signed by the critic. At the left it has a subscription: "THE PHOTO-SECESSION GALLERY. / March thirtieth, 1909."

Maurer had anticipated that New York would not welcome his latest work. Nonetheless he was probably startled by the violent attacks on his new manner. Late in February the *Sun* announced that a number of works by Alfred Maurer would be exhibited at "291," following drawings and photographs of paintings by Henri Matisse. Maurer enjoyed "the distinction," the *Sun* noted, of being "one of the much discussed American painters." In addition, he was "one of the most painted of artists," a portrait of him by Miss Susan Watkins then being on exhibition at the Pennsylvania Academy. The two-column reproduction looked out at the world in candid aplomb. Slouch hat, plaid scarf, cape, and cane, Maurer had put on his uniform for the world.

Soberly but not fearfully did Maurer gaze out on the world from a photograph headed "The First American Post-Impressionist," sent out by the Associated Newspapers' Service. No hint of the coming storm is to be read in the caption:

> Alfred H. Maurer, now recognized as one of the most gifted of the post-impressionist painters, has the distinction of being the first American to master this new form of art. Mr. Maurer has lived in

Paris for the last fourteen years, and his early work in conventional painting won him many prizes, both here and abroad. For seven years he has devoted himself to the new school of art. He . . . is exhibiting his work in New York, with the idea of educating his fellow countrymen to an appreciation for post-impressionism. As is the experience of most pioneers in art, Mr. Maurer met with a storm of ridicule when he exhibited his first impressionistic work in Paris, but this has been overcome by a steadily increasing host of advocates and admirers of what is claimed to be the more sincere, more vital, and more individual expression in painting.

No premonition seemed to haunt him when he wrote on February 16 to his father to send birthday greetings and to give news of himself and his work. He was working hard to get off six paintings of his "latest kind" to Brussels, where he had hopes of doing some business. It looked as if something would come of this exhibition from his talks with the man who selected the pictures, who was also managing the show. He felt hopeful also because several French people had been in to see his paintings and they might be able to help him in the way of exhibiting. So the date neared for his world premiere.

While Alfred Maurer had been waging a one-man revolt, revolt had been blowing up in America. In 1908 "The Eight" had held their unique group exhibition, and the art world was the richer for the work of the "Ash Can School," the "Black Gang" or whatever else artistic conservatives chose to call them. Scorning technical facility and refined themes of tea tables and dressing tables such as swelled the American salons, this oddly assorted intransigent group sought to mirror real life. In that heyday of social reformism when Ida M. Tarbell, Ray Stannard Baker and Lincoln Steffens were exposing the ills of American society and the magazine *Everybody's* had a department, "Little Stories of Real Life," a few artists had felt the pull of reality, human experience, and human misery. So Henri and Luks, John Sloan, Glackens and Jerome Myers, Everett Shinn to a degree, and later Glenn Coleman, and the early George Bellows set down the portrait of dust blowing in windy streets, of dirty and clamorous elevated trains thundering overhead, of street fiestas and shrines in "Little Italy," of half-starved black cats slinking through Greenwich Village's back yards, of the Haymarket, of McSorley's wonderful saloon (no women admitted!), of buxom blondes leaning out of upstairs windows combing their hair, of boys swimming naked in the East River, of the skyline of New York from the harbor, and the million and one sights of the city of a million joys and sorrows. Here were the roots of a native realism, sunk into the soil of a joyful acceptance of humanity.

Paralleling this trend in American art was the secessionist program of Stieglitz and his group. Imbued with scorn of corruption and degradation and possessed of private income, Stieglitz struggled in his highly personal fashion to restore purity to art. He sought to exhibit and reveal the new, the growing, the living, so as to allow the rebels and the pioneers a chance to say what they had to say. His disgust for the impure and the vulgar led him to a particularist isolation when he wrote in his magazine *Camera Work* that *"Art is for the few, and by the few"* [Italics mine—E.McC.]. His group idea, for which he entertained an almost holy awe, would dwindle away from an Augustinian community and he would remain the patriarch of a declining clan in which the chieftain could lord it, because none had the inclination or energy to challenge him. This was later. In the first decade of the twentieth century, the Stieglitz movement and "The Eight" came from similar sources—the ennui of creative spirits with the going academic institutions for art. Soon the duality of the two was revealed. Increasingly Stieglitz's proteges withdrew from the hurly-burly of life—or withdrew from him. For example, when Gertrude Vanderbilt Whitney launched her activities in behalf of living American artists, members of the Stieglitz group remained aloof and continued to remain aloof.

Nonetheless Stieglitz's "291" was an avenue of access into America for modern art. There he showed early masters of photography working as creative artists in the newest medium of personal expression—the science-art photography. Among these were David Octavius Hill, Julia Margaret Cameron, Edward Steichen, Clarence White, Gertrude Käsebier, and himself. Before the date of Alfred Maurer's exhibition, Alfred Stieglitz had shown drawings by Matisse and the sculptor Rodin, Japanese prints by Utamaro, children's art, and Lautrec. After, he would show Cézanne and Renoir lithographs and Picasso drawings, as well as the first experimental, striving modern work of Maurer, Marin, Marsden Hartley, Arthur Dove, Max Weber, Georgia O'Keeffe, and photographer Paul Strand. Standing apart from other groups and programs, he provided, if not a forum in which many new voices could be heard, a rostrum on which a few new artists could stand.

Into the small crowded "291" came Maurer, eager to prove the direction he had chosen. Steichen had visited his studio in Paris and seen small landscapes and still lifes packed in among towering 2x1-meter canvases. Their subjects included night scenes, the boulevards, and people sitting at tables in open-air cafes; and those who recall that first exhibition remember the small panels of street scenes, cafe scenes and night scenes. Fra Dana recollected, also, that she and Maurer went about Paris at night, on the streets and in the cafes, to make notes. "He carried a little notebook," she reported, "and if we were in a cafe, he would sketch the interior, so that he would know how to lay out his canvas and write in the colors he saw. So many of the cafes were white and gold that winter, and brilliantly lighted. The next day he would paint the scene by daylight. They didn't have daylight lighting then and you can't paint at night." Two or three of these notes survive, warped and dingy, with paint peeling. It was these small sketches in oil which Steichen carried over and introduced to Stieglitz. Thus Maurer was launched as a pioneer of modern art in America.

None of those fifteen sketches has been definitely identified. Mrs. Dana's small *Houses* and *Trees* probably were not in the "291" exhibition; for Mrs. Dana had bought them from Alfy in Paris and doubtless took them directly to her Montana ranch home. However, two small panels formerly in the Stieglitz collection might well have been purchases which Stieglitz made at the time of the exhibition and which remained in his possession till his death. The other Maurers in his collection were larger and more ambitious, obviously works of a later date. It is hard to understand today why these paintings struck horror into the hearts of press and public. *Houses* is painted in a palette of primary colors, the roofs being orange-cadmium, while there are two areas of a strong ultramarine blue, one between the houses toward the

left and the other at the base of the tree. Emerald green, deep
earth reds and light cadmium yellow round out the color scheme.
Yet these early "modern" paintings infuriated the critics and well-
nigh broke his father's heart, according to an anecdote related by
one of Stieglitz's Boswells. In his *Emergence of an American Art,*
Jerome Mellquist tells the story.

> One day an older man visited the gallery. He stood a long time,
> gazing and shaking his head. "Who will buy this stuff?" he de-
> manded. There was something spruce and gay about him, with his
> cane and goatee and his crisp attitude as of one who had driven
> first-rate trotters all his life. He did not identify himself, but
> finally, as he was about to leave, he was accosted by Alfred Stieglitz,
> the guardian of the little center. "Mr. Maurer," said Stieglitz, "I
> wouldn't feel so crushed. Your son is all right."
>
> "Who may you be?" Maurer asked.
>
> "I'm the son of your old friend Edward Stieglitz. You used to
> come to the house at 14 East 60th Street, years ago. You and my
> father liked to ride horseback together."
>
> Tears filled the old man's eyes. "And you are Alfred. . . . And
> you seem to understand my son's work."
>
> Yet still he was worried. Once more he inquired why his son did
> such "stuff."
>
> "Don't worry, Mr. Maurer," replied the photographer. "Your son
> will be all right."
>
> Still shaking his head, the father left. Later he said that he had
> "buried" his son.

So much for the struggle between generations, whether of parent and child or of old ideas and new ideas.

Critic Caffin saw Maurer differently. In the brief essay for the
exhibition, he wrote, in part, as follows:

> He has been led to discover other colors in his paint box than
> blacks and drabs and white; also to look for color beyond the walls
> of an artificially darkened studio. He has been drawn out-of-doors
> into the sunshine. There, under the indirect persuasion of Matisse,
> he has found himself in seeing, not only local color, but visions of
> color, evoked from the actual facts, by the play of his imagination
> under the spell of some particular mood. He has ranged himself,

in fact, with the other men of Paris, who . . . are trying in their pictures to substitute interpretation for representation, and whose interpretation eliminates as far as possible the assertion of the concrete, seeking an abstract expression through color harmonies, somewhat as does the musical composer.

In these studies then, for that is what they are—color notes of spiritual impressions received in the presence of nature, he is not aiming at the representation of the landscape, but at the projection on the panel of the color-harmonies with which for a moment nature has inspired him. They are primarily to be judged as little creations of color beauty, with the same detachment from notions of subject matter, that you approach the appreciation of a piece of antique pottery. You may even observe in some of them—I don't know how intentionally on Maurer's part—a dripping application of the color, and the leaving of portions of the ground apparent between the masses of color, that recall the antique potter's method of applying colors and leaving parts of the biscuit of the vase in reserve. In judging them this way, however, one may be conscious sometimes that an object has been so emphasized as to challenge the mind to a question of what it represents, without giving sufficient clew to the answer. A doubt is raised. One is puzzled, and thus the mental operation of conjecture interferes with the free play of the imagination.

But the occasional occurence of these concrete disturbances to the purely abstract impression may serve by contrast to bring out more clearly at what this artist and others, working in the same spirit, are aiming. They would borrow from nature only so much form as may supply a scaffold on which to hang the decoration of a color fantasy. When once we have accepted this point of view, we cease to attach separate importance to the scaffold, and only ask, in return, that the artist will not obtrude it on our notice. If he does, it is at his own peril of disturbing our appreciation of his abstract purpose. The latter, for my own part, seems a natural evolution from the example of Whistler and marks a new and very suggestive note in modern painting.

Thus handsomely did Caffin redeem his unkind words of 1901. Other critics supported him, though less eloquently and less at length. Sadakichi Hartmann observed moderately that Maurer had tired of the academic palette's brown and blue and "made the scarlet departure" to "pink, crimson and ruby-coloured shadows." The *Sun's* Huneker gave the opening forty-eight lines of his column, "Around the Galleries," to the "291's" "duet in fire and shadow," calling Maurer "The Knight of the Burning Pestle" and Marin "the master of mists." The "lead" position went to Maurer:

> A profound peace will overspread the exacerbated souls of them that display threatening grinders when the names of Sorolla and Zuloaga are mentioned. Here is this young Maurer, who went abroad in full possession apparently of his color sense, suddenly become a chromatic fantasy. The catalogue notes that the influence of Henri Matisse shows itself in these extraordinary efforts. Matisse, yes, and also Gauguin, whose strained symbolism has evidently affected the ambitions of the American. . . . We know that Prendergast of Boston can succeed in making clear his vision while working at the same bloodshot optical region. Perhaps Maurer will some day. It is a cruel Eastern garden of writhing arabesques that he puts before us. And yet—but let us wait; such attacks pass. Besides this chap has talent as well as boldness.

Thus was Maurer welcomed in an art world where rebels Sloan and Glackens still used the brown and blue palette he had abandoned some years before. What was the nature of the work which aroused critical and parental ire?

II

LACUNAE are many in Maurer's life and work—lack of information about his youth and early art work, scanty data in regard to his personal life, physical loss of paintings done in Paris from 1897 to 1914, silence which enveloped him on his return to the United States at the outbreak of World War I, fragmentary letters, relative infrequency with which he dated his works. In this instance the lacuna in regard to his transition from naturalism to modernism creates the effect of a life split in half, or of a two-faced artist, one face looking to the past and one to the future. No doubt if more were known of his work in these crucial years, Maurer's evolution would seem less staccato. As it is, a few guideposts serve.

Maurer seems to have painted in a fauvist manner before he became "America's first post-impressionist." Aside from the thumb box panel landscapes which were his first effort to break away from representational art, a few still lifes and a portrait study survive, probably painted in 1907 or 1908. In 1950 a score of hitherto unrecorded Maurers of this period were discovered in Paris, as said before. Four of these are reproduced here (pages 80-81), as well as another newly found Maurer from another source, a landscape dated 1907 (page 79). The photographs and halftones show how Maurer had left behind the smoothly painted surface of his prize-winning arrangement and even the somewhat more broadly brushed-in style of his genre pictures. The stroke is spontaneous and direct, brusque and impetuous, free and luminous. It is possible to read in these photographs how he used subject matter of the outdoor world near Paris where he spent his happiest times. The houses are familiar, and an arbor appears which seems to be the same he later painted in *Teahouse, Châlons* (page 100) in 1911. From the look of the photographs it would appear that Maurer painted some of these newly found works on the ground described in the following paragraph. Details of the actual discovery are more fully documented in the Epilogue.

Fra Dana returned to America early in 1909 from a trip to Paris where Maurer had confided to her his technical secret of "made" canvas, which she kept for forty years tucked away among her personal papers. Some of the works referred to were painted on the ground described in her notes, under the heading *Alfred Maurer's directions for "Made" Canvas.* About this time also Maurer and Eugene Paul Ullman were seeking to discover the technical secrets of the masters, experimenting with tempera and other mediums, an interest which both independently carried on for many years. As Mrs. Dana took down Alfy's dictation, the formula follows:

Stretched linen on frame.
If oil painting is to be used, size canvas with denaline and water and coat with turpentine varnish. Put on thin coat of glue and

water. Do not let dry. Then soak well with a coat or two of glue.
Then coat of denaline. Then coat of glue. Then turpentine varnish.
Then paint with denaline for ground.
Denaline: dextrine and plaster of Paris whiting.
  (dentists' plaster of Paris)
Get powdered colors for under-painting.
Venetian turpentine—½
Ordinary turpentine—½
  (boil, but not quite)
Let dry in shade.
Varnish
Set in sun.

How closely Maurer followed this technic in *Head* (page 82)
and *Still Life,* not reproduced, is not clear. The ground has been
applied to French cardboard, with disastrous warping in the portrait. The denaline-glue-plaster coating has produced a pleasing
matte surface, which is not, however, impervious to abrasion.
Aside from technical considerations, the two paintings (as well as
a still life of a cup and plate and perhaps also a semi-cubist still
life of a cup on a table in which Maurer has employed gold leaf
and a stencil in collage style) give a clue to his palette in the early
years of his rebellion. *Head* is painted in a scheme of strong reds
and greens, cheeks and lips accented in sharp triangular areas,
while the background is thin and transparent. Fauvist color is an
obvious attribute of the still life. The table top is painted in violet
with blue shadows, the compote in blue with deeper blue shadows,
the bowl in rose madder designs on yellow with deep blue shadows, while at the top the background is divided into two areas of
an acrid middle value yellow-green with a blue triangle between.

If these were shown at "291" in 1909 or the next year, they must
have intensified the critics' wrath. At least they bore out Caffin's
reference to Matisse's influence on Maurer. The strongly drawn
line of the edges of planes has an evident resemblance to the flowing Matisse line used as early as 1905 and 1906 for the *Dancers*
commissioned by the Russian collector, S. I. Shchukine. No doubt
he and his traveling companion, I. A. Morisov, had met Maurer
at the Steins'. Thus a circle of cause and effect might well have

operated on Maurer's expression. The influence, however, seems general rather than particular. When the line reappeared in Maurer's painting, as in the girls of the early 1920s and in the later formal heads, it could not be read as other than his own calligraphy.

The *Times* had already commented on the fact that many of Maurer's admirers had found him "sufficiently impressionistic before he became a convert to impressionism" and had referred to his paintings of Le Bal Bullier as indications of how loose and brilliant his brush stroke was. Something of that freedom of touch passed into his early small landscapes and certainly into his larger landscapes, such as *Autumn* and *Poplars*. With broad brush stroke and heavy impasto, he painted nature in an increasingly brighter palette. As he grew more emancipated, he painted directly from the tube or sometimes (it seems) in the fashion of finger painting. This love of the textural qualities produced by impasto he carried on much later, by molding his gesso ground in relief before under-painting and varnishing. With his control of drawing, concern with color, interest in the surface of paint, and preoccupation with form, Maurer possessed the formal attributes of the painter. In his struggle to liberate himself from the past, he felt at first that these are all the artist needs. Under the stress of existence he came to another view, expressed more in practice than in theory, but nonetheless expressed, that the function of the work of art is the communication of experience. To this point of view he came slowly, through sorrow.

Meanwhile he painted, painted, painted, as he always had. In 1910 Maurer—with Brinley, Carles, Dove, Fellowes, Hartley, Marin, Steichen, and Weber—made up the group of "Younger American Painters" at "291," the first group exhibition of American painters that Stieglitz held. Shortly before, Maurer had made a visit to New York; and on March 17 he wrote his mother, informing her of his safe arrival at Boulogne. On April 5 he wrote "Steiglitz" (as he spelled the name on occasion) to inquire how the show had come off, as he had had no word and had not seen anything in print since his return to France. He was much concerned with a flood which had swept through Paris and cleaned the stone bridges up to the high-water mark. He ended with kindest regards to Steichen and Marin, as well as to Stieglitz.

The history of Maurer's life and work is occasionally eked out with an almost miraculous document, unassailable fact, or dated painting. Such is *Teahouse, Châlons* (page 100). In the summer of 1911 Maurer was fishing and painting in the Marne country. In September he was attracted by the tantalizing color of an open-air teahouse in a boxwood garden brilliant with flowers and rose trellis. In quick, hurried strokes he set down his subject, using cardboard with a gesso ground which shows through in certain areas. The tempo of his stroke and the almost pure complementary colors he used are a measure of the mastery he attained in his new style, in which he would continue to grow. How did this key painting, as far as dating is concerned, come to survive?

In the fall of 1911 Mr. and Mrs. A. W. Venino, distant connections of the Maurers—they called the father "Uncle Louis"—visited their "cousin" Alfred in his Paris studio. There they saw the painting leaning against the wall. The one or the other, or perhaps both, fell in love with the gaily painted teahouse. What a brilliant note of color it would make in their home, they would buy it, they said. Maurer tried to dissuade them. "People will think you're crazy," he said. He had learned from his two experiences with the New York press. They liked the picture, and they insisted on having it. Finally, some time later, Alfy brought the painting around to their hotel, in one of the frames he made for his paintings. Because of these circumstances, this painting can with certainty be dated 1911. On such an unpredictable clue hangs the dating of much of Maurer's early modern work.

About this time Gertrude Vanderbilt Whitney was the "angel" of American artists in Paris, and probably about this time she bought the *Flowers* (page 102) now in the collections of the Whitney Museum of American Art. To judge by style, it is later than *Teahouse*. The brush stroke is more rapid, and the areas of unpainted cardboard are skillfully used for textural and tonal effects. The frame, however, resembles the Veninos' frame in weight and decorative motives. It is fortunate that the Maurer story can be strung on a fine cord of conjecture, since external evidence is often missing.

By internal evidence, *In The Vineyard* (page 101) is another late impressionist-fauvist Maurer. Its broadly painted surface goes far in using unpainted areas for overall luminosity, and the division of color into primary, complementary pigments is advanced. Cleaned, the painting is brilliant, even to eyes accustomed to the 1951 medley of abstractionist, expressionist, surrealist, and non-objective painting. Against a cerulean blue sky with white clouds, Maurer placed a tree painted in alizarin crimson with emerald green leaves. Notes of primary color are a cadmium orange cloud, areas of dark cadmium yellow at the top of the tree and below it to the right, and areas of permanent blue surrounding the lower yellow area. Overall are washes of pink. If our eyes today could be washed free of all the visual images of the years between, this would seem a daring palette. So it did in 1913.

At this point we may leave the story of Maurer's aesthetic development and turn to the last external events of his art career before he left Paris in 1914. These are his exhibition at the Folsom Galleries and his participation in the Armory Show. The story of the Armory Show has been told, in part, and from many points of view. Perhaps an archeological expedition would be required to do full justice to the event which shook American art from its base and atomized succeeding generations. Revolt was stirring here. Revolt was rampant abroad, among Europeans and Americans. Maurice Prendergast had brought back tidings of impressionism. Maurer had been the first of the Americans in Paris to throw off naturalism. Fifteen-year-old Karfiol, twenty-four-year-old Weber, Walkowitz, Marin, Steichen, Samuel Halpert, Dove, scores and hundreds of others had been recruited to the modern movement. At home "The Eight" and after them the Independent's fought the good fight of native realism; and in his later lonely eyrie Stieglitz proclaimed his messianic truths. But the Armory Show was something else again. It shook the foundations of the art world, and it involved artists for two generations in controversy, recrimination, and renunciation. In this stirring event, Maurer took only an inactive part.

If the Armory Show was an explosion, it had also the aspects of guerilla warfare. The stay-at-home insurgents, headed by that maker of gentle idylls, Arthur B. Davies, sent out scouts to explore the land in Paris and elsewhere. The late Walt Kuhn was one, and Walter Pach another. Maurer, the great man of the Quarter, the first of the American rebels, was one of the artists in Paris whom Kuhn approached immediately. Wouldn't Maurer help him borrow works for the proposed exhibition, he asked. Maurer was too busy, he told Kuhn. Perhaps he was preparing for the Folsom Galleries exhibition. But the old-timer, as Kuhn called Maurer, did introduce the young American emissary to "the formidable Monsieur Vollard." Vollard was willing to listen but remained noncommittal. Nor could Walter Pach enlist Maurer's active support. Apparently he made contacts for Pach and Kuhn but did no "dirty work" in assembling exhibits such as he did a decade later in the Society of Independent Artists. In the latter, Maurer was a tower of strength, hustling paintings and sculpture, driving nails, cutting linoleum blocks for invitations and posters, and attending the annual balls in costume! Maurer, however, did exhibit in the Armory Show when it opened in February, sending three paintings, No. 53, *Landscape,* No. 54, *Old Faience,* and No. 55, *Autumn.*

Before this took place, he had had his second one-man show, that held at the Folsom Galleries from January 15 to January 29, 1913, and apparently was in New York at that time. There was an accompanying brochure which "reprinted . . . an abstract of introductory remarks contained in the catalogue of the Post-Impressionist Exhibit" then "being held at the Grafton Galleries, London," which had been written by Clive Bell and Roger Fry, leading advocates of modern art. There was no check list of the paintings, however. According to one press account, twenty-seven postimpressionist works were shown. The exhibition would be viewed "with mingled feeling" by "students of art," the reviewer believed. Remaining "mindful of the way in which public taste and art ideals change, even in a single generation," the commentator added that it was "certain many will dislike [the paintings] and . . . some will laugh at them; but to others they will be not only interesting but will give real pleasure." Maurer had begun to make his way to critical tolerance, if not acceptance.

Indeed, the comment makes a fairly impartial case for the artist. It continued:

In painting figures, landscapes, or still life Mr. Maurer is not particular whether he makes the painting look like the object painted; all he seeks to do is to make the observer feel as the object made him feel. Consequently dishes, all "out of drawing," seem about to fall off tables, while trees and fields in landscapes are mere patches of color. In some pictures he has fallen short of his intentions and the beholder is bewildered. Other paintings are a delight because of their color.

One of these color schemes that brings joy is "On the Way to Azy," the paint of which seems to reflect the mood of spring. Another successful post-impressionist work is "Border of the Village," a poor medley presenting a broken down hut amid rocks and vegetation, with houses back of it, the whole arousing a pensive feeling.

Two still life pictures, "The Agate Pitcher" and "Old Faience," are beautiful because of their jewel-like color. "The Poplars," however, is a color discord, and "Autumn" looks as if the artist had placed on a palette all the colors needed to paint an autumn landscape and then had upset the palette on a canvas. The colors are there and beholders with imagination can get a pleasing autumn sensation.

Yet, despite his plus-minus attitude, the critic faced a dilemma. ". . . four pictures painted by Mr. Maurer before he became a convert to the new idea" are academic canvases, "painted in sober grays and subdued flesh tints." They "look dead when compared with the artist's new pictures." That was the artist's choice, life or death.

For his choice he received praise as well as blame. Maurer represented "THE NEW" in the *International Studio's* department "Fashions in Art." With judiciality, the critic wrote:

> There is no gainsaying the fact that the eager quest of novelty is quite as much a mode as is the placid reliance upon precedent. If it be the fashion in certain plutocratic quarters to patronize only that which is hallowed by the past, it is quite as obviously the habit elsewhere solely to tolerate that which is feverishly, not to say flagrantly, modern. The argument is, however, vastly in favor of the latter group. They are at least esthetically alive, not languidly somnolent. They breathe the atmosphere of their own day and

generation and respond to those vital, formative currents, social, scientific and intellectual which are surging about us in splendid unrest. They are animated and experimental in their attitude toward their work, and the future is undoubtedly theirs.

Perhaps the future was to prove theirs, but it would be won arduously and painfully. For the moment the *International Studio* was one of the rare voices lifted in support of Maurer, who "has revealed an increasingly strong grasp of the essentials of the modern movement and has displayed, above all, an individual richness and beauty of coloration which rank him well in the forefront of that courageous little band which has recently brought from overseas the gospel of Expressionism." And so the review was off to definitions of impressionism and expressionism, with a shrewd statement that the latter best defined Maurer's bent.

Less kindly was the Boston *Transcript* later in the year. Of the forty-seven Americans in the 1913 Salon in Paris, Maurer was singled out for dubious comment. He offered, the *Transcript* wrote, "not too impossible still life, and two canvases of more than doubtful signification, each of which bears the noncommittal title, 'Etude.'" If that venerable newspaper had survived to the present day, what would it have made of such titles as *Painting* and *#11?* It continued with a quotation from a French critic, one Louis Vauxcelles, to the effect that Maurer was "hypnotized by the Matisse of 1910. It is worth noting that the imitators get quickly winded in following their models: they are always a year behind."

As for the Armory Show, that came and went. Hundreds of thousands saw the mammoth display in New York and Chicago. Native talent, however, did not take precedence over the imported, and the nine days' wonders were not Maurer and his American fellows, but the novelties like Duchamp's *Nude Descending a Staircase*. Press comment on the exhibition, therefore, does not supply any fragments about Maurer. Indeed Maurer's exhibiting in the United States in 1913 ended in a mix-up. Maurer wrote Stieglitz from Paris in April, regretting that what he had tried to avoid had happened. He continued:

I went to Budworth [the firm of picture shippers] and wrote your name and "return to 291 Fifth Avenue" on the backs of the

two pictures you wanted notifying Budworth of the same. I will
write to my home and find out what was returned there & if they
have them they can be sent to you. Was delighted with the success
of the big show. . . . From the papers things were hot in New York,
was glad to be away from it.

Perhaps this was fortunate for the future, however. It seems that
these paintings which Budworth did not return to "291" survived
for years in the family home at 404 West Forty-third Street and
escaped the general fate of Maurer's French work. Now his years
abroad were moving to their climax. Soon war would come; and
Maurer, one of the innumerable pawns of history, would return
to his native land, never again to see his beloved Paris.

III

MAURER'S FLIGHT from Paris is shrouded in unreality. The facts
are not clear, nor is Maurer's own attitude clear. If he took a
position critical of the forces causing war or if he felt that the
artist is above the battle is a question. Artists of that time separated from our own by two world wars had scarcely felt the
urgency of history nor had they become concerned with their re-
sponsibilities as citizens. Apparently Maurer did not vote after he
returned to his native land, as Winslow Homer earlier had ab-
jured jury service. His world was the studio, that world painted in
symbols by Picasso, Braque and Léger. The studio denied him,
what was left? Such values pervade a letter he wrote to Fra Dana
from Paris on August 17, 1914. Little of the tragedy of history is
expressed, but much of the trials and tribulations of the writer.
Thus, too, the newspaper account of the fishing reels he lost on
the Marne seems unreal, measured by the mass human suffering
of war. Was this ill-judged protective coloration?

Maurer wrote his letter in the white heat of war and invasion.
It is his longest known letter, and it is quoted here only in part,
from excerpts supplied to the author by Mrs. Dana in the spring
of 1948. Perhaps its tone is the tone of the nervously excited person who giggles or laughs from shock. Certainly the fullness of

detail of the letter and the haste with which Maurer wrote it, so soon after the German breakthrough on the Marne, evidence the deep friendship which lasted till death. It follows, with Alfy's medley of English and French, and his punctuation and spelling, in Mrs. Dana's version:

This terrible case of prickly-heat that has broken out on the continent over here is fierce. Everybody has had some kind of experience. I was caught in the country right on the line of mobilization, saw train loads of soldiers going to the front and never thought a thing about it. Was trying to work, thinking of painting, whenever any talked of war to me I was more than convinced it was impossible. Here I was   nights I could hear the trains going by more than usual, and over   night I was trapped.

Was misinformed at the mairie, the mayor was away and could not get back, his clerk was ignorant of my case until I called his attention to it on a poster which was put up around town. He looked through his papers and found a sauf-conduit, which stated I could not use the railroad and this was crossed out—"Il est informé qu'un service d'automobiles sera organisé les 2 et 3 jours de la mobilisation entre ――― et ―――. Il pourra utiliser gratuitement avec sa famille ce moyen de transport sur la présentation du présent sauf-conduit. Le Maire le renseignera sur le moment et le lieu ou il devra se trouver pour obtenir l'accès des automobiles."

I had to go to Epernay, 22 kilometres, no horses, no automobiles. I picked up an auto-taxi on the road   he come from Paris   taken a lady out to Reims and was on his way back—made a deal with him to take me to Epernay where I had to present my sauf-conduit to get a laisser-passer. He was a very decent chauffeur, told me he had two very good days and did not expect too much as I told him I was limited for money, which was the case.

Well, I got to Epernay, showed my sauf-conduit at the mairie, was told by a fresh youngster, "Yes, this is all right, you can return to Paris afoot." I knew my sauf-conduit had to be signed or something done to it so I sought out one of the officials who sent me to the officer in command of the railroad station, he sent me to another official where I found out I was three days too soon, I being a neutral. They were to appear the fifth day of mobilisation.

Here I was my chauffeur engaged to Paris, short of money; when I broke the news to him he was fine, told me not to worry to pay him the trip from Dormans to Epernay and back. I gave him lunch when we returned. He volunteered to take letters to Paris, which he did. He took one to the consulate and one to Lefebre-Foinet [*sic*]. He promised to return Thursday morning and take me to Epernay and back to Paris. When I knew war was declared I was convinced he could not use the highway because everything for the army and I not knowing if I could use the railroad the only thing to do was to try.

I got my ticket because the man knew me. When I got to Epernay the commander of the gare knew nothing of my case, had no understanding of my case. He called in an officer who asked me who I knew in 9 rue Falguière, fortunately he knew everyone I named and told me he was an architect so I got my laisser-passer; even with that I had difficulty in getting my ticket on account of the ticket agent never having seen a laisser-passer. When I got my tickets I almost destroyed them by mistake; here I am in Paris.

My chauffeur appeared one hour after I left, he followed me to Epernay, looked in the lunchroom and saw an old man in the opposite corner. He came to see me in Paris and I settled with him and hope to be of some service to him some day. He really was a white man. He got a document from the consul and some money from Lefebre-Foinet [*sic*].

Another rare record of Maurer's departure from France for the United States is a yellowed newspaper clipping, dated "1914" in his own handwriting but not sourced. Under the heading "Art News and Comment," it states:

Alfred Maurer, who in the old days, when he painted in a style that had a certain kinship to that used by the Frenchman Alfred Stevens, was generally praised by the critics, is now anathematized by them for being a post-impressionist. He has returned to America for his annual short visit.

His summer place in France is in the district near Rheims, and last autumn he had to vacate it in a hurry. After the Germans had retreated from his section of the country he made the journey out to his place to see what had become of his property. He found the kitchen wall had been knocked in, but otherwise the house had suffered little damage, although it had been much peppered with bullets and bits of shrapnel were embedded in his orchard trees. His paintings and his furniture were intact, but he deplores the loss of three fishing reels. Whether the Germans or the Allies got them of course he does not know.

Rumor has said that Maurer was ordered home from Paris by his father, on threat of having financial supplies cut off. This has been controverted, with the statement that Maurer had to return because he was a "German." Such an argument seems ill-founded. Maurer was an American-born citizen, the son of an American-born mother and a naturalized father. His own repugnance to all things German would have made it unlikely that he would be thought of as pro-German, despite a German name. Indeed, his own letter proves that his status as a neutral was recognized without question by the authorities.

That he was a coward to flee from war when he might have remained in France and enlisted for military service is another observation which has been made on what seem to be equally weak grounds. Maurer was only about five feet two inches in height, and in 1914 he was forty-six years old. The United States was not at war with Germany and would not be for almost three years. Perhaps if he had been so inclined, he would have been accepted for military duty; but it seems unlikely.

The final rumor, which like the rest cannot be substantiated at this distance of time and space, when two world wars have swept over Paris, is that Maurer had to leave behind him a sweetheart who committed suicide in despair at their separation. Some vital loss—whatever that loss was or when it took place—preyed on him. The memory of the lost one returned in the image of eyes forever staring which he painted again and again. Looking inward to remembrance, what face did Maurer see?

His old friend, Gertrude Stein, has a word to say about this, a casual, passing word, but a word spoken in friendliness. Together with the critical praise of 1913, this was to be the last kind word Maurer would know for many a year. Gertrude Stein and Alice B. Toklas had managed to return to Paris from England after the outbreak of war. Paris was deserted, or so it seemed. Expatriates were stranded, without ready cash, clamoring at their consulates, pleading to be transported safely "home." Carefree days were over. Paradise was lost to flaming war. An era of illusion had been shattered by the momentum of history. Those unaware of the surge of powerful forces might, or might not, wake from their dream to reality. Let Gertrude Stein end the incident:

> Everybody who had seemed so far away came to see us. Alfy Maurer described being on the Marne at his favorite village, he always fished the Marne, and the mobilization locomotive coming and the germans were coming and he was so frightened and he tried to get a conveyance and finally after terrific efforts he succeeded. As he left Gertrude Stein went with him to the door and came back smiling. Mrs. Whitehead said with some constraint, Gertrude you have always spoken so warmly of Alfy Maurer but how can you like a man who shows himself not only selfish but a coward and at a time like this. He thought only of saving himself and he after all was a neutral. Gertrude Stein burst out laughing. You foolish woman, she said, didn't you understand, of course Alfy had his girl with him and he was scared to death lest she should fall into the hands of the germans.

So Maurer escaped from the territory overrun by the "Boches" and returned as best he could to the safety of New York. If he had known what a no-man's-land of loneliness and bitterness *home* was to prove, would he have chosen the terrors of war? But choices after the event are futile.

Maurer fades into the lost years, baffling and inscrutable years of silence. He lived. He breathed. He ate. He slept. He worked. He amused himself. He knew joy and sorrow. Perhaps he loved, and perhaps he hated. Locked in time and in his unanswering memory lies the tale of this most hermetic chapter of his hermetic life.

NEW YORK

4. *Lost Years*

THESE were years of silence, years lost out of the memory of Maurer's life. Silent years, lost years, but not empty years, they are marked off in the book of years: 1915—finding a home, sinking roots. 1916—exhibiting again. 1917—a blow for independence, then his mother's death. Silence, and the slowly passing years. What filled them, save the immeasurable interminability of time? Shall we say an hour struck off the clock is an hour lived, or a meal consumed is grace added to life? What fills life with meaning when meaning has been snatched away? To endure, to survive, can these nourish the soul? Or does a soul so fed slowly starve and slowly die?

Maurer walked through the years silently. He saw friends, ate with them in New York, visited them in Westport, Tuckahoe, Babylon, Centerport, and elsewhere. He worked: paintings survive from these years. But he walked ghostlike. Recollection tells little of the outer face of his existence, nothing of its inner look. How did he seem to himself? He had come home from the warmth and gaiety of Paris. He had come home to New York in winter, snow in the gutters turning to gray slush, cold winds blowing through the streets. He had come home. What was home? A place he hung his hat. A place he slept. A place where friends sat on the bed to view his paintings. Home is where you hang your art, Alfy might have thought if that had been the day of such popular songs. Home is where you eat the bread of bitterness. Home is where a father of eighty-two tyrannizes over his children, grown to manhood and womanhood, themselves nearing the half-century mark. Home is where you remain a prisoner, bound by unbreakable chains of love, of hate, of pledged loyalty, of dependence, of inescapable custom. Home is that bondage you have been fleeing all your life, that bondage you can never escape until you place the knot around your neck and die.

What was the root of his dependence? Could inner uncertainty already be read in his face? Meredith wrote, "We are betrayed by what is false within." Was Alfred Maurer's need for love the bond which held him prisoner? The silent years do not answer. For their silence let a multitude of unspeaking eyes speak. Forever accusing, forever confronting, the women of his vision answer silently.

The era had been one of illusion; Maurer's escape was illusory. The artist in society, he learned by desperate education, is not a free agent. He is the child of the time and the place in which he is born. He is of as much value to the world as the world sets a value on him. He has work to sell; if there are no buyers, what shall he do? If he live by the fruit of his labor, as Maurer would in time have done, can he escape the twining ties of habit which nurtured his youth? In his middle years Maurer came back to those ties, returning to his native land and his home for refuge from war's disasters. He had believed himself free in Paris, by academic triumph and by aesthetic rebellion. He had found himself humanly in the Quarter's camaraderie. He would return to Paris when the war was over and take up that happy way of life. He would go back to his studio, back to his friends, back to his work, back to whatever felicity he had known there. He would be older and wiser than the boulevardier of Mahonri Young's statuette (page 62), but he would be free, free.

In the interim he took up residence in the family dwelling at 404 West Forty-third Street. He resumed habits of behavior and thought renounced twenty years earlier. *My son . . . doesn't paint the way I taught him,* a mocking whisper ran through the house. Torn away from familiar and friendly ties, bewildered, disori-

ALFRED H. MAURER, ABOUT 1914
A PHOTOGRAPH BY ALFRED STIEGLITZ
COLLECTION: MISS GEORGIA O'KEEFFE

LANDSCAPE: TREE, *ca.* 1916
OIL ON PAPER, MOUNTED ON CARDBOARD, 21½x18 IN.
COLLECTION: MISS RUTH M. LINDSAY

ABSTRACTION: FISHING, *ca.* 1919
OIL ON PAPER, MOUNTED ON CARDBOARD, 21¾x18 IN.
COLLECTION: MR. AND MRS. HUDSON D. WALKER

TWO SISTERS, *ca.* 1921–1923
OIL ON GESSO PANEL, 26¼x18 IN.
COLLECTION: E. WEYHE

ented, lonely, Maurer came to hoard anger and frustration, resentment and hatred. Hostile emotions gathered through the years until they burst out in annihilating action. He believed he would escape again. He would never escape.

Maurer cast about him for a tolerable way of life, temporary though he thought his stay in New York would be. He made a studio for himself in his third floor bedroom and there tried to work. That was not easy. Routines on which he had depended had been lost; his world was in fragments. Faith in the creative act of art must be great to engine artists in days of doom. Can one close eyes and ears and heart to the clamor of the destitute and the dispossessed? Perhaps. Even so, there is no wall so high that distant agony cannot be heard. If Maurer shut himself within a walled garden, nonetheless his soul was troubled—though but for personal reasons. Yet may we not believe also that he was a human being, not unpitying?

He returned to New York, carrying the one suitcase and the change of clothes with which he had fled Paris. He sought to find himself anew. Seeking to reorient himself, he laughed, made jokes, danced, enjoyed wine and spaghetti, and sauerbraten. At forty-six he was not, however, as youthful as he had been. The tempo of his life grew less staccato, his mood grimmer. No longer was he the debonair Alfy of *fin de siècle* Paris. His hair was growing thinner and graying at the temples. His mustache was less flamboyantly trimmed and trained, his eyes less devil-may-care. He was neat and spruce, but not the swashbuckling dandy. So Stieglitz saw him when Maurer visited "291" for companionship and comfort, and so Stieglitz photographed him in a portrait (page 127) more revealing than had yet been made.

Lacking the support of a congenial habit of life, he settled down in the family home which he had left behind long ago. He painted. He met friends, but for the most part outside of "404." When they did visit him there, they sat on the bed. He kept in touch with Fra Dana by correspondence. He saw Dove and the Fuhrs, Elsie and Ernest, whom he had known from art student days and from Paris. Later, when he had discovered the friendly Shady Brook boarding house at Marlboro-on-the Hudson, he made new friends who occasionally visited him on West Forty-third Street. Calling on the Phillipses at the Brevoort in 1915 or 1916, he painted a still life in their room. The subject is a small red Chinese vase with orange flowers, "very sketchy." So he made a bridge between France and America, such as he would continue to build at Shady Brook in *Landscape: Tree* (page 128) and related works.

As time went on, he made a life for himself outside the walls of "404." For long periods he lived with the Doves and the Fuhrs in Westport, and he visited the Phillipses at Tuckahoe and at Babylon, Long Island. At Centerport lived Mr. and Mrs. John L. Miller. Mrs. Miller was the sister of Belle Maurer, his brother Charles' wife. Alfy visited them also. When Dove moved from Westport to Long Island, Maurer spent much time with him at Halesite. After Maurer's death, his walnut bed and wood carving tools came to rest with Dove in the old farmhouse outside of Geneva, in the Dove Block skating rink, and finally in the former post office at Centerport to which Dove and Helen Torr Dove moved from upper New York state.

At Westport Maurer found the fun and excitement which were lacking in his cabined existence in New York. He went fishing with Dove. Young Bill Dove, not yet ten years old, was allowed to accompany them sometimes. Alfy carved and painted and gilded beautiful casting plugs, a few of which survive. These raise the wonder if it was toward sculpture he was tending. Alfy was hectic and gay, loud and boisterous, swearing every other word: he frightened the shy and reserved only child. The two painters who sacrificed success for conscience cherished a deep and mutual affection. In the years after Maurer's death, Dove never spoke of his friend except with deepest grief. He could have told much of Alfy's unwritten history; but remembrance was too painful.

Maurer and the illustrator, Ernest Fuhr, had been students together in New York, and they had taken up their friendship in Paris. Elsie Fuhr met Alfy in 1910, and the Fuhrs saw him there till 1912 when they came back to the United States and also after his own return. He was desperately unhappy because of the drastic change in his life. Soon after his return, they invited him to make his home with them—but on one condition, that all three must work—and he spent six or eight months with them in Westport. They got up at six every morning and started painting. Maurer went out sketching regularly, and he and Dove would invite the late Henry Raleigh, well known illustrator and member of the Westport colony, to go along when they went fishing. Alfy began to regain his gaiety and bounce; and he would go into nearby Saugatuck's Italian quarter to bring back his favorite spaghetti, macaroni, cheese and wine. In the 1920s his preference persisted. When he took friends made at Marlboro out to dinner, it was to the old West Houston Street Italian restaurant, Passerini's.

He sketched and painted. Working mornings and afternoons, he would turn out two or three pictures a day. His facility worried Dove, a meticulous craftsman and careful workman. He often told Alfy that he was too facile, that he should study more and take greater pains with his work. In the feverish heat of work Maurer used any materials at hand. He painted on newsprint with oil paints thinned with kerosene oil, not the most permanent medium, but perhaps at that time sympathetic to the rapid tempo of his emotions. Sometimes there would be heated discussions between Dove and Maurer: should a line be black or should it be red. Maurer drew with color: red suited his purpose as well as black. Dove drew in India ink, using the Waterman fountain pen designed for artists, and filled in his semi-abstract areas with a wash of water color. He saw the line as a line, a free flow of linear statement, not as the containing outline for a form. So the two friends differed, but remained staunch in their devotion.

They differed, too, about the frames Alfy made. Dove, always careful and conscientious in his work, made his own frames, also. He took great pains, however, to miter corners exactly and to finish the wood neatly and appropriately, in color or in aluminum or bronze paint. Maurer knocked his frames together in as great haste as he painted. The late Charles Prendergast criticized Maurer's handiwork; apparently his carpentry did not come up to the consummate craftsmanship of his cabinetmaker grandfather. Yet Alfy's frames, like their maker, have a whimsical if impatient note. For his boyhood friend Riz he created a special design, carving a peach at the top of every frame: *she was* (Alfy said) *such a peach*. The American rhythm is here, as it is in Maurer's rare letters, and as it is, also, in the letters and other writings of Dove. Their native overtones, as authentic as Mark Twain, surely endeared to them both that folklorist, Sherwood Anderson, whom Maurer first met at Westport with Dove.

The memory of simple, enduring, homely experiences persisted in Maurer's transitional *Abstraction: Fishing* (see page 129). Painted in oils on paper, this recaptures the excitement the fisherman-artist felt as he saw the fish rise to his lure. Maurer followed his quarry in rushing brooks, whose tumbling motion he mirrored in paintings like this and one not located, *Tango-minnow*, exhibited at the Independent's in 1920. This kind of painting and this kind of subject, simple in color scheme and hurried in stroke, ends one phase of his work. At Marlboro he became a student of nature and gave up sporting activities. Probably his first efforts to paint again had to deal with the familiar and comprehensible, in easily handled mediums and sizes. His energy might well have been limited: he was discouraged and lonely. Perhaps all he could do, in terms of available physical and moral strength, was to paint hastily on small pieces of paper and trust that what he said would prove of more interest than material or size.

In 1915 or 1916 Maurer found a new home for himself at Shady Brook, the Schramm and Ormsby boarding house on the old post road outside of Marlboro, which took its name from the dammed-up stream on whose pond guests amused themselves, swimming in the summer and ice skating in the winter. The Caywoods had bought the farm in 1874, and the late Mrs. Frederick W. Schramm, Sr. (as she was after her second marriage) had begun her summer vacation business in the 1890s. The main house stands today as it did when Maurer first went there, and members of the family are still managing the boarding house. An old register, on the first line, is headed by Maurer's name and the date "February 12, 1919." But Alfy had gone there earlier, as is proved by landscapes he painted in 1916 and 1917. Why he went there in the first place, no one seems to know. His parents and sister had gone for a number of years to Stamford in the Catskills. However Maurer happened to go to Marlboro in the first instance, he continued to go there because he loved the people and the surroundings. He spent every summer at Shady Brook till his death; and his friend, the painter William F. Waltemath, planned to take Alfy to Marlboro early in August, 1932, only to learn of his suicide from newspaper headlines.

Marlboro is in the heart of a small fruits section. The strawberries and the raspberries are ready to pick the first and second weeks of June, and then the currants. Apples, grapes, and peaches ripen in the fall. This is also a wine country, some of the best New York state vintages being made nearby. Settled in 1734, the village dates back to "Yankee" strains in the westward movement. Like all America, Marlboro has felt the effects of change. In 1913 an Italian family came there, and soon a new immigration was under way. The Italian-Americans began to buy farms and to plant tomatoes, a big crop today. Even in Maurer's time, the rolling hillsides which slope down to the Hudson were terraced; and the terrain has a look not unlike rural France and Italy. No doubt Alfy returned there year after year because the land had the look of that French countryside where he had been happy and free.

At Marlboro he was happier perhaps than anywhere else during his American years. Six open-air bungalows stood in a row—"Rotten Row"—behind the farmhouse; and Alfy had one of these all the years he spent at Shady Brook. Each was a one-room affair with the upper half open but screened and furnished with canvas awnings to be rolled down as shelter from driving rain. The bungalows were frankly meant for summer use only; but Maurer made his a half-year residence, coming up from New York late in April or early in May and remaining until after Election Day. Wild morning glories covered his bungalow.

The routine of his Shady Brook existence was regular and consistent. For years his place was at the head of the long table which stood at the right of the fireplace, set from east to west. His armchair was at the end opposite the fireplace. Here, promptly at 8 A.M., Maurer opened the day for Shady Brook, as it were officially, seating himself for his breakfast and playing host to the guests. After he had eaten, he would walk up to the village for his New York paper (no one recalls what paper it was). On the way he would meet the neighborhood children going to school, if it was the season for school, and they would walk along in a merry group.

Then he would go out sketching, painting furiously and continuously. After the break for the midday meal, he would go back to work at once, lugging his campstool and sketchbox to the trap-rock quarry, or up along Shady Brook to the old mill, or scouting over nearby fields and hillsides. Then the evening meal, and rest and relaxation. He would go down to the ice-cream parlor-*cum*-drugstore at the corner of Main Street and Western Avenue and sketch the customers, or he would bring in five or six girls and treat them. Alfy liked plain vanilla ice-cream best. Or he would sit evenings and talk with Mrs. Schramm and her mother, the late Mrs. Ormsby, who had started the boarding house in the 1890s. "Bonna," the elder woman, was his confidant. No doubt she could have answered many questions about his inner life.

So much a part of Shady Brook did Maurer become that he always left his summer painting kit there when he returned to the city for the winter. When he first went to Marlboro, board and room was $12 a week; but he was given a special rate of $10 a week, almost like a member of the family. Long after rates had to go up, he paid this modest sum. Finally when rising costs made it necessary to raise the rate for him also, the proprietors were much distressed. Today visible memorials of Alfy are few—the pond, the bridge, the view toward the quarry. The bungalows were torn down some years ago; and the old tartarian cherry trees have been cut down. Yet dearly is the remembrance of Alfy treasured by his adopted family. Only in the spring of 1948 did the present owner, Edith Caywood Meckes, a daughter of Mrs. Schramm by her first marriage, give away his old painting coat and the paints and blank compoboard panels which he had left behind him when he went away—forever, it proved—in the fall of 1931.

II

STRENGTHENED and encouraged by old friends and by the pleas-ant new associations of Shady Brook, Maurer began to resume his oldtime routine of painting and exhibiting. Opportunities for exhibition were not plentiful for modern artists, especially with the interruptions caused by the war. Early in 1916, he was invited to show in the Forum Exhibition. He had taken his father to Atlantic City to recover from illness, and Stieglitz wrote him post-chaise for work to enter and a four-hundred-word statement of his aims in painting. On February 4, Alfy replied characteristically:

Four hundred words to explain my aims when they were never to write, not even letters.

I can't do it, so if this wont interfer with my exhibiting I will be delighted.

I suppose Daniels will let you have what you want of my pictures, and if you use ordinary frames whatever expense you go to for me I'll settle on my return.

You see I thought I was caught in America, but worse, now I'm caught in Atlantic City, a dry town. A thirst for whiskie is is hell, but no whiskie for a drink is hell too.

Well, my father is getting better & I'm getting sicker.

They had a big fire here last night, as soon as I get out they can burn the whole damned town

Am coming in to see you as soon as I get back

As ever

A H Maurer

Did Stieglitz relish Maurer's thirst for whisky? Or was it in his later years that the prophet of An American Place subsisted on hot water, lemon juice, and sugar at the Woman's Exchange on Madison Avenue?

Regardless of Maurer's lack of ambition to be a writer, the Forum Exhibition catalogue did contain a note by Maurer. Perhaps a literary friend helped him. Dove took only a quarter of his allotted four hundred words, but Maurer filled a page. The exhibition was held from March 13 to March 25 in the Anderson Galleries at 15 East Fortieth Street; and an elaborate brochure was published, with explanatory notes from the artists repre-sented, except for Marguerite Zorach. Her note was omitted when it came time to print the catalogue because there was not enough paper, or so she was told. Each artist was represented by one re-production and Maurer's was *In The Vineyard* (page 101), a painting which he subsequently gave to E. Weyhe and which for years has hung over the head of Weyhe's bed. This painting was also shown in 1917 in the first exhibition of the Society of Independent Artists.

Besides Maurer, the artists were Ben Benn, Thomas H. Benton, Oscar Bluemner, Andrew Dasburg, Arthur G. Dove, Marsden Hartley, S. Macdonald Wright, John Marin, Henry L. McFee, George F. Of, Man Ray, Morgan Russell, Charles Sheeler, A. Walkowitz, and William and Marguerite Zorach. "What Is Modern Painting?" inquired critic Willard Huntington Wright in a long essay; and there were forewords by the members of the jury of selection, Christian Brinton, Robert Henri, W. H. de B. Nelson, Alfred Stieglitz, John Weichsel, and W. H. Wright. Apparently none of these are condensed to make space for the lone woman exhibitor. *Arts and Decorations* commented on the literary apparatus displayed for an exhibition which attacked literature in painting.

Maurer's note was signed *Alfred Maurer,* without the middle initial. It read:

> My main concern in painting is the beautiful arrangement of color values—that is, harmonized masses of pigment, more or less pure.
>
> For this reason, it is impossible to present an exact transcription of nature, for the color masses in nature are broken up by many minute color notes which tend to eliminate the mass effect. Consequently, I often use the dominating color in a natural object, and ignore the minor notes. By this process the natural *effect* is retained, and at the same time the picture becomes a color entity divorced from mere representation: and I have acquired a volume of color which will take its place in the conception of the picture. This, of course, would be lost if all the details were truthfully set down: the many inconsequent aspects of an object would detract [sic] the eye from the final and pure effect of the work.
>
> In order that I may express myself through the medium of color alone, I have eliminated, as far as possible, the sombre effect of black masses, and have keyed my pictures to a high articulation, so that the reaction to them will be immediate and at the same time joyous and understandable. Black, I believe, has a deadening effect in a pure color gamut, and I am trying to express the emotional

significance of a scene without it, for pure colors are more moving than black, which is a negation of color.

It is necessary for art to differ from nature, or we would at once lose the *raison d'être* of painting. Perhaps art should be the intensification of nature; at least, it should express an inherent feeling which cannot be obtained from nature except through a process of association. Nature, as we all know, is not consciously composed; and therefore it cannot give us a pure aesthetic emotion. I believe that the artist who paints before nature should order his canvases; and in doing this he is unable to adhere exactly to the scene before him. The principles of organization and form, which animated the older painters, must not be ignored. They form the true basis for artistic appreciation. But the modern men can make use of these principles through a different medium. He can find a new method of presentation.

The artist must be free to paint his effects. Nature must not bind him, or he would have to be more interested in the subject-matter before him than in the thing he feels need [*sic*] expression. In my case, where I am interested in the harmonic relation of color volumes, I consider the tonal values first. That is why my pictures differ from the scene which they might seem to represent.

Maurer's formalism was challenged about this time. "The symbol is everything," wrote a reviewer, "and since we do not understand the symbol, our pleasure in the art is limited to the amount of pleasure we are capable of receiving from an obviously calculated arrangement of colors." To Maurer's "post-impressionist" landscapes the review conceded "a kind of simplicity in these apparently inchoate forms and these blobs of strong blues and yellows." It was not the simplicity of a beginner, however, but the simplicity of full sophistication. In conclusion, though willing to grant "a high degree of intellectuality to Mr. Maurer's theory of art," the reviewer asked "if science carried as far as he wishes to carry it can produce the emotion essential to art."

Despite unfavorable criticism, Maurer continued to practice intransigent principles as he had in the Paris secession. He exhibited with the *avant-garde* Forum group, and he affiliated with the Society of Independent Artists. Neither action helped him

conciliate an art world hostile to modern manners. Thus he continued in the forefront of a movement indispensable for needed
change. The history of American art shows how insurgency has
periodically revivified creative effort: in 1825, the National Academy of Design in protest against Trumbull—in 1877, the Society
of American Artists to offset the Academy—in the 1900s, renewed
revolt against academicism. When the Society of American Artists
amalgamated with the Academy in 1906, George Luks refused
election. Now new forces for revolt were needed.

For a generation art rebellion followed two channels, symbolized
by "The Eight" and by Stieglitz. The first was the inheritor of the
native tradition of naturalism, moving from nineteenth century
landscape to city scenes as urban life became the dominant twentieth century culture. The second channeled Europe's aesthetic
rebellion into the American stream. Three days before the United
States declared war on Germany in 1917, the Society of Independent Artists opened its first exhibition. America's entrance
into the war put a period to the Stieglitz program; his gallery was
closed, and *Camera Work* suspended publication. The former
movement was democratic and inclusive, the latter anti-democratic
and exclusive. Almost willy-nilly, Maurer took part in both.

The Independent's had been organized the year before, to provide more exhibition opportunities for artists, with William
Glackens as first president. It was to be no-jury, admission being
contingent only on the payment of a small exhibitor's fee. Critic
Henry McBride, an early friend of modern art, hailed it: "It is
impossible for any Academy, whether royal or democratic, to be
a proper guide for the young." When its first exhibition opened
on April 3, 1917, it filled the two main floors of the Grand Central Palace: myriad paintings hung on four hundred screens. At
the close of the exhibition, the society faced a deficit of $10,000.
The outbreak of war (not foreseen by the artists, probably) cut
down attendance; and expected income from admission fees did
not materialize. The next year John Sloan took over the office of
president, which he held till the society was dissolved at the outset
of World War II. Among the first directors were Walter Pach,
Charles E. Prendergast, George Bellows, Homer Boss, Katherine S.
Dreier, Marcel Duchamp, Regina A. Farrelly, Arnold Friedman,

Charles W. Hawthorne, Rockwell Kent, John Marin, Man Ray, and Maurice Sterne.

"Dissenters who offered the butcher, baker and candlestick maker a chance to display his wares," the Independent's were called. The society actually played a useful role in providing encouragement and incentive for the young and unknown. Not till the Federal Art Project gave employment to some thousands of artists in the mid-1930s did American society create a broader base for art. Great were the difficulties the Independent's met the next year in finding a hall, with 1917's $10,000 deficit overshadowing their laudable program. The exhibition committee thought of Central Park when no hall was available, or a large circus tent. Finally a vacant store was found. In later years the taboo broke down, and exhibitions were held at the Waldorf roof.

The Independent's set a precedent for subsequent groups. Holger Cahill, who later was the Federal Art Project's national director, worked with the society on various publicity schemes, including a Teapot Dome expose, a Josh Nolan stunt, and the hoax in which Maurer took part, painting and sculpturing works for the alleged Indian culture called "Inje-Inje." Later Cahill put his experience with the Independent's to use in a mammoth exhibition he directed in the depths of the depression; this was at Rockefeller Center, then almost completed, and a mile of pictures was hung, gathered by the democratic no-jury system under the auspices of the Salons of America. Washington Square's well-advertised outdoor art fair was another instance of the power of example. In the late 1930s the American Artists Congress, the Artists Union, and other organizations availed themselves of vacant stores on occasion when museums and galleries were not available for their exhibitions. So the Independent's simple platform of exhibition opportunity continued to be of influence.

For Maurer the society was a valuable tie with the outer world. On his return to the United States he had been prostrated with grief and despair. About the time he began to paint once more, Stieglitz closed his gallery. What would Maurer have done through a long, lonely period if he had not had the opportunity at least once a year to exhibit his paintings? After he became a director in 1919, he plunged into the society's activities. He carried and hung paintings, and he made linoleum cuts for posters and invitations, one of which was reproduced in the old *World's* picture section in 1920. Here he found an American version of the Latin Quarter's gaiety and informality.

Maurer exhibited with the Independent's every year from 1917 through 1932, the year of the "swap" exhibition in which he showed *George Washington* (page 239). In 1933 the Independent's seventeenth annual exhibition included a memorial group of Maurer's work. If the exhibition records were detailed, they would no doubt fill in gaps in his artistic evolution. However, entry cards were thumbtacked onto the back of paintings and thus easily detached or lost. Catalogues were not exact as regards titles, and not every artist could afford to pay for a reproduction or cared to do so. Maurer's entries read, interminably, *Head, Head, Head.* Fortunately his painting in the first exhibition was reproduced, and fortunately *In The Vineyard* (page 101) has survived, since it is one of the rare Maurers with a provenance. For a few years father Maurer and brother Charles also exhibited in the Independent's, perhaps as a heckling device for the family's artistic black sheep. In 1917 Louis Maurer showed *The Scout's Salute* and *Rocky Mountain Wild Sheep,* evidently from his Wild West period.

Thus Alfred Maurer began to reestablish himself, working, exhibiting and making a personal life of a sort. If there was a solid emotional center of gravity for his existence, that remains mysterious. Yet with such a daily routine as he had evolved, Maurer filled his days. He was getting back on his feet, spiritually and morally. The inner battles of his soul might yet be won.

III

DEATH and bereavement broke off his life again. On December 16, 1917, his mother died. Only two months before Louisa Stein Maurer and her husband had celebrated their fifty-seventh wedding anniversary. She was a quiet woman, and her life is unrecorded. Alfy loved her dearly: his visits home during his Paris years were for her sake, and for her sake he sought to root himself in America, if but temporarily. How often she arbitrated between father and son, none say. She kept the house, she made a home, Maurer had roots there. With her death his roots were cut, it might be thought. For months he vanished from his accustomed round. No one saw him. No one knew what he thought or felt. His mother had died. He seemed to die.

Was it on her deathbed that the final bond was bound about his life? Maurer loved his mother and believed that his father tyrannized over her, as the son thought the father did over his children. In the home and in the family Alfy was his mother's partisan, as his sister was perhaps her father's. When Louisa Stein Maurer lay dying, she entreated her son to promise he would never leave his father; so the story runs. It is a credible explanation for Maurer's long-continued, seeming dependency on Louis Maurer. If it is true, the deathbed vow was fulfilled in death.

The sadness of little things, of trivial details, of small meaningless incidents nonetheless meaningful, runs through the Maurer tragedy. Louisa Stein Maurer was a kind and faithful wife and a loving and just mother. Her will, dated June 3, 1913, and proved January 2, 1918, attests her as one who had no favorites among her children. Secretly she may have loved one most. When legal formalities were completed, her gross estate was $10,251.48, divided equally among Charles, Alfred and Eugenia. Eugenia Maurer Fuerstenberg was named sole executrix; and the will was witnessed by A. W. and Babette Venino.

Personal bequests are revealing. First, to her son, Alfred, "residing in Paris, France" at the time the will was drawn, she gave and bequeathed her mantel clock, "purchased from A. Frankfeld and Company," and her diamond ring. To her daughter-in-law, Belle Maurer, she left an onyx top brass lamp table, and to Charles the silverware she had "received from Mr. Heppenheimer as a silver wedding present and the golden cup . . . received as a golden wedding present." Eugenie Furstenberg (so the name is spelled in the will) was given the silverware Mrs. Maurer had had from her mother, as well as Louisa Maurer's diamonds, jewelry and wearing apparel and "the cabinet which was made by [her] husband's father for table linen and silverware and the serving table also made" by John Maurer. Her grandson, Alfred Louis

Maurer, received a cash bequest of $500. So Louisa Maurer apportioned her earthly treasures, in a pitiable last casting up of accounts intertwined with grief.

In his sorrow Maurer would care little for such details. To settle his wife's estate Louis Maurer deposed that he owned the house in which they lived and all its furniture and that the contents of the safe deposit box belonged to him "except Fifty (50) shares of stock of the New York Pie Baking Company . . . and . . . a gold medal and a $100.00 United States government second Liberty Loan Bond, which belonged to [his] son Alfred." When the estate was finally settled, Alfred received the clock (appraised at $5), the ring (appraised at $140) and $2,711.40. His small inheritance had come down through his mother from his grandfather Jacob Stein, who died in 1887, leaving his property to his wife Catherine for her life and then to his four children. His estate had included two houses, at 328 and 344 West Seventeenth Street.

During the months when he vanished from the sight and knowledge of his friends, what did Maurer do? Perhaps it was at that time that he made the atypical sketches in water color and gouache which are "sports" in his *oeuvre*. Perhaps he wandered about the city and sought comfort in a stranger's eyes. Perhaps he rode in the subway and stared about him numbly, dazed. Outside himself he may have found tangible, concrete reality, at which to clutch, to which to cling. His notes were never developed; and there are not many of them: An old woman in black with a shapeless black hat perched high on her head. A Negro, black coat buttoned high about his neck, chin dropped on his breast, black hat with downturned brim shading all his face except nostrils and mouth. A man reading a newspaper, in profile, pork pie hat of an earlier mode atop close-cut hair. A girl with round horn-rimmed spectacles, a female Charlie Chaplin, a Cinderella, swollen as if with mumps, clipped in a boyish bob. These fragments of reality he saw and noted. They did not sink deep into his mind or heart; yet somehow they lingered in his memory. A decade later he used their remembered faces as an argument when he was reproached for painting such odd abstract heads. "Don't you ride in the subway?" he asked.

A day would come when sorrow twice befell. Did the sweetheart left behind in Paris die by her own hand? When was this? Who was she? Rumor is contradictory. The answers are locked in Alfy's breast, or in the hearts of old friends who choose silence to revelation. Alfy was dining at Redding Kelly's, with Paris intimates. He had his mail sent there, to keep it safe from prying eyes. The post came. Letters were placed on a salver and handed around. Maurer opened his. It told of the suicide or disappearance of that mysterious woman of whom Gertrude Stein wrote. A last bond was made: he could never go back to that well loved studio where she had waited for him. Would he ever go back to Paris? He never did, although he thought it was but a question of time till he would be free to do so. Failing to return, he wanted to bring his hundreds of paintings from the rue Falguière studio to New York. Always afterward Maurer expressed bitterness because his father would not help underwrite the expense.

Maurer's roots had been cut: they did not die at once, and they never died completely. New tendrils struck out for a new existence, fed on loneliness and hate. Again Maurer struggled to find a way of life. He created this in incessant industry and experiment. At the end he transcended technic; but for a time technical research was his salvation, as to fix his gaze on external reality had been.

IV

FOR MAURER the rupture of war and personal bereavement was almost incurable. He was older than the lost generation, and he was not one of the bright young things. He could not find a way out of an historical impasse in dadaist-surrealist anarchy. He had invested his life in an act of faith. Now faith must sustain him. Faith nourished him for many a long lonely year.

Painting was Maurer's life, as his days at Marlboro show. In a frenzy of work and technical investigation he turned out hundreds of penciled sketch-maps for paintings made after he began to practice Jay Hambidge's dynamic symmetry system. Hambidge had been in Paris about 1900, and Maurer knew him there. In

1921 Hambidge began to issue lessons in loose sheets, complete
with drawings, exercises and diagrams, not unlike the *Q.E.F.*s and
the *Q.E.D.*s of high school geometry. An incomplete set survives
in the Maurer papers. Why an artist of Maurer's experience and
flair should have hoped to solve his problems by mechanical means
is a question. Yet the arguments were seductive, and they enticed
many another American painter, including George Bellows.

Maurer used the Hambidge formulas, however, before Hambidge began to publish his correspondence course in 1921. His
early abstractions, such as the fishing subject illustrated (page
129) and *Tango-minnow,* are not obviously built on mathematical
designs. Construction lines are, however, visible in a series of
heads in water colors and gouache, one of which is dated 1920.
Sketching around Marlboro, Maurer made rapid field notes on
previously prepared pads, ruled off into geometrical patterns
recommended by Hambidge. In a water color and gouache on
another theme, *Mannequin,* the construction lines are not apparent. They show to the naked eye in a drawing, *Two Girls.*
Maurer was seeking aesthetic solutions by slide rule, as it were.
He was also experimenting with mediums and materials as a
means to aesthetic salvation, or was it personal salvation? He made
gesso grounds with rabbit's skin glue and dental plaster, and he
made home-made water colors and pastels. He might have tried
his hand at making paper, if Dard Hunter had not set up his well
known handmade paper manufactory in the old mill farther up
Shady Brook. In Westport Maurer ground colors between carving
casting plugs, and possibly in Marlboro between sketching. For
years his friend Dove ground his own colors, made his oils and
water colors and rolled uneven sticks of pastel.

Maurer's fondness for decorative costume suggested abstractions
like *Mannequin.* He had no wife for whom to pick out hats, but
he could window shop along Fifth Avenue with his women friends
and admire the window displays. Plate glass has a fascination for
the contemporary eye from the French photographic master Atget
to today: reflections in glass are as exciting now as reflections in
water were to the impressionists and Debussy. Maurer turned
men and women in absurd headgear into manikins, painting them
rapidly in modulated complementary colors. A stylized man poses

for a hat model and a couple pose in the latest numbers. In these the critics who berated Alfy for his "Frenchness" have a case; these paintings have the chic of French advertising art. It is unlikely that Maurer was influenced by the poster art of Cassandre; he anticipated it.

While he worked at his lesson sheets, he experimented with color, abandoning traditional divisionism for the color wheel. On a piece of thin cardboard he painted a circle about four and a half inches in diameter, which is divided into twenty-four segments, painted with swatches of pigment. The following colors have been used, if the segments are listed in clock-wise sequence from an arbitrary point. Maurer's abbreviations, spelling and punctuation follow:

Ch. Med. & Ch. Orange; Chrom. Or.; Harrison Red & Or. Ch.; Harrison Red; Harrison R & Garance; Scarlet Lake; Alaz. Crimson; Aliz. Crimson & White; Gar.; Ul. R & Gar.; Ul. B. & Gar.; Spectrum Violet; Ulta. & Garan.; Ulta B.; Cob. B.; Prussian Blue; Prussian B (and) Vert. Emeraude; V. Em. & Per. G.; Vert Emeraude; Emer. G.; Per. Green; Per. G. & Cad. M.; Zinc Yel; Chrom. Med.

To find the complementary for a given color, the painter had simply to take the color directly opposite on the wheel. By counting to the twelfth following color, the reader may do the same. Advocates of permanent pigments may feel a certain horror at Maurer's palette.

He also experimented with building boards like beaver board, Upson board, Pabco board and Homasote. He probably used these because they are cheap and easy to handle. If there was no audience for his work, why stretch canvas? In the old Paris days canvas had been expensive, and he had tacked cardboard on a stretcher instead. It was probably too much work to tack the compoboard panels on stretchers; or perhaps the cost of stretchers was a consideration. He covered the panels, for the most part, with the ground already described. Today the unreinforced panels are often warped, and their ground has cracked or flayed off. Many of them show deterioration of paint, as reported in the section, Maurer's Painting Technics. A common flaw is spotting or "freckling" of the surface, as the pigments seem to "bleed" or "bubble" from airholes in the gesso. He also covered the panels with assorted materials, such as canvas over which he applied the gesso, and bed ticking. Later he used oil cloth, in white, black and pink solid colors, and women's dress fabrics of silk or cotton, in plain colors and in figured designs.

Materials and methods aside, Maurer was primarily concerned with the act of painting. He roamed the countryside, to return to nature as a first principle. He painted variations on a theme, using for subjects the physical world about him. The pond and the dam, the old tartarian cherry trees behind the boarding house, the dance hall, the driveway to the Buckley place (by that time the Goudy place), Buckley's Bridge, a Japanesque footbridge over the brook which led to Dard Hunter's paper mill, these were familiar themes within a stone's throw. He ranged more widely to paint nearby farmhouses and barns, the road to the village and the road to the quarry, high tension wires from Highland, a model T Ford in front of the garage. In spring, summer and fall, he painted minutiae of changing seasons—raspberry bushes ripe for the pickers, corn shocks in the harvested fields, snow on rolling hillsides. Thus he painted the world of Marlboro, as Mount made the sights and scenes of Setauket his "little Italy."

From nature he went to humanity, to the little girls of Italian extraction who picked berries on the hillsides. He painted them without their knowledge, sad-eyed and weary, as documentary photographers later recorded migrant farm workers in the West. They were "like desert flowers," wrote Sherwood Anderson, "flashing into quick beauty" but also mirroring "life twisted, beaten down." When he began to paint these pathetic young girls about 1919 or 1920, he found an outlet for the pathos of his own life. In the same compassionate mood he painted the Shady Brook domestic assistants. One is Claudia, a maid who cleaned his bungalow. Local legend was that she had stabbed her husband in a quarrel, but not seriously. Alfred pretended to be afraid to stay in the bungalow with her, a sample of his humor. Most assuredly he was not frightened of Claudia, as the warm sympathy with which he portrayed her shows. He painted her again, more abstractly: a victim of work and economic insecurity whom he recognized and understood.

He painted many still lifes in tempera and gouache and in oil. Flowers and fruits and the rich harvest of the earth were his theme —beauty of growth, loveliness of the function of living, endurance of organic and biochemical life. At Shady Brook, a bowl of flowers or of fruit always stood on the dining room table. At night Alfy seized this still life triumphantly and triumphantly carried it away to paint the next day. Dahlias and zinnias came from a garden up the road, and roses and various garden posies from Mrs. Schramm's back lawn. Again and again he painted these, with home-grown apples, plums, grapes, pears and little green acorn squashes. Sometimes the garden pinks tired and drooped; he did not.

His paintings began to make an appearance in the world. Each year Maurer sent one or two of his latest to the annual exhibition of the Society of Independent Artists. In 1918 he entered two still lifes, not illustrated in the catalogue or identified. Brother Charlie sent *Mildred* and *Cover Design* and Louis Maurer *Glimpse of the Wild West* and *Maine Moose*. In 1919 Maurer was represented by two unidentified landscapes, and his father by *Fur and Feathers*. Of the latter a reviewer said: "there is no doubt in Louis Maurer's painting . . . that foxes and birds are the subjects. Mr. Maurer is said to paint but one picture a year, and that for the Independent's exhibition. He is now at work on next year's." Apparently *papa* worked hard; in 1920 he showed two items, *Disputed Rights* and *Elk*. That year Charles made his last appearance, with *Landscape* and *The Golden Girl*. Alfy exhibited *Tango-minnow*, from its reproduction a gay, dashing number.

Meanwhile the heckling continued. "Why don't you go to the opening of the Independent's?" asked a young friend, herself a painter. "Every time I go there I find my father in front of my painting, shaking his fists and cursing." Louis Maurer continued to act as his son's severest critic. The legend is multiform. The father would go into his son's bedroom-*cum*-workroom and take the brush out of Maurer's hand to improve his work. He would climb a stepladder and peer through the transom to see what Alfy was doing. He would go into the room, to stand in front of Alfy's paintings and vituperate them. "For fifteen years," Maurer told Holger Cahill as they were hanging the 1922 Independent's, "not a living soul has said a kind word about my pictures." The pleasure of exhibiting in the same show with Alfy soon exhausted itself. In 1921 Louis Maurer showed for the last time, exhibiting *Moose* and *Nocturne,* while for the first time Maurer showed work in the "Girl" series, his two entries each being entitled *Head.* The one illustrated in the Independent's catalogue is related to the *Girl* (page 163) reproduced here. Thereafter Maurer had the field to himself, as far as the Independent's were concerned.

Maurer had already made the acquaintance of E. Weyhe and his right-hand man Carl Zigrosser. Today Weyhe does not recall exactly how the meeting came about; but it came about through Weyhe's interest in Maurer's work, that is certain. On August 31, 1921, Alfy wrote Zigrosser from Marlboro:

> Thanks many times for the check.
>
> Some day soon I may run in to see you for a few minutes, haven't finished up here yet, expect to do some more painting. The best time is coming. Have been having trouble with the paint for the last few weeks. But that's all in a life time some times it goes and some times it don't and when it don't it don't and when it does it does, and that's that.
>
> My best to every body in the place and greese me on Mr. Weyhe when you write him same to you
>
> > As ever
> >
> > Alf

His deliberate misspelling of the German greeting, *grüss,* is symptomatic. No wonder he had been having trouble with the paint, considering the unorthodox technical stunts he attempted.

In 1922 Weyhe bought his first Maurer, the *Girl* (page 163) reproduced. Times were hard. The inflationary prosperity which followed World War I had begun to collapse. Bankruptcies were common; and artists felt the effects of the receding economic tide. Mitchell Kennerley, Stieglitz, and others organized an auction of works by living American artists of the modern persuasion, which was held at the Anderson Galleries on February 23. Maurer showed four of his heads, all oils. Which the veteran bookseller-art dealer bought is not known; but it was one of these, and it brought $125, no doubt a high price for a Maurer in those times.

The silent years were drawing to a close. Names and dates begin to appear again in the Maurer story. About 1920 or 1921 he was painting the backs of his panels a bright red, a "barn red," someone has said, but more likely a light cadmium red. In 1922 he attended the Independent's ball, as well as contributing to a "collaborative" panel of thirty-two silk six-inch squares, each painted by a well known artist. The panel was the front part of a costume worn by Nat Smolin. Others contributing were Bellows, William and Marguerite Zorach, Sloan, Glackens, Henri, Stuart Davis, Al Frueh, Zoltan Hecht, Walter Pach, Theresa Bernstein, Niles Spencer, and Henry Schnakenberg. Alfy danced as gaily as any, but what he wore the records do not tell.

In 1922 Maurer exhibited two heads at the Independent's, and in 1923 each of his two entries was called *Head*. About this year he took a trip to Nassau with Redding Kelly, but again the records are silent. Modern art began to win a hearing. Andrew Dasburg, one of the sixteen artists in the Forum Exhibition, was writing on "Cubism—Its Rise and Influence." A coexhibitor of Maurer's, Dasburg did not mention Alfy at all, though he discussed Sheeler, Man Ray, Hartley, McFee, Marin, Wheelock, Demuth and Max Weber. Was Maurer completely forgotten?

He was soon to be rediscovered. Suddenly a miracle befell him. Thus this decade begun with tears was to close joyfully. Early in 1924 E. Weyhe used his commissions from a "sell-out" of Arthur B. Davies' water colors to purchase the contents of Maurer's studio. Would recognition and success come to Maurer after silence and neglect? In the years remaining could he heal old wounds of loss and loneliness, regain the fire of youthful hope, rebuild his shattered life?

5. *Rediscovery*

ON JANUARY 8, 1924, a miracle befell Maurer, working in silence and loneliness. He was almost fifty-six; only now did he receive tangible encouragement—the first he had had since he returned to the United States. Incredibly, miraculously, E. Weyhe offered to buy the contents of Maurer's studio and to hold an exhibition the next week. Off went a wire to Sherwood Anderson, asking for an introduction to the catalogue; and artist and entrepreneur hurried to the printer. Maurer was to be presented to the world in all the excitement and interest of an artist who had labored for ten years without recognition. Was the long blockade of neglect ended?

Probably there are no miracles. The Weyhe miracle, as Alfy truly felt the sale to be, did not miraculously win understanding for his work. The art press seized on sensational news angles—"shotgun" purchase, "hurry-up" exhibition, "human interest" features in Maurer's history, girls whose haunting sadness he painted incessantly, eclat lent by Sherwood Anderson. In a week Maurer had been given more space than he had had in years. Columns of press notices recalled the glowing academic triumphs of long ago—Carnegie in 1901, Buffalo, St. Louis, Liège and Munich, and the salons of Paris, Berlin and London. Headlines did not, however, win quick appreciation for Maurer's painting. Aesthetically speaking, he was still ahead of his time. Ten years had passed since the Armory Show, and the walls of Jericho were crumbling, but not for Maurer. His was an art personal and particular, within a frame of special reference. Time, and his own growth, belatedly created an audience for him. This would not be in 1924.

How did Weyhe settle on Maurer as an artist to be encouraged and supported? They had become acquainted some years earlier, as the Zigrosser correspondence shows, and Weyhe had bought his first Maurer in 1922. He liked Maurer's painting; and he liked artists. He had some cash on hand as an unexpected return from the Davies exhibition of December, 1923. What better use could he make of it than to assist a serious artist, he asked himself. Now ten years in the United States, the German-born bookseller had prospered; and but recently he had moved into the then newly built bookshop at 794 Lexington Avenue, where he still conducts his book and art business. Decorative tiles gave its facade a modish look, and over the door swung an octagonal sign. Later Maurer painted another sign with a girl's head on either side. In holiday spirit, Weyhe rushed off to Alfy's home and "made the proposal to buy every thing in my studio, every damned picture." When the tumult died down, Weyhe was the richer by "some 255" Maurers, as contemporary accounts gave the figure, and Alfy by something over $2,000, the largest lump sum of money he had received for his work since 1901.

The sale was a high point in Maurer's life. Three letters in the Sherwood Anderson papers reveal the old, gay, ebullient Alfy. "Such a thing to happen in my young life," he wrote from 404 West Forty-third Street, "the blow almost killed Alfy." His father hadn't yet got the news; possibly the son had no inclination to share the good news with him. But he saw "Reds" and Arthur Dove and they "all danced around the boat." This was the first time this ever happened here, Dove said, and he felt very hopeful. As for the art patron "Weyhe says he doesn't care if he never sells them, he simply likes them, and this is the first time he ever did it."

The essay for the catalogue came (see pages 156-157) and the small folders were printed. The exhibition opened Tuesday the fifteenth, or perhaps it was Saturday the nineteenth. The first review was that in Henry McBride's column in the *Herald* the next day. On the twentieth, Alfy wrote to Anderson from "Arthur's Boat." (Dove and his wife were living on the *Mona,* a forty-eight-foot yawl with a small motor, from which the centerboard had been removed to make more living space and which they kept moored in the Harlem River.) Success, a little recognition, a little cash, what tonics they are for the weary soul. Alfy sounded young again and hopeful again. "You know," he wrote, "how grass goes through a goose, well, that's the way this affair with Weyhe has gone, just smooth." Sherwood's foreword was fine, and Alfy assured him he appreciated it fine. He'd like to say a whole lot more about it, but just didn't know how.

The bad time was over, he thought. "It looks like success for me, hope so, at one time I promised myself to strangle success if I ever got hold of it, now, I've changed my mind." It was a good world, a happy world, a world with hope. "Oh! sweet success," he wrote, then added cautiously, "but it's not here yet so I'll shut up." The foreword had been a great help with the exhibition, and Weyhe never tired of quoting it. He wanted to know if Anderson and Maurer had been playmates together. "I told him yes millions of years ago."

Finally the excitement was over. A month later Alfy wrote the last of the known letters to Sherwood Anderson. "Weyhe was delighted," he repeated, "and most so by your foreword and he wants me to ask you if he has about two hundred of them printed on fine paper, would you sign them if he gives you one of my pictures for your trouble." He would and he did. Two hundred and fifty broadsides were printed, one hundred of them with the double autograph of artist and writer (pages 156-157). This item of Maureriana and Andersoniana exists in two states—one on handmade all-rag laid antique paper 15½ inches long and the other on Japanese print paper 14½ inches long. It is headed by a linoleum cut showing one of Maurer's long-necked girls flanked with vases of flowers. Maurer made few prints, except the blocks he cut and printed for his exhibitions at Weyhe's in November, 1924, January, 1926, January, 1927, and April, 1928, though he had tried his hand at etching, using the Phillipses' press in Babylon. Graphic art was not, however, congenial to his restless temperament.

Weyhe's role in the sale has been discussed ever since, pro and con. Stieglitz approved the terms, so they must have met his criteria of fair play for the artist. If the average price per picture was not high, it was higher than zero, which is what Maurer had been receiving for his work for ten years. In Marlboro, teen-age Fred Schramm, Jr., used to feel sorry for Alfy because he sold his paintings (he told the lad) for $3 or $4 each when he made his regular trips to the city every two or three weeks. The truth was that there was no market for his work; he took what he could get. The Weyhe purchase came at a crucial time in Maurer's life. The backing, material and moral, was an incentive for him to continue to work. Weyhe followed the purchase with a verbal commitment to buy twenty or thirty water colors a year from Maurer at a fixed price of $35 each. That he did not realize a fortune on his investment may be judged from the fact that many of these still remain in his keeping. At the time, a quarter of a century ago, they were offered for sale at $75, no exorbitant markup on the cost price, but apparently a going market price. Through this arrangement Maurer was assured of a small regular income with which he could pay room and board at Shady Brook and buy painting materials.

Maurer became "dramatically famous" as "A Modern Byzantine" as soon as the exhibition opened, wrote the *Times*. His "Byzantine manner," his "stiff, stereotyped pattern of elongated forms," was called "dignified and vital in design and extraordinarily beautiful in texture," and his "startled child with tense arms, sophisticated relaxation of a mature woman, . . . old woman with a high, close color [collar?], supporting a bravely smirking head," were admired. The critics did not, however, respond in aesthetic terms, though much space was devoted to news. Henry McBride gave his story the subhead, " 'Third Floor Back' / Story With Moral." The "lead" position in his column was given to Mme. Hermine David; nonetheless, Maurer received twenty inches of type, an amount of space artists today, as then, are glad to have. Let the dean of the art press tell the story:

A. H. Maurer

NOTHING could be more delightful for me to
to think about than an exhibition of the work
of Mr. Alfred Maurer.   These paintings are such
living things, plucked out of the life of modern
cities.   The young girls are like desert flowers,
flashing into quick beauty just caught; the old
women, like gaunt, barren old hills.   I own but
two of his canvases.   Would that I owned two
dozen.

It is several years ago now that a friend, Mr.
Arthur Dove, took me into Maurer's neat little
workshop and I came away owning one of his
street girls.   What a charming companion she has
been.   I have carted her about with me ever since.
On mornings when I have awakened unable to
quite face what I thought the discouragements of
my own life, I have looked up at her hanging on
my wall and a smile has at once begun playing

MAURER—SHERWOOD ANDERSON BROADSIDE, 1924

over my inner self. She sends me out into the streets again believing in the inextinguishable charm and reality of life.

Life twisted, beaten down, perverted often enough, life as it is — in young girls in the back streets of cities, in tired old women — life everywhere having its wonder moments, this poet has caught.

Always the strange half mystic wonder of reality.

Long have I been convinced that Mr. Maurer is one of the really great modern painters. It is evidence of the persistence of life in us all that the subtlety and understanding of this painter is beginning to be recognized.

Two hundred and fifty copies of this broadside by Sherwood Anderson with an original linoleum cut by Alfred Maurer, of which one hundred have been signed, were published by E. Weyhe, 794 Lexington Avenue, New York.

MAURER—SHERWOOD ANDERSON BROADSIDE, 1924

One of those events that happen frequently in novels and some-times on the stage has just occurred in real life, and faint-hearted students of art will be enormously encouraged by it; and faint-hearted art dealers also, since one of the latter has just done a generous deed and seems in a fair way to be recompensed for it.

Listen. This is the tale. Mr. E. Weyhe, the art dealer, has just purchased *en bloc* the entire output of Mr. Alfred Maurer, an artist no longer in the first flush of youth, who has been living in a state of unsalability "on the third floor back of a house in Forty-third Street." Furthermore, Mr. Weyhe placed them promptly on view in the gallery and sold twenty of them before the show was officially announced. Is that not wonderful?

It is so wonderful that it is bewildering. One does not know whether to laugh or to cry. At all events it will be difficult to give a coherent account of what has happened.

As a pioneer spokesman of modern art in America and an early purchaser of Maurer's work, Henry McBride might well have been bewildered. Why should Maurer suddenly "catch on" when he had not caught on before? What an ironic situation when twenty sales were made before the exhibition was officially announced. Like many before and since, he fell back on quotations—using ex-cerpts from Sherwood Anderson's foreword. Critic McBride wrote that Sherwood Anderson had "been dabbling in cubism for some time" and "he had made the acquaintance of Miss Gertrude Stein and got over his first terrors." Yet "it was a great credit" to An-derson "that he was able to read the spiritual message of the strange formula that Mr. Maurer presented; . . . for the artist [had] recently been seeing people in elongated forms." However "life has been doing things of late to Mr. Anderson as well as to our artist, and the willingness to accept life as life, no matter how twisted it might be, brought about the *rapprochement* between them." The foreword was "a gem, a perfect little prose poem," dis-tilling the essence of Dostoievski's *Crime and Punishment*. And so the twenty inches of type was filled out with the Anderson text. Let us, like the *Herald* critic, be grateful for "one American novelist who looked fearlessly at pictures."

II

How ALFY reacted to his press notices one can but guess. On February 10 he wrote the last letter to Gertrude Stein which has survived, heading it "Dear Gertrud." Sherwood Anderson had asked him to send her a clipping of McBride's review. "He thought," Alfy went on, "the terror part of meeting you might be of interest." If he were only at 27 rue de Fleurus, he could talk his head off; his, he added, was a story no fountain pen could write, "so some day." He ended, *comme toujours*, "Until then my love to you and Alice." About this time he had clipped from the *Herald* a two-column reproduction of Jo Davidson's almost life-size portrait of Gertrude Stein, then on exhibition at the Fearon Galleries. The sculptor portrayed her seated, leaning forward, with hands dropped between slightly spread knees. She had not cut her hair in the characteristic grizzled short coiffure of later years but wore it long, piled on top of her head, as Picasso had painted her in 1906. The memory of old friends was dear to Maurer. This faded clipping survived him, preserved in his papers.

If Alfy did not react negatively to his press, another old friend did. Eugene Paul Ullman took up the challenge for him and became embroiled in a heated correspondence with Henry McBride. One of his two vehement letters of protest to the *Herald* was published and answered, and one was not. Ullman later published the whole exchange in a 17x11-inch flier, set in four columns, with a four-column banner head:

THE HOLY INQUISITION

Gertrude Stein, Grand Inquisitor—Henry McBride,
Little Inquisitor—Eugene Paul Ullman, Heretic.

Ullman ended with a four-column two-line head at the bottom:

THE HOLY INQUISITION USES ITS OWN METHODS TO CRUSH INDI-VIDUALITY JUST AS THE ACAD- / EMIES USE THEIR OWN METHODS FOR THE SAME PURPOSE. WITH EACH IT IS A STRUGGLE FOR LIFE.

The burden of Ullman's reproach was that if McBride did not care for his (Ullman's) academic manner of painting, then contrariwise McBride should greatly admire Maurer's non-academic manner of painting. By inference, McBride should do all he could to promote Maurer's abstractionism, as indeed he should have done long before, according to Ullman. Gertrude Stein, an old friend of all three, would not be pleased by his (McBride's) indifference to Maurer. The one-sided war did not seem to have much effect on Maurer's fortunes, nor did the spate of publicity which followed the Weyhe exhibition.

It was indeed a curious situation, commented the *Post's* reviewer, Margaret Breuning, under the heading, "Taking a Plunge in Art," "when a dealer in buying up the entire output of an artist who cannot sell his own works finds that even before the collection is hung on the gallery walls there is a strong demand for the paintings, each moment growing stronger." With the passion of newspapers for a news angle to make art news palatable, the comment gave another interpretation of Weyhe's motives: "E. Weyhe, feeling no doubt that continued successful exhibitions of well-known men were hardly sportsmanlike, took his plunge into the unknown recently in buying en bloc everything that Alfred H. Maurer has done in the last ten years, some 200 pictures in all. And presto change! The pictures were being sold before they were hung."

Without insisting on morals to the story, the reviewer could not but find food for thought in the situation, though she also found time to discuss Maurer as a painter. She continued:

> Mr. Maurer's work has been seen before, but few people appeared to be interested enough in it to buy it, although these few possessors have been enthusiastic about their possessions, notably Sherwood Anderson, who has written a poetic tribute to the power of the artist's work, which serves as an introduction to the exhibition.
>
> Mr. Maurer, after going through conventional art training and receiving conventional honors for his work, decided to find more freedom in expression, a decision that made him one of the pioneers of modern art in this country. It is the quality of intense individual-

ism that first strikes one here, a sort of definite challenge to the world of the right of the artist to speak in the language that best expresses his personal creed, so that there is something aggressive and hostile about some of his work. Labels, consequently, do not fit very well. "Realism," for instance, would be a very bad tag to attach to any of his stark, uncompromising canvases, for there is so little of the outward illusion of reality and so much of its inner power.

Considering the slowness with which Maurer's paintings made their way in the world, the criticism was well taken. His was, as said above, a special and particular art, an art bounded by the limits he chose for himself. At all times in his strangely fragmented development, he worked with integrity and brilliance, according to the criteria he selected. Today "realism" seems an appropriate word for his sad-eyed drooping girls (page 130).

Weyhe had taken the press by surprise. Working in haste and in the heat of enthusiasm, he opened the exhibition on very short notice. Press releases and the paraphernalia of contemporary publicity methods with which the art world today seeks to capture news space were not highly developed then. Even so, there were deadlines and copy had to be in at a given time to make the Sunday editions. Most of the reviews came a week or so late, including that of the *Tribune* critic. He found "The portraits of women, two of whom are shown posing side by side repeatedly, [to] have a strange realism, veiled by a repellent conception of form, a kind of forced naivete." These he called "crude, depressing pictures," though "the landscapes and flower pieces contain some mildly attractive color." So he dismissed Maurer, whom he described as "almost a newcomer" after "his art took a modernistic turn." Yet he had had "somewhat vague but still pleasant recollections of [his] work, seen years ago when he painted in the tradition of such artists as the late William M. Chase."

Maurer's work "suggests an introspective aestheticism which has perhaps never quite arrived at creating its final articulate form but which yet exercises a strange appeal," wrote the *World* on the same day. After recounting the well-advertised facts of Weyhe's purchase and Maurer's old-time academic successes, the review continued:

> The paintings seem to fall into two classes. First those pictures mainly landscapes, in which the artist has used bright clear colors to create a flat design from the elements of the scene. In these the effect is obtained from the clash of the pure colors juxtaposed. In the second class the aim has apparently been to achieve a tonal harmony, in using colors more subtly related. These often reflect an interesting effect on the artist of Negro art and the primitives. The tonal quality in them is not entirely different from that which characterized his old pre-conversion painting, but in those days his figures were drawn in conventional naturalistic style, and now they are made to conform to the arbitrary purposes of his design.

A little later Ralph Flint, in the *Christian Science Monitor*, devoted the first two paragraphs of his column to Maurer, under the heading "More Modernism in New York." Louis Maurer's flute teacher, head of the flute department of the Eastman School of Music in Rochester, had sent the clipping to the Maurers, scribbling "Bravo Mr Maurer. / Mr & Mrs Leonardo de Lorenzo." Like the rest of the critics, the *Monitor's* New York art correspondent related the story of Maurer's early conventional successes, his dramatic conversion to modern art, his long obscurity, the Weyhe sale and exhibition, and his sudden reappearance in the public eye. His resurrection in "the new and attractive Weyhe Galleries illustrates the enthusiasms that attend modern art." For "Whatever else may be denied it, modernism moves forward with unquestionable ardor and enthusiasm, constantly gaining in momentum and assurance, and, what is more to the point, in the number of reported sales along the way." The Flint review added one more question to the long list of those still unanswered. What happened to the letter from Alfred Stieglitz which was displayed in the exhibition? Stieglitz had written to commend Weyhe as one "ready to back his enthusiasm for pictures and books not yet on the passbooks of the institutions."

Next month *The Arts* reproduced a landscape (page 166) and led off its exhibitions department with a mention of the Maurer show. Virgil Barker added the latest news, to the effect that more

GIRL, *ca.* 1921
OIL ON GESSO PANEL, 26x17½ IN.
COLLECTION: E. WEYHE

GIRL IN FLOWERED DRESS, *ca.* 1924
TEMPERA ON FLOWERED DRESS GOODS, ON PANEL, 26x18 IN.
COLLECTION: MR. AND MRS. HUDSON D. WALKER

FLOWERS, *ca.* 1923
OIL ON CANVAS, ON BOARD, WITH GESSO, $29\frac{7}{8}$x$19\frac{3}{4}$ IN.
COLLECTION: E. WEYHE

LANDSCAPE, *ca.* 1923
OIL ON GESSO PANEL, 18x22 IN.
COLLECTION: E. WEYHE

A DOUBLE PAINTING: HEAD (LEFT) AND HEAD (RIGHT), *ca.* 1923
GOUACHE ON THE TWO SIDES OF THE SAME PAPER, 21½x18 IN.
COLLECTION: DR. ELISABETH K. HOYT

than forty paintings had been sold to date, and everybody was happy. The "great gamble on Mr. Weyhe's part" had won out, it gave the critic pleasure to record. Yet the artist's "preliminary gamble . . . had been grimmer and more prolonged." Now "he, too, in a manner of speaking, had won out." The comment continued:

> It is possible that Mr. Weyhe might now prefer to have his part in this affair treated with more discretion. Not that he can for a moment regret doing what he did, but simply that it must have already involved him in complications. He will henceforward be fair game for every unappreciated artist who can in any way get at him with a plea to attempt the same thing again. So that whenever he may feel inclined to he can ruin himself irrevocably for the good of American art.
>
> He did not come a cropper this time because he showed such good judgment as to the appeal of Maurer's painting to a special clientele. It would be a mistake to expect such work to be in any sense popular; it departs too far from common perceptions for that. It depicts the things and people of everyday life—a hillside pasture or a boarding-house female—but these are all seen in a wholly personal way. The purity of his landscape color is delightfully intense; the mentalities of his women disturbingly so. Most of the latter hint at all sorts of frustrations and suppressions, but one girl has not yet had her anticipations so transmogrified.

Maurer's note to Gertrude Stein is the only evidence of reaction to the press barrage. Any publicity is good publicity, he may have reasoned. Whatever he felt about the news accounts, he was cheered and invigorated by the sale and the exhibition. His last letter to Sherwood Anderson continued, in a gay and hopeful tone:

> I'm back again at work painting & frame making, sorry you're so damned far away. I don't know what Reds & Arthur are going to do next summer, I know I would like the South, spent a summer in the Bahamas, it never got too hot for me.
>
> But I'll have to stay near New York. I have to manufacture so much of my materials, and come back and forth carrying pictures

and buying and then a new place is always so interesting that it
cuts in on work. I like to play and play hard.

Weyhe wants me to have an exhibition next year, so I'll have to
keep at it, although I get so much fun out of the painting that I
have no trouble working.

Have not seen Reds & Arthur for several weeks, he's painting
away & doing some fine things. Whenever you come to New York
Sherwood, be sure & come in & see me.

And he signed himself "Yours truly / Alf."

Maurer's rediscovery had come and gone. It did not mean a
great deal in a material or a moral sense, except for the lift it
gave Alfy's spirit. His ten years' work had been purchased, exhibited, and some resold. But was there an audience or a market
for his art? Not in a real sense. The rebel could resolve his dilemma only by more and more work, packing a crowded room
with unseen paintings. Was this the function of the artist in society, to paint for no one?

Louis Maurer was beginning to experience another kind of rediscovery. In 1922 he was ninety, and he played his flute at a
luncheon for Ezra Meeker of the 1852 Oregon Trail fame. All
New Yorkers ninety or over had been invited to attend, and eighteen had come, Louis Maurer with his Böhm-system flute. Again
in 1925, a dinner was held to celebrate Meeker's ninety-fifth birthday, and once more Louis Maurer attended, to gain considerable
linage because of his age. As Currier and Ives prints came back
into favor at the end of the 1920s, he was acclaimed as their sole
surviving artist. In 1927, *Correct Eating* extolled him as a shining
example of old age. Alfred Maurer was not ungenerous. Certainly
he was not counting the days until his aged father should die and
he be freed from the deathbed promise to his mother. Nonetheless he could not have welcomed all the fulsome praise for the art
his father championed, since it was at the opposite pole from that
to which he had given his life.

The horror created by Maurer's two sisters is hard to understand. He painted his theme in many versions and in many manners. Today the two girls look as they must have looked to him,
gentle, confiding, naive, innocent. What repelled the critics of

1924? The youth, the gaucherie, the trusting gaze of the girls? Young they were and gawky, adolescent and awkward, standing with heads thrust forward and stomachs poked out. But they were tender and loving, bright bits of life, as well as fragments of life twisted and beaten down, as Sherwood Anderson saw them. It was their human meaning Maurer sought, whether he painted them singly or in pairs or threes or fours, abstractly or naturalistically. He perceived them as living organisms in a living world, aware and sentient, individual entities in their own right, subjecting existence to their candid gaze. As the years passed, their vision grew increasingly inscrutable. Imperceptibly they pass from childhood to maturity. Their look grows grave, and their brows are laden with a solemnity the children did not know. Whether they uttered their own pain or Maurer's, they speak for the unsmiling hours of life which not all artists record. The dividing line between their childhood and their womanhood is the line that lies between those who have suffered and those who have not. But this is a chapter of the Maurer story still to come.

III

MEANWHILE work remained to Maurer as his means of salvation, as it had been before. The road of work was a less tortured road than that he later trod when ill health and approaching age weighed heavily. Before he returned to Shady Brook for a spring and summer of intensive work, he put in frenzied days to prepare for the eighth annual Independent's, held from March 7 to March 31, 1924. Alfy had been "left flat by the sale of 255 paintings to Weyhe," the *World* reported, and he "had to hurry to get something out for this exhibition," in order not to be left out of the 1,088 exhibits which crowded the Waldorf-Astoria roof garden. He found a solution at the dry goods store, so the account stated, "cloth in which he dresses his two ladies." The item added, "he painted the faces and pasted on the cloth." So much for documents. He glued the cloth to 26x18-inch panels and painted *over* the cloth, allowing the textile to show where surface texture and design would enhance his picture. About a dozen of these dress-goods-covered panels survive.

Inasmuch as he had already covered panels with canvas and bed ticking, he probably did not evolve this inverted college technic solely for the Independent's; it was an extension of previously explored technical means. Sometimes he used a flowered print, as in the panel reproduced (page 164), or a shantung silk with a block-printed geometrical pattern, or again a solid color cotton, as in a particularly handsome and appealing *Girl in Green*. He used a larger than usual panel, 22x18-inch panels being his standard size. He painted in a heavy tempera, with considerable impasto, so that the unpainted areas offer a strong textural contrast.

In the rush of his painting deadline, Alfy found time to do his share of dirty work for the Independent's, of which he had become a director in 1919. With Holger Cahill, Sarah Freedman, Edith Branson, and Mrs. A. S. Baylinson, wife of the longtime secretary of the Society of Independent Artists, he posed for the news photographers, all standing in front of e. e. cummings' abstraction, *Noise No. 12*. Alfy appeared in shirt sleeves: as usual he was working hard.

Now he settled down for a sustained period of painting. Back to Shady Brook he went. The stimulus of sudden sale and exhibition might be temporary, but for the moment it gave him new incentive. He took up the pleasant routine of regular meals, regular work, and friendly converse with the Shady Brook family and the neighbors. He painted his world of Marlboro from every aspect. He would shift his campstool a foot or two in either direction to look at the dam from a fresh point of view. Or he would study the retaining wall and the brook as it tumbled over the dam and under Buckley's Bridge (page 178) to present a dozen versions of the theme. He sat out in front of the boarding house and painted the entrance to the old Buckley place, which Schramm and Ormsby had owned and used for the overflow of their summer boarders.

Type designer Frederic W. Goudy made his home there after he left Deepdene Road in Forest Hills in 1908. There till his death, to the sound of the rushing brook, swollen by heavy rains, Goudy operated his one-man type foundry when he had become disillusioned with commercial type manufacture; and there his

wife, Bertha M. Goudy, performed miracles of hand-set composition for their Village Press. The Maurer and Goudy eras in Marlboro overlap in time; they do not seem to have had much relation
in actuality. The old Goudy house has been made into a Goudy
shrine. Will Shady Brook be honored, save by the pious remembrance of Alfy's old friends? Yet, if there are to be no shrines for
him, even today the mature women with whom he used to walk up
the hill when they were young girls preserve the autographs he
painted for them—"For Rose, on her birthday" wreathed with a
red rose.

He looked farther off to the gently rolling hillside of the quarry,
or he saw plowed and harvested fields. Sometimes, though he
hated the cold and the nuisance of bundling up in heavy winter
garments, he would come up to Shady Brook in the winter and
watch the young things skating on the pond. He stood apart, a
lonely figure, while the young men and women laughed and em-
braced and cheered on Laddie, the collie. He painted then, also
—snow on the rutted road along the brook which led up to Dard
Hunter's mill. Land forms took on sharper outlines. So Maurer
turned toward exact definition and clean-cut outlines. The abstractionism of his later period was not a theoretical or cerebral solution, but a necessity of his way of seeing. Thus, early in his resort
to nature, he revealed the direction he must take, as he revealed
also his hunger for light. So, too, he wanted and needed brilliant
color. The color wheel described proves this, if nothing else; for
the pigments with which he experimented have the virtue of brilliance.

He ranged the countryside and made every acre his own. He was
searching, searching. More confident of himself than he had been
and more encouraged, he found new consolations in his simple life
at Shady Brook. He created a new gaiety in his companionship with
the young girls and young men who came up from the city for
their summer holidays. With them he went swimming in the
pond, and they all played croquet in the long summer evenings.
Where are they now? Some are untimely dead. Most are married,
with children graduating from high school. Wilhelmina, Juliette,
Edith, he frolicked with this trio and loved them. The Caywood
sisters, Edith and Marion, and their half-sisters, Margaret and

Elisabeth Schramm, the Meinung sisters, Jeanne and Eleanor, other pairs of sisters, Marion and Dorothy, and "Midge" and Dorothy, and girls who were not related, Gussie and Myrtle, and many more—these were his friends. And with them the young men, Con and Jack, Earl and Dick, and young Fred tagging along, a "kid" with the older ones.

On Saturday nights the summer boarders danced to the victrola in the old dance hall behind the bungalows. This was the old Mercy Buckley mill, which had been a shoddy mill during the Civil War. It had stood further up the brook (once known as "Jew's Creek," after an earlier inhabitant, Gomez) and it had been moved down bodily to the Schramm and Ormsby place where it was used first as a barn and then as a recreation hall. "I saw Alfy for the first time at one of those Saturday night dances in the 'Old Mill,' " recalls one of those young girls for whom Alfy loved to buy ice-cream and whom he used to paint unknown to them. Her face seems to recur in his paintings. "He loved to dance. Those were the days when men wore plus-fours. Remember? He wore tweed plus-fours and a white sports shirt, open at the neck."

So he lived and so he worked. He painted two girls at the piano, posed against the lattice in the dance hall. He painted the old tartarian cherry trees behind the boarding house. Gnarled and twisted then, now these trees are cut down. They gave him new subject matter and allowed the press to comment favorably on his new work when he showed it in November at Weyhe's. His love of experiment persisted. On black and white oilcloth he painted fflowers, and later he painted a still life on black oilcloth. Meanwhile during this time of intensive preparation for his coming exhibition, he painted on the gesso panels. He used the familiar flowers from the garden, painting the same bouquet over and over till it would fade and droop and wither. But he used new compositional devices, a deep angulated perspective, as in *Flowers* (page 165), to force three dimensions into a flat pattern, as he had done by different means in the early fauvist *Still Life* (previously discussed) or as he would again in *Nude* (page 196). Slowly he came toward creative completion.

Now he began to make his own place. He had found a family in which he was accepted as a well loved son, and he founded a family for himself. Like Henry Adams who dedicated *Mont-Saint-Michel and Chartres* to his niece in spirit ("daughter" will not scan for "son"), Maurer hungered for young, lively, enthusiastic objects on whom to shower tenderness and compassion. He seemed to seek in his "adopted" daughters a resemblance to his own features. Was his life a desperate self-portrait? Yet Maurer was hardly Narcissus: his pain is evident, his pleasure lacking. He had no wife, no child, no hearth. May he be allowed a fantasy, to see in another's face the flowering of his own? So he painted the young girls a quarter of a century ago. So he saw them. So we see them.

In the meanwhile he was working hard, and the work was going well. He was beginning a period of sustained effort which would slowly win him a hearing and an audience, if small. He looked forward to years of fulfillment. The years were no longer silent. Would they now speak with a glad, full-throated joy?

6. Years of Work

MAURER entered on a period of concentrated and fruitful labor. He had lived through years of privation and solitude. He had found a friend who believed in him. Now he could paint and paint, knowing that his paintings would be exhibited and hoping that they would be appreciated and even sold. At last he was about to justify his long years of experiment. At last he could answer the reproaches, spoken and unspoken, with which he had been harassed for fifteen years and more. At last rebellion would be vindicated.

After a summer of sustained work he was ready to exhibit his latest paintings. Eager and enthusiastic, E. Weyhe hastened to present his "find" to the world, instead of waiting till the next year as he had planned. Two red-and-green announcements went forth: *Paintings by Alfred H. Maurer would be on view from November 12 to November 30.* Alfy had cut the linoleum blocks, one showing a seated girl and the other a vase of flowers on a table. He had printed them in deep green on red blotters which soaked up the color till it now looks almost black. He used a simple line drawing style, as he did in the few linoleum-cut prints which survive; his old schooling was reasserting itself. On the green-black background the red lines stand out, strong and emphatic. Pulling

TWO SISTERS, *ca.* 1925
OIL ON GESSO PANEL, $29\frac{3}{4}$x$19\frac{5}{8}$ IN.
COLLECTION: MISS ELIZABETH McCAUSLAND

FLAPPERS, *ca.* 1926
TEMPERA ON GESSO PANEL,
21½x18 IN.
COLLECTION: E. WEYHE

FLOWERS, *ca.* 1926
OIL ON BLACK OILCLOTH,
ON BOARD, 21½x18 IN.
COLLECTION: E. WEYHE

THE OLD TREE, *ca.* 1924
OIL ON CANVAS, ON ACADEMY BOARD, 30X20 IN.
COLLECTION: PHILLIPS MEMORIAL GALLERY

BUCKLEY'S BRIDGE, *ca.* 1926
WATER COLOR AND GOUACHE ON PAPER, 21½x18 IN.
COLLECTION: MR. AND MRS. LOUIS MECKES

the cards by hand or possibly printing them by rubbing the paper with a spoon, he did not achieve a perfect register; for the block's rectangular area is not always lined up parallel with the edges of the card, or with the letter press. He may have worked in haste if Weyhe suddenly decided to move up the exhibition date.

Thus his new work was launched. It aroused "great interest and speculation," wrote the *Sun*. This time the art press had more warning or felt more interest. The *Sun's* news and comment followed closely on the opening on Wednesday the twelfth: "Last year he [had] burst upon the New York art world after languishing in obscurity for more than ten years. Now every one [was] curious to see his most recent work." The beneficial effects of encouragement and kindness were evident: his latest paintings were "different, both in treatment and in choice of subject. His color, if anything, is gayer. There are flower studies that fairly glow with radiance. There are landscapes that are rich in greens and studies of tree trunks lovingly painted with all their gnarled surfaces." He also painted his ubiquitous girls, but "this time in a new medium, gouache."

Brilliant, indeed, are the green leaves of *The Old Tree* (page 177) against a landscape which fairly glows with radiance. Tones of blue and blue-gray in the trunk are lovely against the blue sky and white clouds. The physical weight and substance of paint as material are less sensuously appealing, possibly, in this painting; the gesso ground painted on the canvas which covers the 30x20-inch panel has sucked up the medium, and the surface has little of the "juicy" feel admired in oil painting. This is not an important consideration in this painting, however. The surface has a matte finish from which neither colors nor forms force themselves on the eye. There is an architectural feeling to the surface, indeed, and that critic who wrote later, wishing that Maurer's work might have an architectural "frame," could have used this painting to illustrate his point. In passing, note that Maurer customarily painted on panels of a small size—usually 22 by 18 inches or thereabouts, though sometimes he used a panel 26 by 18 inches or 30 by 20, and rarely 39 by 24, while there is but one 48 by 39.

Such was his drive, or his compulsion, that all his pictures, studied in 8x10 black-and-white photographs, seem large in scale.

It was a large view of nature he took in *The Old Tree;* and this largeness, expressed visually and physically in solid and stable forms, makes the painting memorable. In a day when nature was often seen as a confection, Maurer saw the earth, the land, and the living trees as evidences of the permanence of life. His view of nature was not rooted in centuries-old religious affirmation, as was the Chinese. Nonetheless his view of nature was not small. Cézanne had seen the rocks and pines of Mont-Sainte-Victoire as enduring, ennobling experience. Maurer, one of the inheritors of the wisdom of Cézanne, saw his little landscape large, his small world universal.

The *Times* did not review the exhibition till a week and a half had passed. His girls seemed to escape notice, or perhaps Maurer's new subject matter was more noteworthy. In a brief paragraph, the review read:

> Alfred H. Maurer has deserted his long-necked ladies like antique urns, and has gone out of doors to paint the characterful country just outside of New York, the bright and somewhat cheerless color, gnarled trees, and telegraph poles. Few painters have been so frank about telegraph poles or seen them as so integral a part of modern landscape and modern decoration. The composition is moving and lively, livelier than the color or the subject, with a ground plan not unlike the ground plan of the portraits.

Evidently the underlying Hambidge "blueprint" which Maurer had not completely relinquished could be sensed. Linear pattern aside, his choice of subject matter is significant. In landscapes and in flower paintings, he sought to present observed visual appearances. His life may have forced him to be introspective and subjective, but his bent was toward reality. He had showed this in his early Paris figure studies and genre paintings. He showed it now by an intense interest in the external world. There is no pathos in a hill, a field, a brook, a barn, a rose; only human faces take on pathetic meanings under the stress of sorrow. Maurer struggled not to surrender to the tears of things. The joy of life, the hope of life, the thrust of growth, the conquests made by man's hands and mind—these were immediate and laudable. When he abandoned them, he did so because he must. Meanwhile he painted telegraph poles on the road to the quarry or on the road to the village. Sometimes he painted the high tension wires which carried 70,000 volts of current from Newburgh to Highland, following the ridge road and crossing the Hudson on the old high bridge at Poughkeepsie. These were painted in oil on 30x20-inch canvas- and gesso-covered panels.

His "bright but somewhat cheerless color" is a matter of taste. The flower painting reproduced (page 165) is characteristic of the palette he used at this time for this subject. The background is painted in subdued blue-greens. On a white tablecloth, picked out with blue shadows, stands a light brown vase, whose neutral tone is accentuated by one yellow-green pear contrasted with pears which are green or green flushed with rose. Tiger lilies and hydrangeas, in delicate orange-pink and white, complete the color scheme. If it is bright is a question. Certainly it is not cheerless. Rather the key is sober, quiet, restrained, like a good gray poem.

Maurer had made another bid for recognition, but with no great success. Soon he was to receive news which shook his morale deeply. Before that, however, he showed two paintings in the ninth annual exhibition of the Independent's at the Waldorf-Astoria. For once the Society had departed from its practice of hanging exhibits in the alphabetical order of their exhibitors' names. Three groups were formed, "abstract, representative, and semi, the semis forming the largest group." The *Post's* reviewer, Margaret Breuning, visiting the display before the opening, had to study the art works without the benefit of such an arrangement. Among the first entries seen were Maurer's two "compositions with figures," listed in the catalogue as *The S— S— Sisters* and *The S— S— Sisters' Cousins,* Nos. 683 and 684. Who the "S— S— Sisters" were, or who their cousins were, no one at Shady Brook knows; and the paintings have not been identified.

Fortunately they took the critic's eye; and from the verbal account their central theme and style may be deduced. After recounting how Maurer's work used to be praised—and bought!—by William M. Chase, the reviewer recalled that following "rich promises of conventional merit, [Maurer] had turned vagabond and strayed from the highway in pursuit of such haunting visions as these," in which he painted "faces of emphatic line, synthetized into something resembling a primitive symbol, in reality of the deepest essence of sophistication." He drew "forms pulled out as Euphronios or Douros might have pulled them out to fill an exigent space upon a kylix or amphora" and endowed them with "color of enchanting tenderness, a warm flush, tulips or azalea, something sturdier than the pink of roses; and a warm young green and a yellow, all vital colors and used to enhance the vitality of the forms."

The *Two Sisters* reproduced (page 175) may be taken as characteristic of the category, although there is no way of knowing if it was exhibited at the Independent's in 1925 or anywhere else, then or later. It is one of those 30x20-inch gesso panels Maurer was using at this time; stylistically it appears to have been painted about the same time as the two self-portraits (frontispiece and page 198). Before it was cleaned in the fall of 1948, it was afflicted with "freckles" such as are described in the technical appendix, due to the inferior grade of linseed oil with which Maurer "glazed" his paintings for some time; and its "color of enchanting tenderness" could not be seen. Cleaned, it reveals how Maurer covered under-painting with thin washes of oil color to build solid forms, elongated or not. Against a simple background of light gray and dark gray laid on with considerable textural emphasis, he placed his two girls, one in blue at the left and one in red at the right, and both with long hair of a deep mahogany hue. Flesh tones are painted in a high key of pinks with purplish shadows for modeling. When paintings done in this technic are examined technically, under-painting in gray, black and white is found. The eyes of the two girls are painted in dull black, with no highlights in the pupils, but a suggestion of accents of light in the white of the eyeballs. The blue and red of the girls' dresses are of middle value. This does not, however, suggest the transparent brilliance of the pigments. As in the entire series of heads, the lips are full and carmine red, with strong black outlines.

The two shown at the Independent's were "beautiful paintings," the *Post* continued, "but seeming in search of the right framework, such a framework as a plastered wall with a niche or panel to enframe the painting which is done, apparently in tempera with some kind of varnish or glaze to make it still more a matter of decoration to be linked with architecture and thus divested of the least claim realism could make upon them." Here the critic came close to the basic question of the use of art in contemporary society. Easel painting was reaching its nadir as a rootless, unwanted genre. Its inorganic role and Maurer's unpopular manner partly explain his long odyssey of neglect.

Kind words were followed by harsh events. Alfy had kept his studio in Paris for years, always hoping to return. The purchase and exhibition of his work had given him an incentive to transcend his ties to "404." Suddenly he heard that the contents of his studio had been sold. The news struck home with the force of an edict: *Thou shalt not return.* He had asked for help to bring his paintings to America; he had been refused. Now they were lost forever. His bitterness grew deeper. That his paintings were sold for back rent has been denied by a family spokesman. The official version is that Alfred never asked for help from his father and that the paintings in Paris were sold because of a legal ruling regarding the property of foreigners. Maurer, on the other hand, repeatedly told friends that his father had refused to help him bring his work to the United States. Who should be believed?

II

THE FACT IS, the work is lost and it is difficult to reconstruct this period in his painting. As late as 1931 Maurer had not given up hope of discovering his lost work. Jack Stark, an oldtime friend, hunted for them in Paris, and on his return he tried to see Alfy on his way to the West Coast. He could not find him in the telephone book; a son would not be listed as long as the father lived, the head of the house. Stark wrote Maurer that he had had no success in locating any of the paintings, and not even "Shorty" Lazare knew anything about them. The Quarter had been full of small galleries a few years earlier; but "when the golden period passed, they folded up and went away." The dealers were having a hard time then, at the outset of the depression.

Maurer's paintings could have been saved a little earlier, however. In 1925 or thereabouts Pierre Daura, now a naturalized

American citizen, was strolling along near the famous flea market. He knew the self-styled "dealers in paintings" and stopped in to look around one *barraque*. The place was stacked with canvases, large and small, academic and fauvist, and possibly even the *Jeanne* (page 61) sent over by Lefebvre-Foinet for the 1949 Maurer exhibition. The "vast, voluminous display . . . looked like the life work of some very tormented and very talented artist. There were hundreds and hundreds of them. Framed oils and water colors, drawings, engravings, all subjects and tendencies growing from the Sargent-like school to the post-cubist." The dealer had bought up "all of Maurer's studio."

Daura wanted to buy the whole collection, but he had no money. He tried to raise funds, without success. When he had gotten some capital together, he went back to the dealer only to find that everything had been sold "except three huge big canvases with one figure each—Sargent manner—and two or three small ones." He bought these, and when he moved to the south of France, he took them along. There they have been for almost a quarter of a century. Daura himself, now a member of the faculty of Randolph-Macon Woman's College, came to the United States in 1939 and was not able to return to France till 1947. His home had been pillaged of a great deal of its contents; but he found his Maurers in his studio "rolled in a corner and well preserved." Unfortunately the paintings could not be brought over to America in time for the Maurer exhibition.

How Maurer reacted to his bad news can be imagined. During these years when he worked hard and exhibited every year, critics often mentioned the "bitterness" they found in his painting. Slowly that emotion grew less evident; perhaps he forgot his anger and his hurt; perhaps a larger injury held his attention. Meanwhile he painted and he exhibited and he had his circle of young friends away from home. He used to take the girls and their sweethearts or newly acquired husbands out to dinner. He sent the young women books, *Nize Baby* and *The Book of Tea*, for example. He visited them when they set up housekeeping and enjoyed their young wifely cooking. He helped a young friend whom he called "Myrt" to plan an evening dress, in earth colors to harmonize with her red hair and milk-white skin. He was late getting off the color sample, but at last he wrote:

> Here it is!
> Yellow Ochre, rather late.
> Have a cold but that's no reason for being so behind hand.
> Are you enjoying the book?
> Am getting things together for my show, all upside down and at the same time have the works of the old famibly clock that I'm trying to get to work. Lots of fun seeing the wheels go 'round. Hope your dress is a success.
> My love to you and the rest of the gang.

He had dashed a swatch of color across the top of the note, and he signed himself "As ever / Alfy."

He always wanted his adopted daughters to come to the opening of his annual exhibition at Weyhe's, and he wrote them little notes of personal invitation. He wrote Myrtle again on Tuesday, January 5, enclosing a handful of the announcements of his new exhibition, from January 4 to January 20, 1926. He apologized for sending the invitations after the exhibition had opened:

> Not my fault, not my fault. It's Carl's and the printer's.
> They were sent late to the printer and he didn't work Saturday after the New Year [on Friday] and I didn't get them till today.
> However you don't need these announcements to get in the show, so don't bother carrying them with you.
> These are for the whole bunch
>
> Love and as
>
> ever
>
> Alfy

The announcement he sent out that year was ambitious in design. He still used a line drawing style; but he cut away the block so that the weight of light and dark was nearly equal. The card was printed in black on white, and it was more accurately registered than the red-and-green announcements of November, 1924. Perhaps the printer had locked up Maurer's block with the letter press. The artist composed girl's head and flanking flowers in an overall design. The girl is drawn with dignity and sympathy: her head droops down, sad and weary, and the flowers droop toward her. Exaggerated musculature of throat and neck is evident; the distortion, if that is what it is, enhances the weariness of her head's gesture.

Maurer sought again for understanding of what he said about life and art. Life, in all its sadness and weariness and grief, was beautiful; and he, among others, proclaimed the beauty of life, even in its saddest hours. His was a simple and an innocent aspiration. He was naive, possibly, to hope that his aim would be understood. Why should art speak of sorrow? The work of art, like the sundial, should speak only of shining hours. If he had dressed his themes in elaborate costumes or provided them with complicated librettos, he might have won an audience. He had said long before, in regard to the Steins' Cézanne, who ever heard of a picture being framed unless it was finished. His pictures were finished and framed; the public still could not see them in their own right.

He was not without comfort. Under the heading "The Humanity of Still Life," the *Times* wrote of his exhibition. His name was spelled "Mauer," but the review gave careful attention to his work. His endless experiment was noted, as well as his change to the new subject matter of vases of flowers and telegraph poles. More than that, the critic commented that in whatever he did, his design remained "his steadfast friend." His compositions radiated from a centered point. Moreover the artist emphasized "again the fact that life lies in design and not in subject." As a result, "his flowers are human beings with rich personalities." If Maurer's "aim had been merely realism instead of life, a dead oak leaf would have been brittle instead of unctuous and fat." His "light tablecloth, . . . transparent cerise peach, . . . yellow apple are not sentimental. Instead they burlesque sentimentality. A bunch of flowers with an acid yellow dahlia at its heart" is a criticism of the sentimental attitude. Here Maurer had understanding and sympathy. Why did he not win an audience?

If his life were stated in musical terms, one motive would recur: *He worked and he painted.* He did not obtain acclaim or sales. He worked and he painted. On February 3, 1926, W. R. Valentiner wrote E. Weyhe to ask for the loan of Maurers for an exhibition

to be held in Dresden from May to September. After World War
I Germany had been subjected to a cultural boycott. The proposed exhibition was one of the first steps taken to lower the barriers: in fact, it was to be the first exhibition of modern American
paintings held in middle Europe, and in addition it was to be
international in scope. Again the records are incomplete. Probably it was *Four Sisters* (page 197) which was sent to Germany.
Atypical in size and proportion, this picture represents Maurer's
most ambitious attempt to compose human figures in a group.
This was a design problem which fascinated him and to which he
came back over and over. He painted the two sisters in a long
series from realistic to abstract, he made a few paintings of three
sisters, he drew scores of double nudes, and in the complex twin
heads of his late period, he painted the faces merging and fusing
and breaking apart once more.

In *Four Sisters* he seems to have painted two sets of sisters,
Jeanne and Eleanor and Elisabeth and Margaret. He painted on a
gesso panel 36 by 25½ inches, a shape such as he had used in his
Paris figure studies and genre paintings. The four are placed
against a dark red-brown background, which accentuates the flesh
tones. From left to right, they are dressed in green, figured red
and green, and darker green; the dress of the girl third from the
left cannot be seen. Their hair, from left to right, is red, blonde,
brown and a lighter brown. Apparently the pair of sisters at the
left are the same as he painted in *Two Sisters* (page 130); but they
have undergone a strange sea change and become classic and mon-
umental. All stand with assured ease, looking out at the beholder
with those eyes forever staring.

Probably this painting also is based on under-painting, though
no technical examination of the paint beneath the surface could
be made as it had no surface abrasions. It is not only a key picture, aesthetically speaking; hardy would be he who could deny
its merit and power. It is a key picture in a technical sense also.
A series of photographs exist from the days when *"Vier Frauen"*
was written on the print's back. The early photograph shows the
painting in mint condition, as it left the artist's hands. There is no
mark of spurious "antiquing," such as amateur experts of Maurer
would wish to have believed was his custom and desire. On the

contrary, the faces and arms of the four sisters are spotless; and it was not till about fifteen years after the picture was finished that the drippingly streaked appearance was recorded by the camera. This case and a dozen or more of similar significance suggest the danger of hypotheses invented in a vacuum, without data or analysis.

Maurer was beginning to get about. In February, 1926, the Mattatuck Historical Association in Waterbury, Conn., exhibited his work, with considerable vituperation in the local press. Almost twenty years later the same thing happened in fashionable Greenwich, called the richest community in the United States, when Maurer's paintings were hissed out of town. He began to send paintings hither and thither, to the Little Gallery in Chicago among others. A painting of his turned up at the sale of the collection of Albert Rothart, *Girl Against a Cobalt-Blue Ground,* which went for $50. As usual he exhibited with the Independent's, showing two more paintings, each generically entitled *Head*. His work began to be discussed and reproduced; and *Toledo Topics* called him "The Iconoclast in New York."

So the months went on, and it was summer, and he was once more in Marlboro, painting away as usual, but with time to write Carl Zigrosser a note:

> Hold the paper   will be in in a few weeks   pay Ganso and put it on my account, Please.
> Started at flowers, having a good time. Nights cold. Give Wanda Gag my best and tell her she's welcome
> Will see you soon
>   As ever   Alfy
> P. S. Send my book as soon as it come in

If individuals without a history are happy, as countries without a history are said to be, these were happy days for Maurer. He painted and had a good time. He could buy materials and have the cost put on his account! He could even buy a book. Indeed he did buy many books through Weyhe, expensive art books printed in France by the *pouchoir* method and *Cahiers d'Art* and the like. After his death some of these came to rest with Dove. He cut many large loose sheets from portfolios and albums, using

their superb all-rag paper to draw and paint on. But this was a
little later during the brief winter when he had a model come to
his studio at least once a week to sketch and study.

It was 1926. Maurer was almost sixty. His father was ninety-five.
Wide World sent out a photograph of Louis Maurer standing and
holding a gun in his hands. Another firearm is leaning against the
wall behind him, and above it are targets punctured with shot.
At the left, also behind him, may be seen the branching antlers
of two moose, part of one of his paintings on Wild West subjects.
The caption was headed: "AN EXPERT WITH THE RIFLE AT 95." And
it read: "Louis Maurer, who instructed greenhorns in the Civil
War how to use a rifle, is still an expert shot in his 95th year and
has often entered competitions in the last decade. He is shown
here with one of his favorite guns." If the press photographer did
not have Louis Maurer pose with the gun he had made over
seventy-five years before in Germany, he missed a news angle.

III

JANUARY came again. It was 1927. Again Maurer held an exhibition at Weyhe's. The announcement card was another linoleum block print, with a girl's head against a background of
looped draperies and a vase of flowers. The line is fluent, and a
remarkable effect of light is created with a few strokes. The dates
were January 5 to 20. The *New Yorker* "scooped" the daily papers. Its review was, as usual, sympathetic. Its longtime critic,
Murdock Pemberton, had been attracted by Maurer's story and
then "sold" on his work. He even bought a small Maurer. In a
chatty style he wrote of Maurer as a "symbol of freedom," intro-
ducing his review with a brief digest of the artist's personal history:

> Maurer, if you don't remember, is the artist that was the white
> hope of the mauve decade and was considered along with Chase.
> Then he met Matisse. And what happened to him was nobody's
> business except the bomb squad's. After about a score of years spent
> in picking up the pieces, Weyhe found him and dragged him from
> his studio where he had painted himself in.

Since that time, three years ago, Maurer has caught pace with life and is having a lot of fun. His pictures have sold tremendously and he can turn them out as only a recluse can. This last phase to us is the most interesting. It is a flowering of all the little shoots that have sprung up through the trial periods, retaining the best features of each. His figures and heads in these new canvases have much more warmth. The sun, too, breaks through on his landscapes and, all in all, there seems to have been a truce effected between Maurer and a once unbelieving world. He is one of the few distinctive painters we have turned out having less of the origins about him than most of the disciples.

Maurer has found a new stunt in painting his flowers on black oilcloth. This saves a lot of paint for backgrounds, and if permanent, should just about ruin the linen canvas business. Many a tyro, worrying about what to put back of his composition, should see how Maurer buys it ready-made. Of course, it may be necessary to know how to paint, as Maurer knows, before you get the same brilliant effect.

Maurer's latest "stunt" of painting on oilcloth had caught on. Perhaps his experiments and novelties harmed more than they helped. They provided the press with news angles and allowed them to pass by aesthetic aspects. One of these paintings on black oilcloth has been located, *Flowers* (page 176). It is well painted, the brilliant brushwork becoming visible after cleaning. The *Times* also responded to the "almost mellow bloom [which] illuminates Alfred Maurer's . . . flowers and green bits of fragrant forests." For some reason the mellow bloom was affecting "even his stylistically long-nosed ladies, with their big averted eyes," for they "seem to have buttered their acidulous frustrations with 'enigmatic' smiles." Maurer had perhaps "sweetened their bitterness with a little of the warmth that was lavished upon him by appreciative art critics some three years ago, when Mr. Weyhe rescued him from a heretofore critical oblivion."

The *Times* continued:

Certainly the faces and the high, domish foreheads of these intense women seem less—rather than more, as is usually the case— sharpened by the defeats that are the acrid weeds of those disillusions sown by humdrum existence. One of Mr. Maurer's girls is almost businesslike (about life) as she sits with her man at a wooden table. She and her man might be married, so casually do they disregard each other.

In other words, Mr. Maurer, always an affirmative artist, has become positive in his affirmations. A year ago those affirmations seemed to spring from a sort of splendid anger; now they are beginning to spring from a splendid love. It is silly to say of a grown artist such as Alfred Maurer that he has "grown" in one or two years' time; but it is impossible in his case to avoid the even worse cliché that he is "realizing" his powers at their fullest. The academician, Alfred Maurer, who, when on the approved high-road to a conventional esthetic success, was compared to Chase and picked as his only possible successor, has become Alfred Maurer, a great American artist, who stands alone.

These were brave words. But the great American artist, Alfred Maurer, continued to stand alone. The *Herald-Tribune* did not seem to be persuaded of Maurer's greatness. His two women, flower pictures, and landscapes were noted in a paragraph, with no critical emphasis. Another exhibition had come and gone, and time was passing.

As for the subject described by the *Times,* a couple seated at a table, none of this series has been located. Would that they had; for so far no male subjects have been found in Maurer's paintings of the 1920s except the self-portraits. Could Maurer have painted a couple at a table in the Hill drugstore in Marlboro, or in the Shady Brook dance hall? He did paint scenes with that background, such as *Two Girls at a Piano* or *Flappers* (page 176). The latter is a small gesso panel, in tempera upon which the disfiguring "glaze" of inferior linseed oil was fortunately not placed. There are several studies of this theme in existence, and comparison between those with "varnish" and those without is in favor of the latter. His greens and reds have a deep, lustrous matte finish which is enticing. At the time one was reproduced under the title of *Two Gigolettes.* Whether he, or someone else, gave the picture the title, is a question, as there is a question in regard to the titling of *Flappers.* Whether or not he used such terms, he

loved the kittenlike little girls in all their naivete and assumed
sophistication.

Maurer worked and he painted. He painted and he worked and
he exhibited whenever he had an opportunity to do so. He was
breaking down the barriers of ignorance which had surrounded
his name as a painter in the modern style. In the 1927 Independent's he showed two water colors, each called *Head* and each priced
at $100. This was the first year the society listed prices in their
catalogue. Toward the end of May he sent three water colors to
the thirty-fourth annual exhibition of American art at the Cincinnati Art Museum, among them *Filling Station*. This is one of
the rare dated Maurers, "26" being plainly visible beneath his
name. The view is looking north on U. S. 9-W, the main highway
which follows the west side of the Hudson. Almost a quarter of a
century has passed since then, but the scene is still recognizable.
To this extent Maurer was a documentary painter. Probably today he would have painted a jeep instead of a Model T Ford. His
facile control of water color and his ability to create the effect of
light by apparently simple means are evident. The painting
breathes nostalgia for things past, such a mood as is felt when one
imagines that the problems of existence can be solved by a return
to a simpler way of life.

This same year the Brooklyn Museum held an exhibition of
"Paintings in Oil by the Group of American Painters of Paris"
from April 22 to June 1. "Americans who live in Paris" included
Jules Pascin, Oliver Chaffee, H. C. Lee, C. H. Thorndyke, E. P.
Ullman, Clinton O'Callahan, Gale Turnbull, F. C. Frieseke, Oscar Gieberich, Harold English, and Myron C. Nutting. The guest
exhibitors were Maurer, Glackens, Kenneth Hayes Miller, Rockwell Kent, David Karfunkle, Jean Marchand, and Roderic O'Conor.
Critical comment singled out the following for favorable notice—
Pascin, Maurer, Miller, O'Conor, and Gieberich. Maurer had two
paragraphs of the review's total of seven, Pascin one paragraph
and the rest a listing. Of Maurer the critic wrote:

> To American connoisseurs, the chief surprise of the exhibition
> will be, I believe, the four paintings of Alfred Maurer. Mr. Maurer
> has had a long and strange career, tasting at intervals of success and

enduring neglect for long periods. He began with successes, for it was natural for him to wield the brushes, and his easy manner made him persona grata in the official exhibitions. Suddenly he threw academies overboard and became a rank and daring modernist.

The four paintings in Brooklyn, however, will certainly stir some collectors into taking an interest. They are two flower pieces and two landscapes. They sparkle with color and have a certain intensity that has been missed from the recent Maurer work. Also, there is something unusual, indefinable, about them. Maurer has always endeavored to shun platitudes, and now certainly does.

Time went on, filled with work. Summer came and went. And it was the fall of 1927. At this time Maurer must have rented the studio in the Lincoln Square Arcade Building at the corner of Broadway and Sixty-sixth Street, though friends are vague in regard to the exact date. How else explain the remarkable flowering of his painting revealed in his exhibition in the spring of 1928? He was forced to find a place of his own to work, the story runs, because he could no longer endure his father's climbing up on a stepladder to peek at him through the transom. Release from spiritual espionage released creative forces in Maurer, and he painted energetically. His studio was a small room with a window facing east on Broadway, stacked to the ceiling with pictures, as a photograph taken in the fall of 1928 shows (page 198). The building stood on the site of the farm where Louis and Louisa Maurer had married long before, in 1860, and it was owned by John L. Miller, whose wife was the sister of Maurer's sister-in-law. Apparently Alfy paid about $40 a month rent, no bargain for space in such a firetrap as the building proved to be. He kept the studio through the half-million-dollar fire of January 30, 1931, till his death; and his paintings were removed from it to storage early in August, 1932.

Maurer had more personal freedom now than he had had for years. Friends could come to see him and have a drink in peace. Perhaps he even had a sweetheart there; old friends suggest this. More important than anything else, he could work without interruption or criticism. He had grown very weary of the often-repeated cliches his father loved to utter. He himself did not paint platitudes. He did not wish to have them drummed into his ears. Louis Maurer never ceased being "puzzled at modern art." Even his obituaries rehearsed this favorite remark of his. And he never tired of saying that "its devotees often used [modern art] as a short cut to avoid mastering some of the difficult fundamentals of art as he knew it." He maintained that "the old principles simply could not be flouted." The old principles to which he referred, of course, were a derivative "photographic" renderism, based on drawing from wooden tableaux.

Alfred Maurer, on the contrary, looked to nature and to life for his sources. Now almost sixty, he went back to school to himself. Once a week, or oftener, he had a model come in to pose. Countless sketches, large and small, dashed off in heat and spontaneity or drawn with a relaxed hand and eye, prove him a master draughtsman. He cut up expensive portfolios of art reproductions, including the de luxe Dial portfolio printed in Germany, and on these scraps of paper drew nudes standing, sitting, reclining, alone and in pairs. Sometimes he sketched with quickly drawn brush strokes in thin washes of oil paint. Sometimes he drew in pencil, with soft shadings of tone and value to represent form. Sometimes he drew with a bold black sweep of the pencil, letting volume be suggested by line. Or he drew in ink, with cross hatching or a nervous broken line, not unlike the texture of Degas bronzes.

Only one feature seemed to elude him, the rendering of feet. Many times he drew the feet over, imposing corrections on the first clumsily presented notes. In this respect the tradition of naturalism in which he had his sole formal education for art failed him. The composite of Sargent grand manner, Whistler crepuscule, and Chase bravura did not demand a surgical knowledge of anatomy such as Dr. Rimmer preached at Cooper Union or Eakins at the Pennsylvania Academy. A facile surface representation of appearances sufficed for Chase and his school. Late in life, Maurer sought to correct this lack in his own aesthetic armory. Indeed, might not the early twentieth century revolt against academicism have been a protest, albeit unconscious, and to a degree ineffectual, against the flimsiness of the academicians' technical pretensions?

FOUR HEADS, *ca.* 1930
TEMPERA ON GESSO PANEL, $21\frac{3}{4} \times 18\frac{1}{4}$ IN.
COLLECTION: MR. AND MRS. HUDSON D. WALKER

NUDE, *ca*. 1927

OIL ON GESSO PANEL, 39x24¼ IN.

COLLECTION: MR. AND MRS. HUDSON D. WALKER

FOUR SISTERS, *ca.* 1927
OIL ON GESSO PANEL, 36x25½ IN.
COLLECTION: GEORGE LINCOLN SHASKAN

HEAD, *ca.* 1927
WATER COLOR AND GOUACHE
ON PAPER, 21½x18 IN.
COLLECTION: BERTHA SCHAEFER

SELF-PORTRAIT, *ca.* 1927
OIL ON COMPOBOARD
21½x18 IN.
COLLECTION: PAUL SHASKAN

MAURER IN HIS STUDIO, NOVEMBER, 1928

Maurer, it seems, studied the nude as a subject only this one season, the fall of 1927 and the early spring of 1928. He painted large oils of standing nudes, of which the one reproduced (page 196) is perhaps not the most nostalgic but certainly one of the most imposing. Except for the nude listed in the 1928 catalogue of the Independent's, the nudes shown at Weyhe's are the only work of this kind he exhibited. The painting illustrated here shows less deterioration than many of his oils. Its handsome color and design have not been abraded or attacked by chemical action. One of his large works, a 39x24½-inch panel, it shows the standing figure in multiple perspective, the figure being at eye level and the background of dark screen and tessellated black-and-white floor being seen from above at a sharp angle, as earlier he had painted a flower study (page 165). Where, in his crowded studio, did Alfy find room for perspective at all?

Many of his friends did not know he painted and drew nudes— certainly a facet in the Maurer enigma. Was the taboo of 1893 still operative? Fetishism of a different kind may be read in the subsequent fate of his nudes. About this time Maurer began to be afflicted with hypertrophy of the prostate gland. Painful and enervating physically, his illness undoubtedly had psychological concomitants. He painted out the nudes, slashing away with brush and paint, or he painted over them, transforming breasts and buttocks into women's heads. In *Head in Landscape* (page 208) glowing and voluptuous bodies may be seen, as through masks, lurking behind tortured faces. Was this the torture of self-mutilation?

IV

THE NUDES were not painted out, however, until after the April, 1928, exhibition. For this event, which ran from April 2 to April 14, Maurer cut two linoleum blocks, as he had done for the November, 1924, exhibition. One showed a long-necked girl in a tender pose, bending with a Botticellian air toward the vase of flowers with which Maurer endowed her. The design is freer than previously, and its asymmetrical composition gives space for the forms to breathe. Again he has suffused a simple black-and-white print with light. The other print shows two flappers seated on a bench, perhaps a piano bench, flanked with vertical lines in white, which suggest the folds of drapes. It is a simple device, but effective.

General was the interest expressed by the press in the nudes, "a new departure," and his "over life size self-portrait, a psychological document as well as a marvelous piece of painting." This was, of course, *Self-Portrait with Hat* (frontispiece) which was reproduced in *The Arts* in May, 1928. "There is no question," wrote the Chicago *Post,* which had managed to "scoop" the New York papers by printing its review the day after the exhibition opened, "that this is one of his masterpieces." In oil on a gesso panel 39x23⅞ inches, the self-portrait is Maurer's letter to the world that never wrote to him. He has passed through storm and stress, he has surmounted adversity and isolation, he has conquered the technical and expressive problems of his craft. He faces the world, sober, even somber, but he faces the world. It is he that is the accuser. Those black eyes, unwavering, ask why it is that none has seen and understood.

So immediate is the impact of Maurer's drawing and modeling that it is easy to overlook his constant search for color as a means of expression. The self-portrait is characteristic. The brilliant, sometimes fugitive pigments of his earlier palette have yielded place to a muted color scheme. He has posed himself against a green and green-blue background, in the simple formula he preferred. His soft hat, poked into the shape he loved, is a warm gray in color. His white shirt, open at the neck, is modeled with blue and pink shadows, and his untied bow tie is dark blue with light blue dots. Hot flesh tones, dark red lips much darker than he painted the lips of women, outlines of mouth and nose drawn in black, highlights of raised dots of yellow on his spectacle frames— these colors complete his palette. It is the palette of nature, with that added *x* of psychological content.

The *Self-Portrait* (page 198) without hat, a smaller work, is imbued with the same intensity, as it uses a similar color scheme. Its dark green background is picked out with white and light gray dots, like magnified divisionist points. The bow tie is tied this time, and yellow highlights may be noted on the spectacle frames. Again the beholder is impressed by the power of the face, the revelation of character, the impact of personality. Note, too, how Maurer has drawn his own features in *Head* (page 198). If he was not Narcissus, still he read in dome of forehead, high cheekbones, long jaw, and curving lips a story of form he found forever alluring. In his "niece in spirit," he found the same look.

"This year" [Maurer had painted] "some highly amusing little genre pieces," the press noted, "glimpses of modern interiors with flappers, painted in a brilliant and highly personal style." He also showed "some flower pieces and still lifes with fruit that are remarkable for their solidity and brilliance of color." More than that, "as the years go on Maurer's painting has taken on a richness and a vibrance and a freedom of handling. Thru his mastery and directness of technique there no longer is a barrier between his intention and execution; there is, to be sure, experiment, constant experiment, but no faltering. He knows definitely what he wants to do and he does it."

Not all the early reviews responded so favorably to Maurer's 1928 exhibition. The *Times* damned him with "plus-minus" comment, the main objection being to his cross-eyed women. The *Herald-Tribune* mentioned that Maurer was "known for his inimitable studies of children, which he paints according to a kind of formula." It continued:

Although he has enlarged his repertory a little so that it includes some recent nudes and a large self-portrait, he has really enlarged his range but little. One of the most commendable qualities he has is a feeling for color. He manages it so that it glows with the richness of enamel, putting it to the service of his quaint ideas with flowing precision. In the main, Mr. Maurer depends upon the same models, the little girls who are probably twins, and who occur and recur singly and in twos, sometimes in blue frocks, sometimes in yellow, and occasionally appear in canvases which their faces swallow up altogether. Whatever may be the artist's purpose the effect he produces is that of a kind of caricature rather than of serious portraiture.

A week later, the New York *Post* discussed the "familiar aspects" and the "surprisingly new" features of the exhibition; ". . . the usual long-faced ladies of equine expression in gay dresses" were noted, and attention was called to "a nude, both sensitively and solidly painted, endowed with bodily tension and life in her easy gesture of poise against the richness of enameled hues that belong to Mr. Maurer's palette." The *Post* continued:

> There are still lifes, fruits and flowers with beauty of surface and great charm in their relation of forms and contours. The color, above all, is something quite individual, both in its depth and rich- ness and its lustrous quality. Mr. Ziegrosser [*sic*], who is the tutelary genius of this gallery, informs me that the artist grinds his own colors, a fact which may account for their enamel-like quality. But it is also in the juxtaposition of his color and his unexpected rela- tions of brilliant notes that Mr. Maurer delights one. He plays on an instrument of a few deep plangent tones, but from it he produces a rich, seductive melody that is irresistible once listened to. Color means so many different things in the hands of each artist who uses it that it is useless to describe it or explain its effect. It must be seen and appreciated to be understood.
>
> It is only a few years ago that Mr. Maurer was rescued from his garret seclusion, where he and any number of good canvases were languishing. Now that he is again selling his work and creating it rapidly, there is a gayety [*sic*] apparent in all his paintings—a verve and sparkle that give it animation and relieve it from a haunting sadness that used to be its keynote.

For the first time Maurer received extended critical considera- tion in *The Arts*. He had been mentioned a few times in the 1920s, and one of his landscapes had been reproduced in 1924. His fifth annual exhibition at Weyhe's brought forth favorable comment from Virgil Barker, an exacting member of that exact- ing magazine's editorial staff. Maurer was given a column of type and two reproductions, *Nude* (page 196) and *Self-Portrait with Hat* (frontispiece). One of our serious critics and an early exponent of the significance of the American tradition for American artists, Barker wrote at length. His comment is given in full; it represents, probably, the most mature criticism Maurer had had up to that point. It follows:

> The occasion of my first acquaintance with the paintings of Mr. Maurer was in March of 1924, when the accumulation of years was

displayed. The circumstances surrounding this exhibition were such as to remain in the memory now four years later. At that time the most striking trait of Mr. Maurer's work was intensity, which manifested itself technically in a somewhat disturbing conception of human character.

Both manifestations were still present in the recent work exhibited at Weyhe's during the first half of April; and they were so unmistakably the same that they would have given an impression of the artist having stood still had it not been for the addition of another factor which effectively contradicted the half-formed judgment.

This added element is, I should say, simply ease of expression. As I recall the earlier exhibition, the artist was then in the grip of unmodified reaction against something; and at the time I was not sure whether his was only another raw rebellion against academicism as an exterior force, the end of which is barrenness, or was an inward struggle against the academicism of his own nature which when victorious brings into being a truly personal art. After seeing the recent exhibition, I felt that Mr. Maurer's revolt was of the latter fruitful kind because of the perceptibly increased freedom in his work.

For this there was another reason also. Along with the gain in ease, whether as cause or effect does not much matter, was discernible a greater degree of consistency in thought, which was made all the more plain for the increased range of subject-matter to which it was applied. The pictures of the nude constituted the prime novelty of the exhibition here recorded; the activity of design to be noted in them seemed to me to be due to the artist's more vigorous attack upon form for its own sake.

It is true that Mr. Maurer's vision and psychology are as far as ever from the usual; but for successful expression in art psychological normality is less important than psychological consistency. It is also true that what Mr. Maurer has to say is so definitely different that comparatively few people will relish it; but the fact that a personal quality of utterance is limited does not abate its originality.

To me Mr. Maurer's greatest danger, to which he has succumbed in the large Self Portrait, seems to be over emphasis—a danger which he shares with a whole age of headlines and electric signs and

jazz. It would be silly to urge restraint upon those who have nothing to restrain; but where real power exists there is still some virtue
in understatement.

Emphasis by understatement, selection by exclusion, these are
standard formal principles. In an age torn by economic crisis and
war, the rules have a schoolbook sound. Emphasis by overstate-
ment, selection by inclusion, these have been practiced in life in
an era full of violence, suffering, and chaos. Why should not art
hold up its mirror to these also? For fifty years and more, expressionism has followed a straight line of development. Van Gogh,
the fauves, the Blue Rider group in Germany, Marsden Hartley
of the Stieglitz group—the roots were there. Even in 1913, Maurer
had been called an expressionist. His language was—as Virgil
Barker understood it—a personal speech, not an intellectual system. He had to state his content of experience in terms of its own
inner intensity. How many American painters in 1928 felt so
deeply about what they had to say?

If the "quiet desperation" of Thoreau's phrase had been Maurer's mood, restraint might have been his method. Emily Dickinson
foresaw his dilemma: *Mirth is the mail of anguish.* Quiet Maurer
may have been, in regard to illness and personal loss, and desperate he may have been. Anguished he was, assuredly, and he wore
mirth to armor his anguish. Look at his eyes as he saw himself.
Those are eyes which suffer. His concern was not to be the historian of jazz age and prohibition era, but of one human being,
Alfred Maurer. From the depths of his being he shouted of his
terror and pity: his was a cry from the soul. The world is not
pleased to hear screams of agony rising from the throats of those
who die in the act of daily living. Maurer remained unheard.

7. *Fulfillment*

THE TIME left Maurer was short. After 1928 he had three years for work. Whether or not his death-wish was of long standing, he must have had a premonition of the briefness of time, which his own act made tragically true. If illness affected his creative effort quantitatively, qualitatively his aesthetic statement grew ever more powerful. In these years Maurer found himself. After his long and lonely vigil in the wilderness, he fused theme and language into a single communication. Accepting the necessity of the narrow choice he had made, he made that choice noble. The artist, if he live joyously, may record the laughter of life. If his circumstance be adverse, he may record adversity and yet transcend it. Maurer mastered his bitter lesson. For him life was filled with the tears of things, but at the last he metamorphosed tears into brilliant and shining jewels.

The final chapter of Maurer's life was marked by an intensely dramatic expression. Whether looking into his own soul or into that approaching future of eternity, Maurer scanned the spiritual horizon of existence with a fierce and concentrated gaze as if to draw forth from the unknown answers to all the questions he had been asking all his years. From his self-portraits he fixed somber and brooding eyes on the onlooker. To his armory of vision he added all the pairs of eyes of all his somber and brooding women. His piercing gaze proved not an obsession but a means of survival. *The eyes of Alfred Maurer's women never close.* He saw the words in print, he read them written on the retina of his mind. *Wide open windows in the pale rosy stucco of their physiognomies, these eyes . . . terrible in the dead straightness of their stare, . . . seem to challenge . . .* What? Time? Fate? Or all the faces of existence on which he found no answering look?

Maurer grew older, stooped, tired. He wore his clothes with less of an air, and they were not as well pressed as they had been. In November, 1928, he posed for the press in his Lincoln Square Arcade Building studio (page 198) in front of two paintings, with scores of others stacked in racks up to the ceiling. Strength, resiliency, gaiety have been drained from his slight body and poured into his work. Yet the work itself looks forth confidently. Maurer has come to the point in his life at which his painting speaks for him. On that he must stand. He has lived sixty years and he has been an artist more than half of his life. If now he must make excuses, what a sorry end to rebellion and suffering. He stands in his studio, weary, aging, alone, and leaves the rest to history. Look a year or so ahead, and see the son posed with Louis Maurer in the father's third-floor studio at 404 West Forty-third Street (page 27). The fable of his life is written plain. Yet Alfy was not a man to enjoy rivalry and competition. He was compassionate and tender, and generous with his fellow artists. Even the Broadway shooting gallery camera saw (page 222) that he was a man of good will.

Maurer's last years were filled with unrecorded work, illness, and Louis Maurer's rise to fame. Maurer did not hold another exhibition at Weyhe's until 1931, his last one-man show. He continued to exhibit every year in the Independent's and continued to receive kind words from the press. But his life drew in its boundaries. His disease became increasingly painful as kidney damage progressed. He could not get about the Marlboro countryside as freely as he had, and he gave up his after-supper croquet games. He did not dance as he had before; and when he spent Christmas Eve with the Doves, he sat by abstemiously while the others drank "red ink." Was painting over the nudes also connected with his disease?

THE FLORENTINES, *ca.* 1929

OIL ON CANVAS, ON PLASTER BOARD, 26x18 IN.

COLLECTION: PHILLIPS MEMORIAL GALLERY

HEAD IN LANDSCAPE, *ca*. 1929
OIL ON GESSO PANEL,
39X23¾ IN.
COLLECTION: MR. AND MRS.
ROY R. NEUBERGER

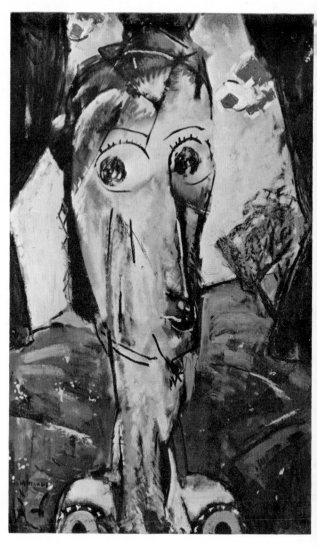

HEAD, *ca*. 1928
OIL ON GESSO PANEL, 39X24 IN.
COLLECTION: MR. AND MRS. HUDSON D. WALKER

208

TWO HEADS, *ca.* 1928
OIL ON GESSO PANEL, 48x39⅛ IN.
COLLECTION: MR. AND MRS. HUDSON D. WALKER

TWO HEADS, 1930
OIL ON GESSO PANEL, 21½x18 IN.
COLLECTION: BERTHA SCHAEFER GALLERY

His channel of life was work. He had sent a *Nude* and a *Head*, each priced at $200, to the 1928 Independent's. He began to paint masterly still lifes in a cubist-abstractionist style. How far he had left behind the glowingly decorative naturalistic flowers. Far from Paris and far from the followers of Picasso and Braque, he evolved a personal idiom in which paint is used freely for sensuous surface qualities and in which form is freely designed in space. He left behind the bondage of gesso, under-painting, and "glazing," to paint directly. Sometimes he achieved the effect of directness by using earlier oils as a base. At least on them his colors, applied almost as they came from the tube, could not sink into a greedily hungry plaster ground.

He continued to work in series, as he had done with girls, vases of flowers, and gnarled trees. He used an apparatus of table, vase, picture on wall, fruit in a dish, and the rest, and rearranged his composition over and over. Sometimes he would deck the table with black-and-white linoleum prints. Other times he draped a fish in a plate and decorated the background with a fish-motif wallpaper, a touch of his old whimsy. The still lifes show progression from recognizable subject to abstract expression. In the *Still Life*, owned by the Brooklyn Museum, he simplified, or "abstracted," the *Green Striped Bowl* and left only a strong Prussian blue form with deep green shadows, an area of burgundy red slashed with deep green stripes, and a contrasting area of light green-yellow. Later his still lifes again became texturally complex and intricate, with paper doilies used for lacelike stencils.

The success of his still lifes was attested by the *Times*, which wrote: "Maurer is quite at his best in a still-life composed of a white plate with a scrawled pattern in red and blue, some solid toothsome pears that cast deep blue shadows of eccentric shape and a billowing fabric of many colors. The bitter yellow that serves him as a gallant banner, flaunting itself above the other colors in his scheme, defiant against crimson, is used more extensively in his picture, 'Two Girls,' where the long faces and high foreheads, the pinched and starved anatomies seem to justify the choice of this strangely disconcerting color."

The reference was not to *Two Heads* (page 209); but it applies except for color. A profoundly brooding air pervades this largest of Maurer's paintings, excluding his early 2x1-meter canvases. Four times larger than life, the two faces look out from a dark green background, their hair green-black and their eyes black. Crimson lips and hot flesh tones stand out against blue and white checks, and the outlines are in black. Modeling and texture have been carried toward greater simplification than in *Self-Portrait with Hat* (frontispiece). Almost three times larger than life, *Head* (page 208) uses a similar scheme. In both, weight and mass create monumentality. Line is pure and form is pure; but it is human personality with which Maurer is concerned rather than formalism. His inheritance from Botticelli has been transmuted into his own coin, as has his legacy from Whistler and Chase, and his association with Matisse and Picasso and the Steins.

He painted and he exhibited. In 1929 he sent two heads to the Independent's, each priced at $100. Perhaps these were his powerful, staring gouaches. He sent out work in the traveling exhibitions organized by the College Art Association, including the self-portrait and *Flappers* (page 176); and the former was shown at the Atlantic City Municipal Art Gallery in 1929. Finally, some of his paintings were lent by Weyhe to an exhibition of furniture and interiors at Modernage. Maurer was seeking to get his work out into the world through all possible channels.

The years were passing. Alfy and Paris friends, Elsie and Ernest Fuhr, the Glackens, the Prestons, were together for the last time on New Year's Eve, 1929. Death was beginning to dissolve old ties. Yet death would not dissolve one bond which Maurer found ever more painful to endure, the tie which bound him to his father. Could not Maurer have returned to Paris in the early 1920s, using the small legacy from his mother, or at least after 1924, on the small annual income guaranteed him by Weyhe? Americans in Paris who received small allotments in American dollars could live on a princely scale; $20 or $25 a week was great wealth. Had hate woven bonds for Maurer as indissoluble as those of love?

He painted and exhibited. In 1930 he sent two heads to the Independent's, each priced at $850. Perhaps these were the large *Two Heads* and *Head* above mentioned. Looking back to the great depression, one cannot but wonder at the innocence or ignorance which allowed Alfy to put such prices on his work. Financiers and artists were solving their problems by jumping out of windows in the financial district skyscrapers or off bridges. The United States was moving toward a "stockpile" of millions of unemployed. What use was art when there were no nickels for apples? Maurer had always remained curiously aloof from life. He never voted in this country, remaining at Marlboro till after Election Day, though his legal residence was New York. He understood the suffering of the individual, extending his own misery into the lives of others and identifying himself emotionally with the oppressed whose unhappiness he could read written in their eyes. Probably he never learned the deep social causes of suffering. So he put these prices on his paintings at a time when nothing was being sold, not even bread.

Yet by ultimate values, the prices were modest. To the extent that the artist is the spokesman of the rights of man, as well as the rights of the artist, Maurer maintained the right of fair pay for honest work. In fact, Henry McBride wrote sympathetically in the *Sun* of Maurer's entries in the 1930 Independent's. Among noticeable pictures in the display, the critic mentioned first "the contribution by Alfy Maurer." He had "at the first sight of the big 'Head' by him . . . burst as heartily as any philistine into laughter." It was, he hastened to add, "sympathetic laughter—with reservations." He went on to explain:

It is so wild a picture that I even wondered, for a moment, that the Independents took it in. It is one of those long, narrow heads to which Mr. Maurer has accustomed us; and which meant so much to Sherwood Anderson. The eyes, ears and other features of this head occur at random. There is something frantic in the arrangement of the items, as though they had been assembled by a highly nervous person in the midst of a cyclone. At the same time, there is what we call "organization" in this picture and a breadth of treatment that could come only from an expert. Mr. Maurer is to be commended therefore for his courage in defying conventions and in relying upon his "vision." There are so few among our artists who are willing to risk their reputations for a principle.

Maurer had left his days of mirthfulness behind. But the end of his life was rounded out with comedy. The day before McBride bestowed his modified praise, a nightclub hostess approached a Maurer with strenuous criticism. Under a two-column head, "June Day Sees Herself / Then Slashes Picture," the *Telegram* wrote in the style of the gay thirties:

June Day, who admits that she is the "Texas Guinan of Paris," took one look at a portrait of her in the Independent Artists' show today and yelled right out loud.

She seized a knife from an innocent bystander who was sharpening a pencil as he soaked up art in the Grand Central Palace.

"I'll show that bum," yelled the red-headed Miss Day, and she proceeded to have a private riot of her own right then and there.

FINALLY RESTRAINED.

She slashed the picture across the face. She raised her arm for another swing. Attendants and spectators bore down upon her to protect the art of Alfred H. Maurer.

The painter hove into view, surveyed the situation with consternation and prudently departed for the gentlemen's dressing room, where he remained barricaded until Miss Day was led vociferously from the gallery.

"That guy," shrieked the departing Miss Day, "couldn't even paint a barn."

PAINTER MOURNS.

After she was gone, as attendants gathered in sorrowful consultation about the slashed portrait, Maurer strode forth to contemplate his art.

"What did a night club singer expect?" he demanded. "A madonna?"

Maurer, a chipper little man of 61, has his studio at 1,947 Broadway. It was there that he painted an impressionistic portrait of Miss Day, who lives at the Hotel Lombardy on Park Ave. and holds forth as czarina of whoopee at the Night Boat, a night club at 117 W. 48 St.

"I didn't let her see it. I told her I would surprise her with it in the show. It seems that I did.

PAINTED AS SEEN.

"Certainly it isn't an academic portrait. It is Miss Day—a red-headed night club singer—as I saw her beneath her lipstick."

Miss Day disagreed.

"I never looked that dopey even with a hangover," she commented politely.

The one-column cut of June Day does not provide a clue as to what painting was slashed. A cloche hat hides her hair; the millinery of the period itself makes the wearer look "dopey." Was this a scheme to obtain publicity for the nightclub? Or for the Independent's? The hoax might have appealed to Alfy, sunk though he was in his personal depression.

II

WHILE Maurer worked alone and without recognition, Louis Maurer was experiencing a resurrection. It was not a rebirth of fame; fame he had never had in terms of public acclaim and reputation. He had had a hard-earned financial success and the satisfactions of economic security and leisure. He had not been known as a painter of importance during the years in which he devoted himself to painting after his retirement from business; and in his early printmaking days, he had not been publicized as an artist. The makers of the Currier and Ives designs were craftsmen producing a commodity for which there was a popular market at popular prices. No aura of art surrounded their work. Thus Louis Maurer had never fed on the bright magic thing, glory. Now he would.

In 1928 Harry T. Peters met Louis Maurer. The late sportsman-print connoisseur had been collecting Currier and Ives prints for a number of years. He began to plan to put the rewards of his years of collecting into book form; and in 1929 he published his two-volume *Currier & Ives: Printmakers to the American People,* with a check list of all known prints. In the course of his researches, collector Peters learned that Louis Maurer was still alive. A friendship was struck up, the two talking German together and reliving former times. The Peters book was issued by subscription at $40 a copy, after publishers had refused it as a bad publishing risk. It came out late in 1929; by January, 1930, single copies were selling at $250, and by April for $375. It was published at the psychological moment. America had been "rediscovered" by Waldo Frank and by hundreds of expatriate artists, writers and musicians who had had to return to the United States when the "crash" cut off allowances from home.

Louis Maurer, as the sole surviving artist who had worked for Currier and Ives, was also "rediscovered." He had a biographical section in the book, and he was discovered in person. The revival of Louis Maurer was excellent feature and human interest news for the press, a factor which by no means interfered with the revival of Currier and Ives. Special articles and interviews appeared in quantity, illustrated with photographs of Louis Maurer standing in front of Currier and Ives prints or sitting in an armchair in front of them, smiling at dinners given to launch the books which began to appear about these printmakers, posing in the studio at "404" in front of paintings he had made of Buffalo Bill and General Custer, almost half a century earlier. The furore paid handsome dividends of public approval and attention to Louis Maurer. To Alfred Maurer, harassed by illness and saddened by lack of success, the fanfare sounded no harmonious note. Moreover, his father, when interviewed, lost no opportunity to deride his son's "modernistic" art. Thus the father-son war ceased to be private.

Maurer continued to work. Whatever the difficulties of these years, he was ready by January, 1931, to hold an exhibition of his latest work. To greet the New Year, he wrote Laura Canade Zigrosser, whom he saluted as "Maglaura." "Ha!" he shouted, "What a fine name for a flower." Her Christmas greetings he returned with a "me, too, here too, to you." Like Dove, Alfy never lost his ear for the American language. He added: "Am coming over soon, was so mad this Christmas I shot Sato Clause in the pants, and I was so excited I didn't know he coming in, in place of going out." Was it *papa* Maurer's foghorn playing on Christmas Eve which made Maurer mad, or his flute playing on New Year's?

Maurer's last one-man show was held at Weyhe's from January 12 to 26. The announcement was not decorated with a linoleum cut print but with a half-tone cut of a very handsome still life of table top and vase, with a painting propped up against the wall behind the table. Apparently the work exhibited was selected with care not to present novel or "repellent" themes; for the powerful double heads of 1930, some of which are dated, were not mentioned by the art press. The *Herald-Tribune* wrote:

> A number of new still life designs mark the principal development of the last year in the work of Alfred Maurer. . . . These venture further in the direction of pure abstraction than Mr. Maurer has yet progressed and reveal in their best form a new sensitiveness toward color as well. Here is a painter who, throughout the years, has tacked an irregular course, finding strange new adventures at every turn. The study of a young woman, painted in a Whistlerian effect of appropriate subtlety and charm, dates back many years, but it serves eloquently to illustrate the point of departure from which all his later work evolved. There are several of those inimitable heads of girls in the show which blossomed so abundantly from his brush a year ago, but on the whole the present occasion concerns itself with inanimate objects. What Mr. Maurer makes of his fruit and his books is wholly subtle and a little vague, but the way the items are arranged on the canvas and brushed in with a soft, indefinite accent, is certainly the result of an outlook of his own. It is to their advantage, moreover, that Mr. Maurer has refrained from glazing them over as he has done with dubious success in his paintings in the past. And the thought occurs that all of his pictures would be benefited by larger frames.

The *New Yorker,* a longtime supporter of Maurer, wrote cordially, ending with a rebuke for those who cling to the past and reject the contemporary:

> With considerable shrewdness, the Weyhe Gallery also shows Maurer's early masterpieces of the Chase period. Probably Weyhe didn't intend to be ironic, but we think this part of the exhibit a fine bit of evidence for the cause of Modernism. The timid may be won over to a newer form of painting if they can be convinced that at one time Maurer could paint as prettily as any of the calendar artists.

The *World* also stressed this moral sympathetically though not accurately, since the painting described is not the arrangement for which Maurer won the Carnegie prize. The comment follows:

> There hangs in the Weyhe Galleries a painting by Alfred Maurer that won a gold medal in a Carnegie international exhibition about twenty-five years ago. It is a full-length figure of a comely woman gowned for the street. The original might count on welcome in select company. This picture now finds itself on view with a galaxy of recent paintings by Maurer, with women of angular faces and elongated necks in the majority. Maurer has subjected anatomy to self-expression in his maturer life. The comely figure and those of the painter's present ideals are hung in contrast to show how he has progressed in his art. No doubt is left that in the act of creation he has drawn subjects from a realm not on the map, but where evolution works full time.

To the ambivalence of such criticisms, Maurer might have replied with Emily Dickinson's "Demur—you're straightway dangerous / And handled with a chain." The reviewers were, it is evident, attracted to Maurer's work. They wished to understand his expression, and they applauded his single-mindedness in remaining true to his convictions. At the same time they were teased by an uneasy sense that there is something suspect in rebellion. The status quo, even in the harmless area of aesthetics, must be maintained. Let revolt stir in the ateliers, and the guardians of the republic of art rally to defend what is. How else can the reviews' "plus-minus" tone be interpreted?

As Maurer's last exhibition drew to its close, his father prepared to hold his first one-man exhibition. This was to be of Currier and Ives prints which he had drawn; and it was to be held at the Old Print Shop on Lexington Avenue. The event was announced in a tastefully designed broadside, illustrated with two medallion portraits of Louis Maurer, and also in a two-column advertisement of the exhibition of "America's Oldest Living Artist and Surviving Member of the Staff of Currier & Ives." By a curious irony, the date set for Louis Maurer's world premiere was January 26, the day on which Alfred Maurer's exhibition closed. Earlier that month the father had been indisposed. When the date came, he

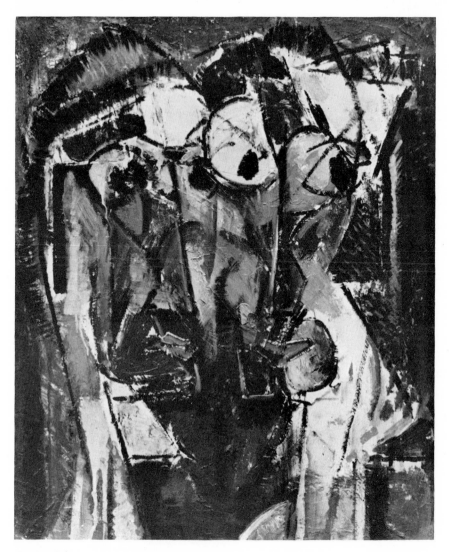

TWO HEADS, *ca.* 1931
OIL ON BOARD, 21½X18 IN.
COLLECTION: BERTHA SCHAEFER GALLERY

TWIN HEADS, *ca.* 1930
OIL ON CANVAS, ON BOARD, WITH GESSO, 26½×18 IN.
COLLECTION: MR. AND MRS. HUDSON D. WALKER

STILL LIFE WITH DOILY, *ca.* 1930. OIL ON UPSON BOARD, $17\frac{3}{4}$x$21\frac{1}{2}$ IN.
COLLECTION: PHILLIPS MEMORIAL GALLERY

STILL LIFE WITH PEARS, *ca.* 1931–1932. OIL ON COMPOBOARD, $25\frac{1}{2}$x$35\frac{7}{8}$ IN.
COLLECTION: ADDISON GALLERY OF AMERICAN ART

HEAD OF A MAN, *ca.* 1930
WATER COLOR AND GOUACHE
ON PAPER, 18½×13 IN.
COLLECTION:
BERTHA SCHAEFER GALLERY

MAURER
IN HIS
LAST YEARS,
ABOUT 1931

HEAD, *ca.* 1929
WATER COLOR AND GOUACHE
ON PAPER, 21¼×18 IN.
COLLECTION: MR. AND MRS.
SETH DENNIS

could not attend the opening, to prove in person that the smiling, bowtie-bedecked, goatee-adorned old man shown on the broadside existed in the flesh, seventy-seven years older than the flowing-haired youth pictured at the outset of his career as a Currier and Ives artist. He was represented, instead, by his son, Charles L. Maurer.

The human interest aspects of the story were a "natural" for the press. The *Herald-Tribune, World, Times, Post,* and *Sun,* repeatedly gave space to the event. The *Sun* led all the rest with an eight-column spread on its "Antiques and Interior Decorations" page, calling Louis Maurer "A Printmaker to the People" in a two-column head. Reproductions of his prints appeared, and a two-column cut of Louis Maurer on his bay Rock, with which he had won a blue ribbon at the first New York Horse Show in 1883. The New York Steuben Club reprinted the *Sun's* story in its magazine, and the *Literary Digest* collected plums from the press under the title "The Oldest Artist in America." This latter was illustrated with three reproductions. And on the day after his ninety-ninth birthday the *Brooklyn Eagle* gave a page in its magazine section to Louis Maurer, with a two-column cut of his painting of West Forty-third Street and a four-column cut of him standing beside another of his paintings. Such was fame.

So Louis Maurer came to his ninety-ninth birthday, his spirit fed on acclaim and rediscovery. The occasion was celebrated at the family home, and he was showered with letters and telegrams of congratulation. All day long old friends called, and a party for relatives and intimates finished the celebration. On the day before, the *Herald-Tribune* carried an "advance" story, in a good position in the first column of a left-hand inside page, with a two-column cut of Louis Maurer, standing flute in hand beside the family grand piano at which his daughter, Eugenia Maurer Fuerstenberg, was seated, ready to accompany him. Subheads on the story read:

Disapproves of Dry Law

———

Dislikes Modernism in Art,
Though It Gave Son Prize

The error of fact in the second bank, that modernism gave Alfred Maurer the Carnegie prize, when it was academicism, does not change the inference that Louis Maurer had said a great deal to the interviewer and that his talk was aimed at his son. The interview stated:

> Modern painting does not appeal to Mr. Maurer, who passed years of hard study to perfect the fine draughtsmanship that is evident in prints of his work. "Modern painters veer too much toward the grotesque," he declared. "They refuse to spend the time and energy in studying drawing. They lack perspective. Good draughtsmanship is the foundation of all good art work."
>
> Mr. Maurer's son, Alfred J. [*sic*] Maurer, is a modern painter, one of whose works "An Arrangement" won the Carnegie prize in 1901. That painting hangs today above the fireplace in Mr. Maurer's parlor in the brownstone house.

The error in Maurer's name is significant: he had exhibited enough so that the *Herald-Tribune's* "morgue" must have had a file for him. More significant is the fact that the interviewer showed no curiosity as to the age of the son of a man lacking one year of one hundred. Was Alfy still in the nursery? Most important is the father's rationalization of his veiled attacks on his son, in the guise of attacks on modern art. How can Alfred Maurer's undoubted mastery of draughtsmanship, which he had rejected in its superficial academic applications, be squared with the charge that "modern" artists cannot draw?

The father took triumph in his stride. He attended the opening of the Third International Antiques Exposition at the Grand Central Palace, where some $25,000,000 worth of *objets d'art* were on display. He made good copy as he autographed a print he had signed seventy years earlier, and as he toured the booths with Harry Shaw Newman, Old Print Shop entrepreneur. He had a letter from the American Consulate in Stuttgart, addressed to "Mr Louis Maurer / Famous Painter and Lithographer / Brownstone front house / W 43rd Street at a stone's throw from 10th Ave / New York City / Vereinigte Staaten."

In April an exhibition of the prints was held at Stern Brothers' department store, announced in a large and imposing advertisement. Again the artist was the guest of honor. He was interviewed by high school students who aspired to journalism as a career, and the interview survives in Stuyvesant High School's *Caliper* for April, 1931. Town Hall invited him and his daughter to attend a dress rehearsal of a pageant on New York history; and Elisabeth Marbury of Sutton Place, then a Democratic national committee member for New York state, wrote to say she would love to meet Louis Maurer. She was herself seventy-four, so she suggested sending her car for him if he ever went out.

Louis Maurer also appeared on the sports pages, in a cartoon "Strange As It Seems" by John Hix. With Tom Greenhill, "who punched the bag continuously for seventy-two hours," and with a cheese made at Oberammergau, whose name has seventy-one letters, he appeared, captioned "Louis Maurer is an active artist at the age of 99." The League for Political Education wrote to thank him for making a personal appearance at Town Hall. And so the year 1931 went for Louis Maurer, closing with a letter of thanks to George Peixotto, who had offered to make a portrait of him.

The year had not opened auspiciously for Alfred Maurer. Would it close more happily? On January 30 fire had broken out in the Lincoln Square Arcade Building, the first in twenty-six years to require the fire department's "9-99" call. More than one hundred and fifty tenants were made homeless, "mostly sculptors, artists, writers, and theatrical people, some of whom fled to the street clutching pictures and plaster busts." Damage was estimated at between half a million and a million dollars, including art losses. The late A. S. Baylinson lost the work of twenty-five years. According to the *Herald-Tribune,* "a number of Alfred Maurer's works were burned," while Sue Hastings "was forced to abandon 500 wooden marionettes and ten small stages which she valued at $40,000."

The report seems to be erroneous in regard to Maurer. If any of his paintings were burned, he must have cleaned them out of the studio when he went back after the fire damage was repaired. None of the paintings studied shows signs of burning, though some are water-stained. It was the psychological effect of the disaster rather than the physical which was tragic for Maurer. *His life's work was lost,* but not by fire. It might have been better if it had been destroyed. It was lost because it had no existence except in his memory and those crowded racks. No one saw the paintings, no one loved them, no one understood them. Why had he painted them? Why did he live? Why did his father live? Why did his father receive praise and adulation, and he none? Life took on the aspect of a foe to be fought by all means. He hurled images violently on paper and panel, violently he assaulted the symbols in his paintings. Events of the outer world were planned to injure him. Accidental and irrelevant incidents wounded him more and more. What a witless, stupid world it was, to shower fame on the old-fashioned academic art of his father and pass him by, pioneer of modern art that he had been.

Even Harry T. Peters, who admired the old father and who did not care for the son, discriminated between Louis Maurer's graphic art, which has merit, and his later work, which does not. He was preparing to bring out a sequel to the Currier and Ives book, to be called *America on Stone: Other Printmakers to the American People,* and he wrote Louis Maurer about the plan:

> Hoping this finds you well and before it is publicly out and you get it from someone else, I am sending you a circular of my latest book. Unfortunately I cannot promise you that you will appear on every page of this, as you did in my other two, but nevertheless you will appear in many places and I go on and tell your story again and Heppenheimer & Maurer.
>
> I am reproducing one of Mr. Heppenheimer's, "Stone Mountain Railroad." Also, did I not love you so much, I would reproduce a print which you did when it was Heppenheimer & Maurer, which is a show card for some children's clothes. It is a real sweet little print, giving the sizes, numbers and prices of some amusing children's suits of about the 70's, but I love you far too much to show any of your commercial work.

"Did I not love you so much . . ." *Did I not hate you so much.* . . . Was this the mood in which Alfred Maurer lived his last years? Alive he was: no death certificate had yet been written. The usual vital functions of respiration, digestion, circulation, and elimination were maintained, though the latter was impaired.

He might have asked: Why does man live except to live? When his being is turned into work alone, is that life? Yet work was Maurer's life, and through his work his life was noble.

III

MAURER wrote his fable of a father in many psychological paintings. There is a series of these, mounted on cardboard 28x22 inches and backed with pages from the February 16, 1930, *Times* magazine section—visual witness of the father-son war which raged hidden for many years and at the last burst into suicide. If there were no report of enmity between Louis Maurer and Alfred Maurer, these alone would give pause. In them, as in the movie art, motion is the fourth dimension of time-space. The face changes: it is distorted out of recognizable guise. The eyes roll: emblems of fantasy are added to nature. The chronicle progresses to destruction.

Cat-man *Head* (page 222) and *Head of a Man* (page 222) retain elements of nature—feline and/or human pointed ears and whiskers and the father's forehead, eyes, nose, mouth, and goatee. As the duel went on, cat and man lose their identities. Against a striped background (the Stars and Stripes?) a head is posed full face, with curling sidelocks, goatee, and similar characteristics. Yet the familiar whole has altered. One eye has slipped upward and almost disappeared. The nose moves up and down. The goatee wags as one looks at the painting.

The eyes ... never close. ... Terrible in the dead straightness of their stare, they seem to challenge all who look at them. Eyes, eyes, eyes, roll from side to side, ten or more pairs of them, in a patterned necklace of unfriendly peering. The nose moves, too, and the lips, all from side to side, and the chin drops down and lifts up, as if in incessant scolding. To record the never-still apparition of his antagonist, Maurer painted in a frenzy of haste, using fingers to eke out brush. In profile and in full face, he vented frustration in wishful death-dealing images. The face, seen full on, shimmers and shivers like a tree blown by the wind; the eyes, the nose, the brow, are blown back and forth. The curling hair

is serrated and saw-toothed; it waves, also. Forms dissolve and
fuse again and disappear. In another profile, the head is pierced
with wooden slivers, a modern substitute for St. Sebastian's arrows.
The saint in Renaissance art was the hero; in Maurer's art the
arrows are heroic.

The duel continued. Its visible mark is read not alone in paintings by which Maurer released pent-up emotions; it is read also
in a multiplicity of manners. These were many and varied. He
oscillated between styles in a way which might be interpreted as
instability, had not his life been such as to interrupt continuous
growth. Maurer's was not, however, the multiplicity of a soul,
which, like Henry Adams', had lost faith and found nothing else.
His was the multiplicity of the individual without a social base.
That base might be a function in society, it might be an established and respected means of earning a livelihood, or it might
be marriage and parenthood. None of these proofs of security
was vouchsafed Maurer. By those middle-class values by which
he was judged, at home assuredly and probably elsewhere, he
stood condemned: an outcast and a failure. He had none of the
little man's consolations—home, modest income, wife and child.
He had staked everything on art. Art had failed, or so it seemed.
Stoicism could not console him.

He was preoccupied with the purpose of life. He was not an
unintelligent, inarticulate type, not a sheerly "intuitive" personality such as some like to believe the artist to be. On the contrary,
his work presents much evidence of thought and planning. To
resolve his dilemma, inwardly he scrutinized and evaluated his
life. *What is the goal of existence?* he asked. *Is the moral world
fissionable?* he would have queried, had the word been current.
Union, division, merging, fragmenting, oneness, aloneness—perhaps so he described his need to be a member of the human community. Duality confronted him; silence or speech, communication
or the dreadful loneliness of one who talks to none except himself.
The dichotomy was not a question of verbal opposites. In life the
duality was real, as it was real in Maurer's work.

Might his alternation of styles have been due to his search for
a suitable idiom? This seems a partial explanation. Many Maurers create a sense of incompletion, which was not the incomple-

tion of a limited subject matter (though he never attempted the grand manner or wished to people his narrow stage with many actors), but which was rather the incompletion of a human being unsure of his objective. Being uncertain, did Maurer distribute his risks through variety? Yet, though fragmented emotionally and aesthetically he might be, he succeeded in channeling his life's endeavor between straight, deep walls. By the end of the 1920s, his experimenting was over and the unfortunate "glazes" had been put aside. He had left behind coquetting with variety, if that was what his investigations had been. With heightened tension he sought to communicate the enigma of one man's life. Time was growing short for speech; time called for action not experiment, for statement not search. What should he say now of that acre of life which he had made his own?

Not the small, the incidental, the casual, the trivial, did Maurer take as his theme. He chose the enduring, the permanent, the meaningful, the heroic. Art had abandoned its heroes, its madonnas, its crucified Christs, its kings and its queens, its spiritual and its temporal symbols. Art had become the pursuit of playthings and of toys, of decorations and of embellishments. Art did not speak for the vast and eternal aspirations of mankind. The artist in modern times faces many questions. What can art speak of today? How can the deep, undying hopes of the human race find a voice as in the great periods of the past? What themes speak for our democratic time as a fixed iconography did for ages of faith? What is the common experience of humanity if it is not suffering and strength to transcend suffering? What is vaster than suffering, or more lasting? What endures longer than the spirit of man?

Maurer proclaimed endurance and monumentality. His was a declaration of faith in the persistence of the creative act. Such was the gauntlet he threw down to those who make art and humanity small. Human being as symbol became the content of his painting, and his symbol overcomes his doubts as to the meaning of existence. In his last statements, he has resolved suffering into a calm though sober asseveration that the will to live must triumph.

The completion of his paintings is a triumph. Physically slight and depleted by illness, Maurer put his last strength into large panels. He was compelled to paint large, because he saw life large and life calls for a large arena of action. So Maurer transmuted suffering into an imperishable document of the journey of his soul through loneliness, despair, anger, pain. How much suffering must the artist, sensitive and sentient, endure for the sake of a putative affirmation? No more, and no less, than all human beings. Throughout history, that has been too much.

Pain on pain was loaded on Maurer. His tempo grew feverish. His content changed. He sought catharsis, calling forth tortured and twisted shapes, transforming the real into the symbol, compressing inner tension into outer form. The faces of his vision became fierce, challenging, foreboding, warrior-like. Imperceptibly, they change to haunted faces. Ghostlike, they lose flesh and color. They are skulls. They are bones without articulation. Who can breathe on dead bones to give them life?

Now communication became his major theme. Two heads forever move toward each other. Forever they move apart. They reach out to embrace and kiss. They withdraw. Do they ever meet? Do they ever speak? Is there a language both understand? Fusion-disintegration, union-dissolution, are these twin faces of one truth, that unity is the goal of all our search? Maurer knew the truth of apart-ness, now he sought the truth of with-ness. He had undergone the painful erosion of the soul wrought by loneliness. He had seen the years eaten away in silence, and the faces and forms of the world change. How can unity be won? Is there a two-way road fission can travel? Can U-238 put together what it has shattered?

How was unity achieved? Maurer sometimes used kinetic methods, like the montage of multiple images. In flashes of thought-sight, he saw eyes turn inward in a two-dimensional movement. On face, gesture, glance, superimpose face, gesture, glance. Will that be life? He was searching, searching, still. Was he searching for the comfort of human company? The faces endlessly meet and separate, kiss and stab each other with their gaze, join and declare war. They are at times Old Testament characters, bearded and garbed in ritual. Rarely they declare an armistice, to assess each other's gains. It is to the death they war. At the end, though the faces seek to tear themselves asunder, they are one. Two, forever shackled, stare demoniacally. By opposites, Maurer has spoken of the freedom of the soul.

Maurer's thought turned ever inward. His faces turned ever inward. Yet they spoke not in the aside's muted verse nor in understatement's gentle rhetoric. In art, even as in life, Maurer shouted and raged in these paintings, his last acts of faith. Violent, theatrical, over-emphatic, he confessed to the world (if the world would hear) all he had loved and lost, all he had suffered and hated. He told his story with baroque gestures, and with the cadence of murderous drama. From the stage he had set the real characters had vanished—young women of Shady Brook, family of father, mother and child, Louis Maurer and Alfred Maurer. In his paintings, only imaginary characters walk. Wrapped in soliloquy, the twin heroes muse and declaim, sightless eyes fixed on the audience which does not exist.

For thirty years Maurer has been searching, searching. He has explored academicism's wasteland and modern art's uncharted wilderness. None has listened, spellbound, to his report of adventures. Without compass or north star he has wandered alone. At the end, to what will he come home?

8. *Illness and Death*

ALFRED MAURER'S life was drawing to its close. His days raced to the last day when he would knot the rope about his neck and step out of time into eternity. His hermetic history has been written, except its closing. Little of work was left him, nothing of hope. Should not the story of man's life end on its highest note? Yet what is higher than life's conclusion? If that be suicide, the self-willed, self-wrought act takes the pitch of all the forces which set the soul vibrating. To shroud Maurer's dying in secrecy serves him ill. His death by his own hand was (he felt) the best act of his life. His act commends him to our mercy.

"Sound, Sound the Trump of Fame!" trumpeted the Old Print Shop broadside announcing a "Twofold Celebration" from February 19 to March 12, to mark "The 200th Anniversary of the Birth of GEORGE WASHINGTON" on February 22, 1732, and "The 100th Birthday of LOUIS MAURER" who had been born on February 21, 1832. The twofold celebration was to be signalized by exhibiting "67 lithographs of Washington—all they published—portraits and scenes 'from cradle to grave.' Mr. Currier and Mr. Ives are pleased to learn that these have been assembled for the first time and they are guarded for posterity by Mr. George Kayser, of Scarsdale, N. Y." In addition, "Mr. Currier and Mr.

Ives are also exhibiting as a timely gesture the last-known life portrait of Washington illustrated above, a drawing by Dr. Dick, the personal physician who cut the pendulum of a clock at Mt. Vernon to mark the moment of Washington's death."

Louis Maurer was to be commemorated by the display of "A fine group of the lithographs of famous running and trotting horses by Mr. Maurer, the last surviving artist of the Currier staff, a centenarian, an outstanding contributor to the American turf record, an accomplished horseman." This comprised "40 prints, loaned by Miss A. S. Colgate, of New York." Finally, the broadside concluded "Mr. Currier and Mr. Ives have elected to exhibit this diverting panorama at The OLD PRINT SHOP . . . And Would Bespeak An Overflowing Attendance!" No doubt the attendance was overflowing; publicity was.

Even the sophisticated *New Yorker* could not resist a news angle. "Talk of the Town" put Louis Maurer under one word, "Artist," and gave him nine inches of space. Recalling that "404" had been built long before "that part of town was dubbed Hell's Kitchen," the account listed the members of Louis Maurer's menage—"himself; a son, Alfred, aged sixty-four; a daughter, fifty-nine, and her husband; an Irish housekeeper; and a huge yellow tomcat named Goldie. Another son, seventy, lives uptown." The account added: "Both sons are artists."

Celebration of the centenary had been in progress for some time. Louis Maurer's flute teacher, Leonardo De Lorenzo, had written a eulogy of the centenarian for the *Metronome* and on January 25 had sent a first draft for its subject's approval. It contained much information about historic flute players and historic personages who were born or who had died in 1832. On February 1 the *American* featured "America's Oldest Living Artist" on its front page, with a two-column cut. "SCORNS MODERNISTS" the caption began. "He doesn't think much of modern art," the account read, "thus disagreeing with his son, Alfred, a well-known artist in his own right." The father "doesn't paint any longer . . . [but] he still feels he deserves consideration as an artist." In a bathrobe, Louis Maurer had posed beside his portrait of Buffalo Bill.

Louis Maurer was first-rate rotogravure material. The *Times* gave space only matched by that given visiting royalty. "America's Oldest Artist" had posed, seated, wearing the bathrobe which appears in many photographs, and holding a framed print on his lap. A favorite picture was that of Louis Maurer taken at the Stern's exhibition the year before, showing him sitting in front of Currier and Ives prints. The *Herald-Tribune* also ran an advance story, announcing the forthcoming event. As usual, Louis Maurer worked in adverse comment on Alfred Maurer's art. "He reads about modern painting," the account ran, "but isn't greatly impressed with it." The interview continued with fact and error: "His son, Alfred Maurer, a modern painter, has managed to allay some of his father's prejudices against it, for he tells with pride of Alfred winning the Carnegie prize more than thirty years ago for 'An Arrangement.' The picture hangs in Mr. Maurer's Victorian parlor."

The *Post* with great generosity devoted twenty-nine inches to the occasion. Among other items, the account records the father-son rivalry:

> If the boom in Currier & Ives prints had occurred when he [Louis Maurer] was a stripling of sixty and a newly fledged pupil of Chase it might have done him some practical good. As it was, his oil paintings achieved no fame. Indeed, he did them entirely for his own pleasure. They hang on the walls of some of his friends' houses and his own, where they form a striking contrast to some of the earlier canvases of his son, Alfred. The later, "post-modernistic" works of Alfred Maurer are not in evidence in his father's collection. The old gentleman shakes his head when he contemplates the latest phase of Alfred, who, as a matter of fact, is one of the most brilliant and distinguished artists in America.

So the procession was off. The *Times* printed an advance notice of the exhibition to follow up its roto feature. The *Art Digest* discussed the event in two successive issues. And on the day before Louis Maurer's one-hundredth birthday the *Times* printed a further notice. Again *papa* derided his son's modernism:

> In matters of art, Mr. Maurer has faith in the older forms. Modern art, he says, puzzles him. He thinks that some of its devotees

use it as a short cut to avoid mastering some of the hard essentials of art. He believes that the principles which have been worked out through the centuries cannot be flouted, "but," he said, smiling, "people always want to try new things. It has always been that way."

The *Herald-Tribune* gave the announcement less space but used a one-column cut.

Louis Maurer received his greatest attention in the *Sun*. Fortunately the day before his birthday fell on Saturday. The first page of the "Antiques and Interior Decorations" department was allotted to Geo. Washington, the father of his country. An eight-column caption covered four two-column cuts of Washington portraits by John Wollaston, William Williams, Gilbert Stuart, and the pastel portrait by Dr. Dick. The leading article was headed: "COMMEMORATION OF WASHINGTON / TEACHES NEED FOR ARISTOCRACY." The page was adorned with cuts of figures of Washington in glass and of a wood carving, perhaps by Samuel McIntire. The entire page (including advertisements) was given over to the celebration of the two-hundredth anniversary of the birth of Washington, especially as commemorated in salable works of art and memorabilia.

The second page, also headed "Antiques and Interior Decorations," was largely devoted to Louis Maurer, starting off with a two-column head: "Again Maurer — — — and Washington." A three-column cut, which was captioned "Honor to the Grand Old Man of American Lithography," showed Louis Maurer standing beside the well known print, *Preparing for Market*. The "Last of the Old Artists" and "The Last of the Old Printmakers," the *Sun* called him, adding that Louis Maurer was still a "brisk, keen, glowing little man."

The late Edward Alden Jewell chafed at the fanfare, it seems. The *Times'* Sunday art page led off with a three-column head: "City Is Deluged with Washingtonia." Samuel F. B. Morse and Louis Maurer were honored in exhibitions; and the critic observed noncommittally that the "still chipper extant chief celebrant, Louis Maurer, whose ideas flowed so lavishly into the print shop of Messrs. Currier and Ives back in the good old days . . . [had] outlived most of his cronies, [to obtain] the hundredth anni-

versary of his birth today." George Peixotto's drawing was reproduced with the notice.

The celebration continued, with stress on *oldest* and *last*. No
evaluation was made, however, of the aesthetic worth of Louis
Maurer's work, aside from documentary content and patriotic
appeal. Probably no such judgment needed to be made. If biggest
is best, then oldest and last are best. By assumption, old age is
per se meritorious; and by assumption, virtue, wisdom, kindliness,
good will and charity automatically reside in the aged. Ergo: Louis
Maurer became a hero of the press.

Let us say without consulting the weather bureau that Sunday,
February 21, 1932—the one-hundredth birthday of Karl Ludwig
Maurer and the day before the two-hundredth birthday of George
Washington—dawned bright and clear. Fate would not be so un-
kind as to withhold good weather. The house at 404 West Forty-
third Street was thronged with "friends and admirers who called
at the home during the afternoon to bring . . . their felicitations."
The "dean of American artists" was "erect and clear-eyed" as "he
shook hands and talked with each guest." Hundreds of telegrams
and letters of congratulation had come, with quantities of flowers.
"One spray of 100 roses was locked up in [Louis Maurer's] study
. . . Before the reception began Mr. Maurer, surrounded by his
family and a few close friends, formally cut the birthday cake set
with one large candle which had been sent him by admirers."
Finally, "as a supreme favor, toward the end of the reception, the
venerable artist, over the objections of his family, got his cherished
flute and played several selections."

In the receiving line were "Mr. Maurer's two sons, Charles, a
mining engineer, and Alfred, himself an artist, and his daughter,
Mrs. Eugenia Fuerstenberg." Also at Louis Maurer's side "was
his nurse, Mrs. Patricia McClory, who has been with him for several years and who never tired of praising his invariable cheerful-
ness." The *Herald-Tribune* added a detail or two, notably that
Louis Maurer's "physician ordered him to retire to his own room
to prevent an attack of hysteria that seemed imminent." So Louis
Maurer's first century ended, in glory and exhaustion. He had
attained his goal, to live to be one hundred years old.

II

WHAT of Alfred Maurer? The New Year had come and gone. A few Paris friends had visited Alfy at "404" and had to listen, perforce, to Louis Maurer play the flute. Maurer's old friend, Mahonri Young, had seen him for the last time a few days before Christmas. Maurer was coming out of Weyhe's, Young was going in. "Alfy, you look fine." "Hon, I'm a very sick man." Was he sick at heart, also?

Maurer had eight months to live. He would spend two of them in the hospital. He could no longer put off surgical treatment for prostatic hypertrophy. Two months had been consumed in the Louis Maurer centennial celebrations, while Alfy stood by passively, an onlooker. Before he went to the hospital, however, Maurer had work to finish. Several paintings had been on his mind, the large *Still Life* (page 221) and possibly the *Two Heads* here reproduced (page 240). He had an idea he had to set down in paint as an outgrowth of the ceremonies of February 21 and February 22.

He, Alfred Maurer, would paint George Washington. Modern though he was and derided though he was, he could do better than the daubs dragged out of attics to grace Washington's two-hundredth anniversary. So Maurer argued, so he acted. His portrait was finished in time for the sixteenth annual exhibition of the Independent's, which opened April 2. *George Washington* (page 239) is a large painting on a 39x24-inch panel, in which he used all his mastery of drawing and design and all his knowledge of color and space, to project a luminous monumentality.

The sixteenth annual was a "swap" exhibition in which artists bartered paintings and sculptures for goods or services. The depression was almost three years old. Instead of a chicken in every pot, there was an apple seller on every corner. A starving artist had jumped from a bridge in despair, the *Art Digest* noted. In all walks of life the suicide rate was climbing rapidly. The economic base of the exhibition was valid; but such is the reputation of

Bohemia that the *Post* reported the event with emphasis on its comic aspects. The head read:

SIX CANS OF SOUP
PRICE OF PAINTING

———

Some Canvases Quoted Low
as One Poodle Dog at
Artists' Exhibition

———

BANJO   WILL   BUY   REAL   ART

Though generous in space, the *Post* account did not mention many artists by name. It spoke of a painter who would "swap" a painting for a vacuum cleaner and another who would "swap" art work for a saddle horse. Sculptor Chaim Gross and painter Rainey Bennett, less well known than now, were among the artists with offerings. Bennett's requirements were modest; he would trade for a banjo. Chaim Gross had already bartered *Jazz Dancers* (a sculpture in wood) for a couch, two chairs, two bookcases, a coffee table, and a telephone table. He would trade finished sculptures for stone or wood which he could carve.

Whether or not the exhibition made exchanges of art for goods, it made news. "What Will You Swap for a Painting or Statue?" queried one eight-column ribbon head. The rotogravure artist must have worked on the layout; it is done up in ovals and swirls of black outlines, with pictures of the artists and their offerings, including Maurer, Chaim Gross and Adolf Wolff, with work to be traded. For Maurer the caption read: "Mr. Alfred Maurer Standing Beside His Painting, Which He Calls 'George Washington,' and Which He Will Trade for $500 Worth of Clothing or Other Articles to That Value." Valued at $500, he would let it go for the equivalent in clothing.

Maurer could not compete with the Louis Maurer-*cum*-George Washington story; but he did well. The *Post* reproduced *George Washington* as a two-column cut, six and a half inches high, with a caption: "New Angles on Washington." Had the city editor assigned the art critic to write heads? The *Post* added that Maurer, in line with the bartering program of the show, had said he might

GEORGE WASHINGTON, 1932

OIL ON MASONITE, 39¼×24¼ IN. COLLECTION: MR. AND MRS. JAN DE GRAAF

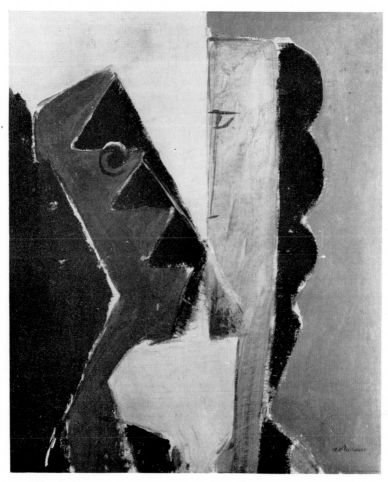

TWO HEADS, *ca.* 1930–1931
OIL ON GESSO PANEL, 21½x18 IN.
COLLECTION: J. B. NEUMANN

TWO HEADS, *ca.* 1930
OIL ON COMPOBOARD, 21½x18 IN.
COLLECTION: BERKSHIRE MUSEUM

TWO HEADS, *ca.* 1931
OIL ON GESSO PANEL, 21¼×18 IN.
COLLECTION: J. B. NEUMANN

accept the offer of a canned goods firm to make an exchange. In general, the press pointed up the contrast between father and son, calling Louis Maurer "America's oldest living artist" and the "last of the painters of the famous Currier and Ives lithographs" and Alfred Maurer "a well-known artist" and "a cubist." The painting proved a puzzle. It was "an abstract painting of George Washington." According to one report, Maurer himself had explained: "George can't be seen, he's got to be felt." Perhaps vision has improved in the past seventeen years: observers today have said that Maurer's George Washington is more like Washington than any colonial portrait in expressing the dignity of his historic role.

Maurer did not "swap" the painting for clothing or for canned goods. In a last act of friendship, he gave it to a friend who admired it greatly. Many years later it left the friend's hands. Now *George Washington* has come to rest in a West Coast collection, Maurer's last work and an undoubted masterpiece. It is the answer to those who used to argue that Maurer's art did not win favor because of its "foreignness." Through the symbolism of an unmistakable American symbol, Maurer uttered his universal message of man's invincible courage.

In suave grays, tans, mauves, yellow-browns, whites, with accents of purple and violet, with heroic nose and eyes drawn in black touched with green, and with flesh tones glazed in a wash of lavender, he composed a montage of shapes, forms and directions. Diagonals create a pyramidal volume, on which is superimposed the rectangle of powerful jaw and brow. Varied textures enrich the surface—flat areas of paint applied with palette knife, areas scrubbed in, glazed black bar across the face, gesso left bare of paint. With all his skill and technical aids, what does Maurer say?

He says that paint is beautiful and form lovely. He says that the dialect of painting—fauvism, cubism, abstractionism, expressionism, realism, whatever it be—must not mask meaning. What is that meaning aside from the artist's personal history? It is the history of man, seen through one significant individual. Maurer's Washington is more like Washington than Washington. Maurer's last painting is more like Maurer than Maurer. All his life he sought what is true and **noble** and lasting. In a trite and hackneyed figure out of conventional schoolbooks, he found the true, the noble, the lasting.

"George Washington, symbol of our country's beginnings," Maurer mused, "a commodity sold over the counter, like a pound of sausage!" He saw the old portraits, the glass images, the anniversary celebrations, the newspaper displays. He saw the advertisements and the sales, he saw the wooden-faced father of our country, a puppet without life or dignity. So . . . "I will paint the true George Washington. I will paint him free from tainting and corrupting entanglements. I will paint him as big as the years from Valley Forge to now. I will paint him as the unvanquished. He knew the tears of things. He suffered the bleeding feet of untrained warriors, the lack of guns and powder, treachery behind the lines, traitors at home, faint-hearted lieutenants. All that he overcame.

"Not the wars of the soul hidden from all others. Not the wounds which are invisible. Not the conflict lost in silence. Not inner and private battles. Not these will I paint. I will paint man's hope, in the wars and victories of life."

Maurer put the destructive, seething emotions of all his years into one tremendous, positive symbol. He had created symbols for anger, for personal warfare, for the good-evil duel between father and son, for the chasm between man and man. He had taken the shapes of nature and molded them into the shapes of his imagining. He had seen faces turn into skulls, and he had painted skull-like heads as if in dreadful forevision of the death he would contrive for himself (page 242). Half in love with death, he had made skulls the images of imagined death which he could bring to pass only by his own death. At the last, a century-long life robbed him of the skull he coveted.

To the anonymous and faceless dead, he sought to add a look of agony. *I like a look of agony,* cried Emily Dickinson, *because I know it's true.* I know it's true, Maurer cried. He sought a look ever more true. He sought the face after crucifixion. It was not enough, he had learned, to destroy outer enemies by wish or act: the enemy within must be conquered. Life has a meaning beyond enmity and hostility. That meaning he sought. He sought the identity of the human individual with his foe. He sought the incorruptible hero, the imperishable one who has mastered himself. Maurer won self-conquest by direct and brutal rope. Others find easier ways. Yet, before he took his last, despairing step, he found his heroic symbol in George Washington.

III

MAURER entered Beth Israel Hospital on April 21, his sixty-fifth birthday. What impelled him to select the anniversary date for admission to the hospital? He had known of his condition for some years, as the records show. He could have had the operation sooner. Why did he wait for his birthday to come around? Was it the memory of his father's one-hundredth birthday cake, with one candle standing for one hundred years, which decided him?

His illness was diagnosed as benign hypertrophy of the prostate gland. A two-stage operation was performed by Dr. Seymour F. X. Wilhelm—bilateral vasectomy and suprapubic cystotomy on April 22 and second stage prostatectomy on April 30. Maurer was discharged from the hospital on June 29 in excellent general condition. No carcinoma was revealed by pathological examination; and the postoperative course was uncomplicated. The abdominal incision was slow in healing, because the condition had been of long standing and Maurer's general resistance had been lowered by kidney damage. After his return to 404 West Forty-third Street, Maurer was mentally depressed. Perhaps, despite assurances of surgeon and physician, he believed he had cancer. There is a rumor, which cannot be checked, that he tried earlier to take his life. Friends who visited him in the hospital found him despondent and unwilling to leave. Yet others visited him; and with them he planned to travel to Shady Brook that summer, as gay and affectionate as ever.

Alone and faced with the question as to whether or not his illness would recur—what layman ever believes his medical advisor?—Maurer brooded on his life. On his inner ear he heard the Böhm-system flute jangle out of tune.

The son is also an artist. The son is also an artist. . . . So Maurer's thoughts rang an incessant tune.

The son is a man named Alfred Maurer, Alfred Maurer whispered to himself. The son is a man who won medals and prizes to renounce them all. The son is a man who labored for thirty years to win understanding for modern art. The son is a man who found the love of his being turned to hate.

The son is also an artist. The son is also an artist. The son is also an artist. . . .

"I am an artist who could not make a success.

"I am an artist who could not win acclaim.

"I am an artist who could not make a living.

"I am an artist who could not have a wife or child or home.

"I am an artist. . . ."

So Alfred Maurer brooded through long nights, while his incision drained and he wondered if he would ever again be his old virile self. How count time in hospital nights? The nights are dark, and the world is dark, and the future is dark. What hope is there? Is it the hope of life to be? Or the hope of a blessed end to life?

In June, while Maurer was still in the hospital, his friend, William F. Waltemath, a painter whom he had met in Marlboro, persuaded Robert Ulrich Godsoe to go with him to the Lincoln Square Arcade Building studio to see Maurer's work. At that time Godsoe was directing exhibitions for the Gotham Outdoor Gallery, planning a series for hotels, bookshops, restaurants, and theater lobbies "to take art out of the cloister, and show it in places where it can most easily be seen and most readily appreciated," as well as to enable artists to show their work at moderate cost. Godsoe was besieged by artists who wanted a showing even if chances of sales were slight. Finally he had given in to Waltemath's entreaties and they had gone to Maurer's studio.

"It looks like a young man's painting," he cried and he agreed at once to include Maurer in his schedule. But before this could happen, Maurer was dead, and Godsoe had never met the artist he so fervently admired. Godsoe did, however, show Maurer almost immediately, in September, 1932. Ever, thereafter, as long as he had a gallery of his own, he exhibited Maurer along with his "living" artists. All in all, Godsoe was bowled over by Maurer; and when he held the Maurer memorial exhibition at the Uptown

Gallery in 1934, he did not hesitate to acclaim him as America's greatest painter, living or dead.

Meanwhile Maurer's story was drawing to its end. On June 29 he left the hospital and went "home." Louis Maurer, having achieved his ambition to live to be one hundred years old, was failing fast. The father was installed in the back parlor, to which he had been removed some years before from the second floor master bedroom. Maurer returned to his third floor bedroom and his walnut bed. He did not recover rapidly: the suprapubic fistula did not heal as fast as was hoped. Perhaps his will to live was not as great at sixty-five as his father's had been at one hundred. When his father died on July 19, Alfred Maurer was confined to his bed; and the news of his father's death was not broken to him immediately. Nor was he able to attend his father's funeral.

As in life, in death Louis Maurer received considerable news coverage. The *Times, Herald-Tribune, Sun, American, World-Telegram* and *Art Digest* all played the tune, *The son is also an artist,* with occasional grace notes on the father's dislike for modern art. So Louis Maurer died and was buried, ripe with years and honors.

The sixteen days between Louis Maurer's death and Alfred's are the most mysterious of Maurer's life. Marlboro friends who visited Alfy at "404" included Juliette and Richard Warnken, Mrs. Frederick W. Schramm, Sr., of Shady Brook, and William F. Waltemath. Maurer had been moved downstairs (so there would be less stair-climbing for his nurse) and put into his father's room. Here he received callers, sitting up in bed and delighting in the paper dolls they brought him because "he loved nonsense." A week before he died, he was as "cheerful and lovely as usual." All this time he was making plans to open a studio in Paris once more.

On August 4, a Thursday, Waltemath came to see Maurer and to arrange to take him to Marlboro for the summer. This was in the morning. Waltemath left the house and walked eastward on Forty-third Street toward Grand Central Station. He had more time than he needed to catch his train and turned back. He thought, "I'll see him in a few days" and so turned away again. At one o'clock Maurer got out of bed and walked upstairs. His sister was not at home at the time. So her husband found Alfy's body

hanging from the frame of the door between his longtime bedroom and the bath. "I never realized he was so small a man," said
a friend long after. Maurer had died of asphyxiation.

There is no need for documents now. Alfred Maurer's hermetic
tale is ended. Nothing of praise or blame can be added. Whether
or not he had as much linage for obituaries as his father, whether
or not they invoked the ghost, *son of Currier & Ives artist,* is in-
different. His long war ended, Alfy lay at peace in the Riverside
Memorial Chapel at Amsterdam Avenue and Sixty-seventh Street.
Like Louis Maurer, he was to be buried in Greenwood Cemetery,
Brooklyn. Before the services, old friends went to the funeral
home: "It was cold and unloving, and no one from the family
was there." So Alfy took his leave of a life he had loved but
learned to hate. On August 12 his paintings were carted off to
storage. Thus ends his story.

LET ALFRED MAURER'S epitaph be written by one who loved
him. Those who die untimely are not dead in the remembrance of
friends. Five years after, Arthur Dove wrote:

> *. . . Alfy [has] been on our minds so much in the last few weeks
> —We have moved to this new address in Geneva and have this
> huge hall as a studio. It is about 50 x 70—*
>
> *Alfy's bench with our combined tools at one corner and his
> bed at the far corner with one of his paintings over it—*
>
> *We are not settled—We had to sell the old farm house—taxes.—
> Alfy would have loved it.*
>
> *I wake in the middle of the night often and rail at Alfy for tak-
> ing himself away from us—We loved him so.—and then I think it
> is all right the way he wanted it. Helen seems to compare every-
> thing to the way I feel about Alfy.*
>
> *I think we knew each other better than anyone up to the last
> visit. I knew then he had no interests left here. Could feel him
> being brave and clowning the whole thing, and yet being in a
> hurry to take off.*
>
> *It was no surprise after that day.—And no death has ever hurt
> so much when life was so beautiful and had such possibilities leav-
> ing out the career-conscious side of it.*

Helen has taken down in her quick writing some time ago a talk that Alfy and I had about painting. It was fun then, fine now.

You probably realized that day at your house that I was choking at those last ones of Alfy's.

It would be nice to separate those from the rest—There was a sheerness about them that broke me—I hadn't seen them before— A sort of Good Bye.

I try never to regret anything—If you love enough there should be none. Only wanting their way.

If he could only walk in I would be the happiest person on earth. He might too for a change from what he might call his heaven.

Epilogue

THE MAURER STORY does not close with Alfred Maurer's death. His work survives. What shall be its fate? From the moment he died till now there have been endeavors to assess its value and to restore it to the world. In June, 1932, Robert Ulrich Godsoe had promised to hold an exhibition of Maurer's paintings. After Maurer's death, his sister, Mrs. Eugenia M. Fuerstenberg, had to make judicious disposal of the art estates of Alfred Maurer and of Louis Maurer. In the press of business detail, she was glad indeed to find an admirer of her brother's work who would take over the task of exhibiting and selling the paintings, and she therefore authorized the young enthusiast to act as her agent.

Maurer had been dead and buried only a month when some of his paintings were included in a Godsoe-organized exhibition at the Towers Hotel in Brooklyn. In the fall of 1932 the College Art Association chose Maurer as one of "Six Painters," for a traveling exhibition which opened its circuit in Guild Hall, East Hampton, Long Island. In the *Times* Edward Alden Jewell prophesied "it is altogether likely that some one will organize a retrospective exhibition." The late critic did not care for the Maurers included except *Three Sisters,* which he reproduced; but he admired Maurer's last canvases which he saw in the Towers Hotel exhibition and which he called "peculiarly fresh, vigorous, inventive and—so far as the subject matter [still life] permits—original." The *Herald-Tribune* wrote that "Maurer showed his latent powers" and added "it is indeed time that a full exhibition of his many phases be seen." Later the *Sun* discussed Maurer's tragic death and confessed to an uneasy fear that Maurer had had too much education in France to flourish here. "The abstract art that the younger Maurer practiced is understood by the few," Henry McBride stated, "but it is still very far from being an American fashion. Maurer got no sympathetic help from the community."

In the *New Republic* the late Paul Rosenfeld wrote of "The Maurer 'Little Girl.' " A spokesman for the modern movement and long a member of the Stieglitz group, Rosenfeld put forth the most advanced group's attitude toward Maurer. "There would be no point," he wrote, "in claiming that in Alfred Maurer the world had passed a great painter by. One cannot, with the best will, see him as an original force." Maurer did not achieve independence in his work, the critic felt, and "this spirit of organic dependency [is] so characteristic of the minor artist." Nonetheless Maurer "was a much neglected artist, thrust aside by, and for the sake of, workers far less serious, significant and delightful than himself . . . But possibly Alfred Maurer should have lived to be a hundred years old, too."

Such was the art world's epitaph for Alfred Maurer. Yet, as in life he could not be silenced, in death he sought to return to notice. Immediately after Maurer's death, his friend William Waltemath and Robert Godsoe began negotiations with the Whitney Museum of American Art for a memorial exhibition. As early as September 12, Godsoe had shown Karl R. Free and C. Adolph Glassgold, of the museum's curatorial staff, a number of Maurers. And on October 17, Hermon More, now the Whitney's director and then curator, wrote Charles Maurer that the exhibition had been scheduled for January 16 to February 15, 1933.

On October 31, the late Juliana Force, then the museum's head, wrote Maurer's brother, stating she was sorry "to hear from Mr. Robert Ulrich Godsoe, who writes as adviser and general representative of the Maurer family, that the members of the Maurer family have decided that they do not wish a memorial exhibition

of the late Alfred Maurer's work to be held at this Museum." She
ended by wishing the exhibition, wherever held, success. On November 1, Karl Free wrote Waltemath, expressing regret that
"this exhibition could not be arranged, as it would be a fitting
and dignified Memorial to the name of an admirable artist." He
added: "We know that you have spent much of your time and
energy in your kind endeavour to carry the exhibition through;
and I can assure you that we appreciate to the full, the great
assistance you have given us in this matter."

Fortunately this correspondence survived. Juliana Force had a
habit of cleaning out her files from time to time; and her later
negotiations with the Maurer family went the way of many other
letters. Because of the Whitney's yeoman service to the cause of
American artists, living and dead, it is a felicitous circumstance
that in this instance the facts are documented. Attached to the
correspondence is a note, probably by Karl Free: "In the autumn
of 1932, following Maurer's death, we tried to negotiate for an
exhibition of his work, but because of difficulties arising with the
family and the representative appointed by them, it became inad-
visable to continue negotiations. More than a year later when the
Maurer family wished to re-open the matter, our schedule had
been so arranged that it was impossible to include this exhibition." It would be seventeen years before a Maurer retrospective
was held at the Whitney, in 1949.

Meanwhile Maurer got about. In 1933 the College Art Association sent out a traveling exhibition, "Entering the 20th Century." Maurer was represented by *Woman in White,* which the
press had mentioned at the time of his last one-man exhibition
in 1931 and which was now much admired and illustrated. In
April, the seventeenth annual Independent's gave him a memorial display of ten paintings; and he was also included in the
Hotel Roosevelt exhibition organized by Robert Godsoe. So Maurer's work continued to be exhibited and discussed. But no miracles took place.

Maurer made his first retrospective appearance at the Uptown
Gallery in New York, in 1934, in a memorial exhibition organized by Robert Godsoe. Early in the year Mrs. Fuerstenberg
had been in correspondence with the Museum of Modern Art and

with the Whitney, urging the one or the other to hold a comprehensive display of her brother's work. Why her proposal was rejected is not quite clear. The Museum of Modern Art's file of correspondence for that period is in storage and cannot be consulted. As for the Whitney, Mrs. Force must have had one of her house cleaning spells in regard to the Maurer file. Neither museum held the exhibition, though the Whitney would have liked to do so then, and later.

The *New Yorker,* reviewing the exhibition, commented that it was to the Whitney's credit, it had made an effort to hold such an exhibition. "Unfortunately," Lewis Mumford continued, "the Maurer family, which possesses this treasure hoard of unknown and unsold pictures, did not see fit to give its gifted black sheep the honor of such a public show. This only adds one more touch of irony to the tragic fate of the man himself." A family spokesman replied by annotating a typed transcript of this review as follows: "Due to outside interference the Whitney Museum who were arranging a memorial exhibition turned it down." Four years later Mrs. Fuerstenberg wrote Mrs. Force, again to urge a retrospective showing of Maurer's work. Again the exhibition did not take place.

Before the Uptown Gallery exhibition opened, Maurer had been included in the College Art Association traveling exhibition, "American Painters since 1900," which was booked for a year. It also opened in East Hampton, then traveled to Toledo and Springfield, Mass., before making a New York appearance. Afterwards it visited Louisville, Manchester, N. H., Buffalo and Rochester. So Maurer was getting around.

The cover for the retrospective's catalogue read as follows: "Memorial Exhibition / Works of / The Late / Alfred Maurer / Oils and Gouaches / Covering Work of / Thirty-Five Years / Uptown Gallery / Continental Club / 249 West End Avenue, New York City / Direction Robert Ulrich Godsoe / October 30th–December 3rd / 1934." The eight-page brochure contained a short essay by the exhibition's entrepreneur, a list of seventy-nine paintings, and reproductions of *Self-Portrait with Hat* (frontispiece) and *Four Sisters* (page 197). It noted that the exhibition also included portfolios of water colors and studies.

"I consider Alfred Maurer to have been the greatest American painter of all time," Robert Godsoe began his manifesto, in which he attacked current assumptions of criticism and aesthetics. He pointed out the improbability that Maurer had played the "sedulous ape" to Picasso, Braque, and Modigliani; and in dramatic and emphatic sentences he called for just appreciation of the artist. "I charge the American public with his suicide," he cried. In such a spirit he threw down his gauntlet for Alfred Maurer.

Ten years had passed since the Weyhe "debut." Sensational aspects had been added to the Maurer story, such as his father's great age and Maurer's manner of dying. The *Art Digest* told the story as a news feature: but its article began with an evaluation. "Of unusual significance is the Alfred Maurer Memorial Exhibition . . . for the life of Alfred Maurer is a sort of epitome of American art." *Mid-Week Pictorial* reproduced his abstractions; and the *World-Telegram* wrote: "Today the brash note his works trumpeted forth has become familiar with frequent repetition. The wave of modernism that broke on American shores at the turn of the century and swept Maurer along with it had receded and merged with the large ocean of art and art developments."

In the *Herald-Tribune,* Carlyle Burrows devoted a double feature to the "Memorials to Luks and Alfred Maurer." Commenting that more early academic Maurers might have been included to give the memorial scope, the critic wrote: "His was a dynamic and searching personality, and in these later works one may see how he strove . . . to articulate his new-felt impressions. . . . Had Maurer gone on in his early manner he would probably have been extremely successful; as it was he had yet to win general acceptance when he put a tragic end to his career. The present memorial will help revive interest in this singular and able artist."

The *Times* also featured the two memorials, though the opening of the renovated Walters Art Gallery in Baltimore took the lead. Edward Alden Jewell commented on the lack of exhibits to show Maurer's continuous evolution and took a forthright stand against the fallacy of attributing Maurer's modernism to imitation, stating "Maurer was a logical product of his time. . . . If often, or for the most part, his essays in abstractionism and 'expressionism' appear to us inscrutable, there is enough vitality in this work to keep it . . . above the obscure ruck of sham and addle-pated incompetence." Nonetheless, the late critic seldom had "a sense of contact with anything that goes far beneath the surface. His color is usually frenetic and raw; his drawing clamorous and impatient of subtlety. Now and then, through the years, an arresting brush effort has emerged. . . . Perhaps a hundred years hence Maurer's rebellious affirmation may appear established upon summits that today look woefully enmeshed in fog."

A week later the author gave a column of type and two two-column cuts to Maurer in the Springfield (Massachusetts) *Sunday Union and Republican*. I had first seen Maurers when visiting Arthur and Helen Torr Dove in their old farmhouse outside Geneva, N. Y., in the summer of 1933. Soon after that there appeared *The Autobiography of Alice B. Toklas*, with fragmentary documents of Alfy. So the review began with an appropriate quotation from Gertrude Stein. It recorded biographical facts and recommended that the work be judged on its merits. With an enthusiasm perhaps not as emphatic as Robert Godsoe's, the writer concluded: "Whether Alfred Maurer is the greatest American artist of all time does not seem very important in comparison with the indubitable fact that he is a great American artist."

"All in all, then, this is a moving and terrible exhibition," wrote Lewis Mumford in the *New Yorker*. In regard to Maurer's relation to the modern movement, he pointed out that "In 1908 [*sic*] Mr. Alfred Stieglitz showed Maurer's new work at '291,' and at that moment American art began to move at right angles to its previous course." He added that Maurer had worked in isolation and therefore had not been a leader in terms of immediately influencing other painters. Yet, "Though it is too early to place Maurer—if only because acquaintance with his work as a whole comes so tardily—one can hardly doubt that he will count among the leaders of his generation rather than among the camp followers."

So the Maurer memorial came and went. To young Godsoe, "New York, with the exception of Mr. Mumford, was lukewarm." The paintings remained in his charge. In the depths of the depression he sought to keep open his Gallery-Secession at 49 West Twelfth Street, as a clearing house for painters, sculptors, writers, dancers and composers, and he continued to include Maurer as a "living" artist with young contemporaries. Miracles remained non-existent, though he sold some of Maurer's paintings, usually to painters.

In 1935 Maurer came back to life in an academic incarnation. The Carnegie Institute held "An Exhibition of Paintings Which Have Received Prize Awards in International Exhibitions at Carnegie Institute." Maurer's *An Arrangement* (page 56), the 1901 first prize painting, was one of the works located for the occasion. Off it went, early in January, 1935, insured for $2,000. Alfred Maurer once more could enter the Carnegie, from which, according to legend, he had been forever barred at the time of his conversion to modernism. He took his place with Sir James Shannon, J. Alden Weir, Childe Hassam, Cecilia Beaux, Frank W. Benson, Ben Foster, Edmund C. Tarbell, W. Elmer Schofield, Edward W. Redfield, Emil Carlsen, John W. Alexander, Gifford Beal, Abbott W. Thayer, Daniel Garber, and many an other academician whose way of life he had rejected almost as soon as he had won the prize.

About the same time, the Whitney Museum of American Art held its exhibition, "Abstract Painting in America," in which art made equally strange bedfellows. Of over a hundred entries, Maurer had five, in regard to which the *New Yorker* commented: "Unfortunately, the representation of Alfred Maurer is inadequate." So the timetable went.

Since critics are said rarely to influence the course of history, a bit of autobiography may be permitted. In the spring of 1935 the Berkshire Museum in Pittsfield, Massachusetts, organized the first one-man show of Maurer's work held in a museum. The exhibition was undertaken by the then director, Laura M. Bragg, one of the rare disinterested and civic-minded personalities of the art world. In the lonely though beautiful Berkshires she launched Maurer, having been introduced to his work through the author's review. Not alone did she exhibit Maurer: she *bought* two Maurers for the Berkshire Museum's permanent collections, an oil, *Two Heads* (page 241) and a water color, *Abstraction*. As far as has been discovered, these are the first Maurers to be directly acquired by a museum.

Time passed. The Brooklyn Museum included Maurer in its

eighth biennial exhibition of water colors, pastels and drawings and reproduced a double nude in the Brooklyn Institute of Arts and Sciences' 1935 annual report. From time to time the art press made casual reference to Maurer. Still no miracle rescued him from oblivion.

In 1937 he found a new friend, Hudson D. Walker, at that time directing a gallery on East Fifty-seventh Street. It was William F. Waltemath who brought Maurer to Walker's attention, as earlier he had made the liaison between Maurer and Robert Godsoe. Maurer made his first appearance in the Hudson D. Walker Gallery with "an impasto semi-abstraction," as the *Times* described the painting. He was in the company of the late Marsden Hartley, another wanderer from the Stieglitz fold, and of younger painters and sculptors. Maurer appeared again, a month later, in a group exhibition of landscapes at the Boyer Galleries, and a passing mention by Howard Devree was the clue which led the author to the two Maurer genre paintings in the Soviet Union (page 59). The *Times* critic wrote: "The late Alfred Maurer, who by the way was the one American artist whom I was able to find represented in the Museum of Western Art in Moscow, makes his impact felt in the tree paintings in the present show." Writing again of the Boyer exhibition, Critic Devree amplified his comment: "Alfred Maurer's inclusion in the group is accomplished by means of a bright yellow-green autumn landscape, a bold, free portrait of a gnarled tree trunk and a landscape in which a clay road and a line of telegraph poles work into a vigorous design."

Later in the year a 1909 Maurer landscape was shown at An American Place, in an exhibition called, "Beginnings and Landmarks: '291' 1905–1917." It was a painting exhibited in 1910 at "291." The curious relations between Stieglitz and the artists he sponsored are suggested in this incident. He had not shown Maurer's work for over a quarter of a century; yet he was glad to claim credit for having "launched" Maurer. Perhaps the *last* gallery which shows an artist deserves the credit for encouraging and supporting him rather than the *first?*

From November 22 to December 11, 1937, oils and gouaches by Maurer were on view at the Hudson D. Walker Gallery, in a one-man exhibition. In the vicissitudes which overtake records, it may be that the author has the sole surviving list of what was exhibited then. It is a carbon copy of a typed list, on manila paper, now fraying at the edges, and with some typographical errors to give it eclat from the collector's point of view. The check list includes twenty-three items, such as *An Arrangement* (page 56), *Self-Portrait* (not so described, but that in which Maurer wears a hat), and *The Florentines* (page 207). Still lifes and abstract heads are also listed, with some nudes and similar subjects.

The art press responded with interest but with no appreciable effect on sales or reputation. The *Post* used a one-column cut of the self-portrait and spoke of the importance of seeing "a good selection such as this to appreciate his high caliber as craftsman and designer." Henry McBride began dramatically: "Alfred Maurer is dead but his pictures are still asking questions." He added: "It may be too soon to answer these questions definitely. It certainly is too soon to answer the most important one, i.e., as to the ability of these pictures to please on their own intrinsic merit; for as yet it is impossible to separate them from the charm of the dead man who painted them. But that they have the power to go on asking the question is something." The dean of New York art critics gave Maurer twenty-two inches of type and ended: "So I have decided that Alfy Maurer will go on asking his questions. I do not think he will be dropped."

The *World-Telegram,* on its Saturday art page, stated that "These canvases by Maurer are head and shoulders above the abstractions done by any other American, in our opinion." The *World-Telegram* critic, Emily Genauer, added: "His life was of such stuff as popular novels are made, and perhaps one day the whole story of it will be told." Then, as now, critics could not help but respond to the human overtones of the Maurer story.

The duality of Alfred Maurer's work continued to harass the press. In the *Times* Howard Devree recalled again the Maurers in the Museum of Modern Western Art in Moscow, displayed "along with Mary Cassatt!" Maurer's paintings "stir up very mixed emotional responses," he wrote, "but responses they do undeniably stir." Much of Maurer's work seemed to the *Times* critic "meaningless and even superficial; much of it jarring and repercussive without very rewarding outcome. But strong and unforgettable much of it is." In the *Herald-Tribune* Carlyle Burrows concluded that "The showing tends to revive interest in a strange and wistful and peculiarly talented personality."

The author, in New York correspondence to the *Republican,* wrote at length of the exhibition, reproducing an abstraction and *An Arrangement* (page 56), each two columns wide. The work was, the review stated, "the armor [Maurer] forged against the world's blows, . . . an extraordinary document in the history of American civilization." In "Gallery Notes" in *Parnassus,* she added that "In the search for an American tradition, men like Maurer should not be overlooked." *Art News* gave the "lead" position in its "New Exhibitions of the Week" to "Alfred Maurer, American Pioneer of the Modern School," ending with the conclusion that "The self-portrait is . . . relentless in its presentation and stirring in its revelation of a victim of the conflicts of his time."

It was 1938. Walt Kuhn was renouncing the ardors which had involved him twenty-five years before in the Armory Show. "Twenty-Five Years of American Art" were on view at the Montclair (N. J.) Art Museum, from Wayman Adams to Grant Wood, with Maurer alphabetically halfway between. The Art Institute of Chicago was preparing a survey of its half century of support to American art and sought to locate Maurer's "Girl in White" [*Woman in White*], which had been exhibited at the Art Institute in 1901. A half century earlier revolt had blown up through the art world; now tempests of war thundered and surged. So the years passed, and art seemed dwarfed in a world fragmented by death.

Yet, such is the human will for survival, that art continued to be conserved even amid the disasters of war. In 1941 Hudson D. Walker, who had closed his gallery, purchased from the Alfred Maurer estate the paintings which had been in storage and in and out of art galleries for almost a decade. Thus the surviving Maurer relatives were able to close their accounts. For eight years the collection was housed in the Walkers' Forest Hills home. Since 1949 the majority of the paintings and drawings have been on loan to the University of Minnesota in Minneapolis. So much of

Maurer has been saved for whatever judgment posterity may make.

Polar privacy encompassed not alone the life and death of that single hound, Alfred Maurer, but the dreams and hopes of every individual. No private hope was possible in a world in which death had been elevated to a public rite. The years passed, and war englobed the human race. How shall man think of the arts of peace when all his skill is turned to war? Two world wars swept over Alfred Maurer and obliterated not alone the work left behind in Paris but the remembrance of him. War swept over the cherished aspirations of painters and poets and composers and scientists, war swept over mankind and left a decade of destruction. In historic terms should the resurrection of one man's life and work be considered important? Too many millions died with no hope of rebirth. Too many dreams were lost forever. How vast must a work of art be to equal the death of one child?

Yet somehow the summoning back to life of Alfred Maurer went on. In June, 1943, the Buchholz Gallery held a large retrospective. Maurer's press continued to support him—*Art News, World-Telegram, Herald-Tribune, Times.* From the latter's reproduction, *Four Sisters* (page 197) looked out with eyes that never close, asking never-answered questions. To some the questions could not be answered because the questions were incomplete. Edward Alden Jewell explained Maurer's slowness to arrive by the artist's failure (as the critic saw it) to assimilate his French source. "This American," he wrote, "fell for modernism and failed to rise, the heights he should have reached remaining merely potential."

List the years. 1944: the Cincinnati Art Museum held an exhibition, "Pictures for Peace," a selection of works shown originally in the Armory Show, and in this Maurer was represented by *Landscape with Tree.* Noting the exhibition, the *Art Digest* added a footnote: "But last month an exhibition of Maurer's paintings at the Greenwich, Connecticut, Library, was forced from the walls by residents of the wealthiest city per capita in the United States, because they didn't understand them and were offended." At the other pole, Maurer was not modern enough for the Museum of Modern Art: a Maurer received by the museum in the

Mrs. John D. Rockefeller, Jr., bequest of 1935 was sold at auction.

In 1946 the Whitney Museum of American Art celebrated "Pioneers of Modern Art in America" by a retrospective glance; and Maurer, as the first American convert to fauvism, had won his historic niche. That fall Maurer made a new friend, Bertha Schaefer, who showed his work for the first time. Maurer, wrote Howard Devree, had "gone too long without adequate recognition," and the critic suggested that "the Whitney or the Museum of Modern Art might well consider . . . a comprehensive exhibition." The *Sun* noted that "the artist emerges . . . with increased distinction. He will not be forgotten." 1947: a second Maurer exhibition was held at the Bertha Schaefer Gallery, and meanwhile Maurers were turning up at auction, bargains if buyers wished to gamble on art futures.

In January, 1948, the project for the Maurer study, exhibition and biography was undertaken by the Walker Art Center, with a committee comprised of D. S. Defenbacher, Hudson D. Walker and the author, in consultation with Hermon More and Lloyd Goodrich of the Whitney Museum of American Art. Thus, after long years, the story of Alfred Maurer was to be put before the public. In the fall of 1949 his work was presented in the first full-scale comprehensive exhibition at the Walker Art Center and the Whitney Museum of American Art. The retrospective traveled throughout the country in 1950 and 1951, being shown in the Institute of Contemporary Art, Boston, the Milwaukee Art Institute, the St. Paul Gallery and School of Art, the San Francisco Museum, the Portland (Oregon) Art Museum, and the Baltimore Museum of Art.

To lay an essential foundation of knowledge a Maurer archive was assembled. The Walker Art Center had all available Maurers photographed and recorded, within practical limits of time and distance. Two collections, belonging to old friends in Montana and Florida, were photographed and recorded by researchers on the ground. Museums, private collectors, and dealers in the United States and elsewhere have generously cooperated in supplying data and photographs for the archive, which includes Maurers in Paris, Leningrad and Honolulu, as well as all parts of the United States.

A large part of Maurer's lifework vanished when the contents of his rue Falguière studio were sold. Fortunately about fifty paintings of pre-Paris and Paris days survive, augmented by a score of paintings located in Paris late in 1950. Some were shown in the 1949 retrospective. Some are reproduced in this biography. How many have been lost is uncertain. From 1914 to 1924, despite difficulties and discouragements, Maurer painted at least a thousand pictures. This does not include those which he destroyed, painted out or painted over. In his European years he might have painted two thousand works. In thirty years perhaps he produced five thousand works, exclusive of drawings. Of this putative total, almost a thousand oils, temperas, water colors, and gouaches have been recorded, while there are also drawings and sketches, uncounted, and some notebooks.

The 1950 "find" consists of landscapes, still lifes, and a portrait or two, most of them painted on the small wood 8x10-inch panels previously described. A few are larger—18 by 12¾ inches, 12¾ by 25¾, 22½ by 25¾, 31 by 25—and are on cardboard. All reveal the rapid, loose brushstroke which characterized Maurer's "new" style when he broke with academic naturalism and began to explore the novelties of postimpressionism and fauvism. The discovery of these long lost works was expedited by the Maurer exhibition. A resident of Paris, who wishes to remain anonymous, saw the "excellent catalogue" (as our Paris informant writes) and was "thrilled . . . because he remembered having seen similar pictures with a small dealer." A few months later, he succeeded "in buying a lot and later bought some others at sales at the Hotel Drouet. . . . He asked the dealer where he got the pictures and the dealer told him that he had them for a very long time . . . and does not remember where he got them." So much of Maurer survived two wars. No doubt more examples of his work will come to notice as time passes.

The study has been aided by two "accidents" which fortunately preserved from destruction great numbers of paintings. The first was E. Weyhe's purchase of the contents of Maurer's studio in 1924, and the second Hudson D. Walker's purchase in 1941 of the paintings remaining in the Alfred Maurer estate. Together the two collections present a rich cross-section of Maurer's work except for the lack of paintings to record Maurer's transition from naturalism to abstractionism.

It is fortunate that visual documents are plentiful. For there are few documents of other kinds, and they are not revealing. Such as they are, they comprise a handful of letters from Maurer to the Steins, to Stieglitz, to Sherwood Anderson, to his parents, and part of a letter written from Paris after the German armies broke through early in 1914, in addition to early press notices pasted into an unfinished scrapbook and loose clippings. For his ideas on art, we must go to his work; Maurer wrote no art manifestos to avow his aesthetic creed. Documentation of the man is equally scanty. To round out the portrait, personal recollections have been obtained by interview and correspondence from old friends who loved Alfy. These sources are listed in the Reference Appendix.

Such is the background for our adventure in the rediscovery of Alfred Maurer. Already it is evident that the total range of works recorded, exhibited, and illustrated gives a new view of Maurer as an artist. Even those who have known his work for years, and believed they knew all of it, have been impressed by his scope and intensity of communication. Seen in a line of development, particular expressions which formerly were thought to be eccentric or outre are found to be steps in a natural evolution. For exhibition and biography, the choice of works shown and reproduced was made with the objective of showing the gamut of his achievement, not of selecting isolated works of individual brilliance. Our hope to restore a "lost" American artist to his tradition now seems to have been justified.

Here we take our farewell of Alfred Maurer, commending him to time and its ultimate judgments. They can be no harsher than those he knew in life.

REFERENCE APPENDIX

Chronology

1868   Alfred Henry Maurer born on April 21, the second child of Louis and Louisa (Stein) Maurer, at 512 West Fifty-seventh Street, New York, New York. Maurer family soon moved to 404 West Forty-third Street.

1882–   Was known to be attending Public School 58 at 317 West Fifty-second Street, New York.

1884   Left school to go to work in family lithographic business; also worked for the firm of A. Lenhard, Elm and Reade Streets.
Studied with Edgar Ward at the National Academy of Design and in Ward's Sunday morning classes, held in the Tenth Street Studio Building.

1890   Painted first known work, a water color, *Covered Bridge.* (page 28).

1893   Visited the World's Columbian Exposition in Chicago, with his mother, sister, and Roselle Fitzpatrick.

1894–   Drew and painted academic portraits, figure studies, and landscapes.

1897   Sailed for Paris on November 13, on the *Rotterdam.* Studied briefly at the Academie Julian; thereafter worked alone.

1900   Listed in Pennsylvania Academy of the Fine Arts catalogue at 19 rue de Daguerre, Paris, said by old friends to be a damp, dark ground-floor studio.

1901   Returned to New York to visit his parents; listed in Pennsylvania Academy catalogue at 404 West Forty-third Street, New York.

Awarded first prize of $1,500 and gold medal by Carnegie Institute, Pittsburgh, for *An Arrangement* (page 56).

Awarded bronze medal at Pan-American Exposition, Buffalo, N. Y.

1902   Listed in Pennsylvania catalogue at 318 West Forty-second Street, a studio building.

In May returned to Paris and found a new studio at 9 rue Falguière.

1903   *The Peacock* purchased by the Wilstach Collection, Philadelphia.

1904   Awarded silver medal, Louisiana Purchase Exposition, St. Louis.

On April 21, his thirty-sixth birthday, broke with academicism.

About this time, met the Steins.

1905   Awarded gold medal, Internationale Kunstausstellung, Munich.

Awarded bronze medal, Exposition Internationale des Beaux-Arts, Liége.

1906   To Italy, where he especially admired Botticelli.

1907–   Painted first impressionist-fauvist works, notably 8x10-inch
1908   oils, on wood thumb box panels.

1908   Helped organize American "secession" in Paris.

1909   Held first one-man exhibition, opening March 30, at the Photo-Secession Gallery, 291 Fifth Avenue, New York, where Alfred Stieglitz gave John Marin double billing with Maurer.

1910   Represented in first group exhibition of contemporary American painters held at "291"—with Dove, Weber, Hartley, and others.

1912   Two Maurers of the early 1900s sold in William M. Chase auction.

Visited by Walt Kuhn and Walter Pach, in Paris, to enlist Maurer's aid in assembling work for the so-called "Armory Show."

1913   One-man exhibition at the Folsom Galleries, New York, January 15 to 29.

Exhibited in the Armory Show, February 15 to March 15.

Apparently in New York at this time; then back to Paris.

1914 Returned to the United States at the outbreak of World War I.

1915 Worked in Westport, Connecticut, about this time; there saw old Paris friends, the Doves and the Fuhrs.

Also about this time began to visit Shady Brook, the oldtime boarding house at Marlboro-on-the-Hudson, New York.

1916 Showed in the Forum Exhibition of Modern American Painters, March 13 to 25.

In this year painted postimpressionist landscapes of Marlboro subjects, as *Landscape: Tree* (page 128).

1917 Showed in first annual exhibition of the Society of Independent Artists; thereafter exhibited with this group every year through 1932; elected a director in 1919; honored by memorial exhibition in 1933.

1919 Began to paint his "sad girls" series about this time (page 130).

1921 Used exercises from Jay Hambidge "dynamic symmetry" correspondence course as guides for quick sketches of the Marlboro countryside.

1922 Included in auction organized by Mitchell Kennerley and Alfred Stieglitz, "Works of Art by Living American Artists of the Modern Schools," at the Anderson Galleries, February 23; E. Weyhe bought his first Maurer from this sale.

1924 On January 8, Weyhe bought the contents of Maurer's studio, "some 255 paintings."

Maurer's first one-man show since 1913 held at Weyhe Gallery, 794 Lexington, opening January 15; Sherwood Anderson wrote the introduction for his catalogue; included in the exhibition were landscapes as well as girls.

For the 1924 Independent's, painted figure studies on dress goods fabrics.

Maurer's second exhibition held at Weyhe's in November; thereafter, exhibitions held there in January, 1926, January, 1927, April, 1928, and January, 1931. Included in the November, 1924, exhibition were gnarled trees, telegraph poles, and brilliant flower studies.

1925 Showed paintings from "two sisters" series at the Independent's, as *Two Sisters* (page 175).

About this time, heard that the contents of his Paris studio had been sold for back rent.

1926   Maurer's work, shown in Waterbury, Connecticut, not well
received.

1927   Paintings done on black oilcloth shown at Weyhe's in January
exhibition; also portraits of women with "high, domish foreheads."

Included in "Paintings in Oil by the Group of American
Painters of Paris," Brooklyn Museum, April 22 to June 1.

About this time rented a studio in the Lincoln Square Arcade
Building, Broadway and Sixty-sixth Street.

1928   Exhibited large *Self-Portrait with Hat* (frontispiece) and
Nude (page 196) in annual exhibition at Weyhe's.

About this time, illness slowed down Maurer's production,
while ninety-six-year-old Louis Maurer was rediscovered as an
early Currier and Ives artist.

1929   Sent paintings from "head" series to Independent's.

1930   Exhibited "psychological" heads at Independent's.

1931   Held last one-man show at Weyhe's, in January. In February,
Louis Maurer, aged ninety-nine, held his first one-man show,
of Currier and Ives prints, at Old Print Shop, 150 Lexington
Avenue.

1932   On February 21 and 22, Louis Maurer celebrated his one-
hundredth birthday, along with George Washington's two-
hundredth anniversary, at the Old Print Shop.

Maurer's last painting, *George Washington* (page 239) shown
at the Independent's in April.

Admitted to Beth Israel Hospital on April 21, his sixty-fourth
birthday.

Discharged in "excellent general condition" on June 29.

On July 19, Louis Maurer died at the age of one hundred.
On August 4, Alfred Maurer hanged himself in the family
home.

Maurer's Painting Technics

NOWHERE has myth been more prevalent than in regard to Maurer's methods of painting. A cult has grown up among admirers who say: ONE, Maurer painted in such a way that his paintings dare not be subjected to ordinary cleaning; TWO, Maurer meant his paintings to look as they do today, covered with a dirty, yellowish film and spotted with "freckles." Where his paintings have gone for thirty and forty years without any physical care, bundled away in storage or left hanging without attention to wedges or the proper fastening of the canvas to the stretcher, they have taken on a dim, dusky look and sometimes they sag and crack, as any canvas would. When cleaned, they are startling in their brilliance and freshness. That the fresh, brilliant painting looks different from the dirty, dingy one is no argument in favor of the proposition that Maurer wanted his paintings to look dirty and dingy. It is simply an argument in favor of modern, scientific care of paintings.

The Maurer project has been fortunate in having what amounts to a laboratory to study the artist's work in. Hundreds of paintings in the Walker and Weyhe collections were at hand for physical examination. As these were photographed and recorded, the author had an unusual opportunity to study the physical deterioration which in too many instances had set in. In the paintings done in the United States after 1914, the deterioration is of two main kinds—"tackiness" with spotting and actual flaking off of paint and supporting gesso ground.

In addition, a considerable number of paintings, both of Maurer's Paris and American periods, have been studied, from the point of view of the professional restorer, by Ingrid-Märta Held, staff restorer of paintings for the Walker Art Center. As a by-product of having paintings put into a condition as close as possible to their original state, we have learned a number of things about Maurer's method of working, not the least of which is that in the hands of an expert most of his paintings may be safely cleaned and, if necessary, restored.

Maurer's early paintings were all in oil, except for the water colors and the pastel reproduced (pages 28, 29, and 28). Whether he painted on canvas or on cardboard on a stretcher, he painted in a rather thin manner. In our file of photographs, there are comparison photographs which emphatically point out the contrast between soot-begrimed paintings and clean paintings. *Landscape* (page 30) is one, as is the *Self-Portrait* (page 55). The Carnegie prize-winner. *An Arrangement* (page 56), is another early work which has benefited from professional care, as are the genre subjects painted a few years later, such as *The Rendezvous* and *Cafe Scene*. Evidences of damage and retouching were found in cleaning some early oils. This would indicate that Maurer, like every artist who works in perishable materials, has felt the ravages of time. All the more argument for scientific care of his works before it is too late.

At some time during his Paris years Maurer took up with the "made" canvas described by Mrs. Dana and recorded in Chapter 3. Most of the paintings of his French period (except the early figure studies and genre paintings which got to the United States) have vanished. Therefore it is hard to assay the state of works painted on this ground. *Still Life,* painted about 1908, is one of the few examples we have to attest to the wearing qualities of the material used. The ground has suffered from chipping, a danger with dental plaster, but a minor damage capable of repair. Another painting of this period, *Head* (of an as yet unidentified woman) *ca.* 1908 (page 82), has undergone a serious warping of the cardboard support on which ground and pigment were placed. One imagines that the warp is due to the unequal tensile strength or "pull" of the cardboard and of the numerous coats of glue. Warp, of course, is not desirable for durability or beauty.

In a sense, Maurer's experimentalism destroyed his effect. Insofar as continuing experimentation made him employ impermanent materials and methods, this is a fact to be noted by lovers of art. In general, it seems true that anybody possessed of a passion for collecting Maurers will be safe if he chooses on the basis of existing knowledge, avoiding the "tacky" and flaking paintings and having other works cleaned if they need it.

The paintings made in the United States also use a dental plaster ground, though not as elaborate in composition as the "made" canvas of the French formula. Rabbit's-skin glue and dental plaster were the ingredients of the gesso which he applied to panels of beaver board, Upson board, Homasote, Pabco board and gypsum board, or to fabrics glued over panels, such as canvas, mattress ticking, oilcloth, and dress goods. This ground also is likely to chip; and there are a number of instances of abrasion or flaking off. On the whole, this does not seem as noteworthy as discoloration and spotting. The latter are due to his practice of "varnishing" tempera underpaintings with linseed oil, a linseed oil which Sheldon Keck, Brooklyn Museum staff restorer, has stated to be of inferior quality, and which turned dark and gummy and so obscured the pigments beneath. In certain paintings, airholes or pinholes in the ground have absorbed a proportionally greater quantity of pigment, which in turn produces a fine crop of "freckles."

These airholes are not unpleasant to the eye in the unglazed tempera panels, such as *Four Heads* (page 195). Where the "glaze" of linseed oil has been used, however, the airholes seem to produce a chemical change; and the resulting spots cannot be cleaned out when the yellowed, gummy, oxidized linseed oil is removed. In this case the only solution is a moderate amount of restoration. Occasionally there will be one noticeable "freckle," as in the direct center of the vase in *Flowers* (page 165). This painting was cleaned and photographed, as were the others mentioned; but the single black spot proved especially distracting and the minimum of restoration was done, as with the other paintings. By this procedure cleaning achieved the desirable result of putting Maurer's work into mint condition as it was when it left his hands.

We have been particularly fortunate to have a number of photographs of Maurer's paintings as they appeared when newly completed. Among these are *Nude* (page 196), *Self-Portrait with Hat* (frontispiece), *Four Sisters* (page 197) and *Girl* (page 163). Most of them were taken about 1928, a turning point in Maurer's evolution. They are among the last of the paintings he subjected to his unorthodox and impermanent "glaze" of linseed oil. None of the early photographs shows the darkened tones and spotting registered in the photographs made in the spring of 1948 when we began to record the Maurers as they are today. The photographs made of these works after they were cleaned are remarkably close to the early photographs. In a few instances we have a series of photographs taken at intervals during twenty years, and these are valuable as showing the advance of deterioration.

Not all the Maurers have escaped inexpert cleaning. Some paintings have come to the author's attention where the commercial restorer's hand is all too evident. In some cases the owners themselves have resorted to "home" methods with rather bad results. Maurer's gesso ground will dissolve if the paintings are washed with water, a common method for home cleaning of paintings, though not recommended. Since most Maurers present an oily face to the world, a collector may not know what is underneath. This is a plea to leave cleaning to professionals, for the sake of art.

Maurer experimented not only with grounds and supports but also with pigment, using mixed mediums, grinding his own dry colors, and making his own tempera paints. It is not always possible, therefore, to "wash" off a given painting with one solvent. The paintings must be approached with great care and caution, and extremely small areas worked on at one time. Acetone and weak ammonia may clean the faces, as in *Two Sisters* (page 175); but the reds and greens Maurer used forbid the use of this solvent on areas like the dress at the right. Because some Maurers have been treated with more energy than discretion, technical examination has revealed the fact that injudicious cleaning in the past has done damage which has in turn been covered up by more varnish and repaint. That in so short a time as twenty years Maurer's paintings have already needed to be repaired is a further argument for making such repairs scientifically.

As too often, the results of professional study will be ignored by those who know more about Maurer than he knew about himself. Yet Maurer was the first person to admit that he had his technical headaches, as when he wrote to Carl Zigrosser in the summer of 1921, "Have been having trouble with the paint for the last few weeks. But that's all in a life time some times it goes and some times it don't and when it don't it don't and when it does it does, and that's that."

Perhaps it is not too much to hope that owners and admirers of Maurer may attain an equally philosophic attitude toward the reality that not every painting he painted is a monument of physical durability and permanence. With a thousand or more surviving, we can grant the artist the right to trial flights in materials and methods and the right to technical failures as well as successes.

Sources and Acknowledgments

THE MAURER STUDY—comprising this biography, as well as the 1949 retrospective exhibition with its accompanying catalogue—is based on diversified research and wide cooperation. Lenders to the exhibition generously parted with their Maurers for many months and were cordially thanked at that time. Author and sponsoring institutions also owe a debt of thanks to the individuals who provided information about the artist. All who cooperated in restoring Alfred Maurer to public notice deserve credit. Interpretation of the data is, of course, the writer's charge.

First to be thanked is the Walker Art Center, for undertaking a program of sustained duration and scope and for subsidizing research. If art books, by virtue of a limited audience, are noncommercial publishing ventures, then our educational institutions fulfill an essential function in supporting projects like the Maurer study. Not all museums so define their social responsibility. All the more reason why the Walker Art Center's support should be recorded with heartiest appreciation. The enthusiastic participation of its director, D. S. Defenbacher, and of its assistant director, William M. Friedman, should be noted, as well as the staff's keen interest.

The support of the Whitney Museum of American Art was not reserved for the exhibition alone but extended to the biography. Director Hermon More was able to shed light on the question of negotiations with the Whitney in the 1930s for a Maurer memorial; and the encouragement of the associate director, Lloyd Goodrich, has been as always inspiring. With his wide knowledge of American art and his customary generous spirit, he read and helpfully criticized the first draft in detail. Also valuable were suggestions made by Miss Rosalind Irvine, assistant curator, on the basis of her collateral research in contemporary American painting.

Of individuals, first to be thanked is Mrs. Eugenia Maurer Fuerstenberg. She, with her nephew, Alfred Louis Maurer, generously placed her Maurer materials at the author's disposal. In granting access to family files, she carried on her long campaign to gain an audience for her brother's work. Family connections who supplied biographical data include Mr. and Mrs. A. W. Venino and Mr. and Mrs. John L. Miller.

Of those who knew Maurer only posthumously and yet have believed steadfastly in his creative worth, first to be named is Hudson D. Walker. For over a dozen years, ever since he came to know Maurer's painting through William F. Waltemath, he has worked to obtain understanding for this "unknown" American artist, as he has worked to obtain understanding for hundreds of living American artists. Thanks are also due Ione Gaul Walker, who gave her studio so that the hundreds of Maurers in the Walker collection might be set up, photographed, measured, recorded, and studied.

Unseen friends of Maurer were also indispensable. With two who knew him well in Paris and thereafter, the author carried on considerable correspondence; and the Walker Art Center sent researchers to them to record all possible data. These are Mrs. J. H. Phillips (née Grace Leighton) of Tampa, Florida, whose collection Miss Alida Conover recorded and had photographed, and the late Mrs. E. L. Dana of Great Falls, Montana, whose collection Miss Clara Nelson recorded and had photographed. The author's correspondence with them, especially Mrs. Phillips, has been most valuable. Friends from Marlboro, like the painter William F. Waltemath, and many friends from Shady Brook, have been unfailingly cooperative, notably the late Mrs. F. W. Schramm, Sr., Mrs. Louis Meckes, and Mr. and Mrs. Fred W. Schramm, Jr. Other friends from Marlboro days are mentioned later, in the list of those interviewed.

For professional help, we are indebted to the library researches of Miss Muriel F. Baldwin, then acting chief, art division, New York Public Library; Mrs. Ina Cassirer, art division, New York Public Library; the Frick Reference Library; the Yale University Library, which provided photostats of letters from Maurer to Gertrude and

Leo Stein; and the Newberry Library, which gave access to letters from Maurer to Sherwood Anderson. The technical assistance of Ingrid-Märta Held, staff restorer of paintings for the Walker Art Center, has been invaluable. Dr. Lawrence Q. Crawley and Dr. Elisabeth K. Hoyt brought expert medical knowledge to bear on the question of Maurer's last illness and general health. Holger Cahill is to be thanked for reading the manuscript in its first version and for editorial suggestions.

Basic research was begun by amassing an archive of Maurer's paintings. This fell into two parts, photographing the work and recording it. First of all, we should thank museums, collectors and dealers who kindly filled out American Art Research Council forms sent to almost two hundred known owners and who often supplied photographs of their paintings. Thanks are due to the Embassy of the Soviet Union, Washington, D. C., and the U. S. S. R. Society for Cultural Relations with Foreign Countries, Moscow, for data on and photographs of two Maurers now in the collections of the State Hermitage in Leningrad. Thanks are due the Metropolitan Museum of Art for the photograph of Louis Maurer's painting of West Forty-third Street and due the Museum of Modern Art for the photograph of Mahonri Young's statuette of Maurer. Charles Sterling, *curateur detaché*, department of paintings, the Louvre, is to be thanked for his kindness in obtaining for us photographs of the paintings reproduced on pages 80 and 81.

The main body of photographs to record Maurer's surviving work was taken by Oliver Baker of New York, who showed great enthusiasm in an essential but often routine task. We may also thank Miss Berenice Abbott for making prints from negatives in the Maurer materials, including a copy negative of an otherwise unrecorded Stieglitz portrait of Maurer and two negatives of the 1901 Carnegie medal. Staff Photographer John Szarkowski of the Walker Art Center brought the archive up to date by photographing Maurers sent to Minneapolis for the retrospective. Other photographers are acknowledged with blanket thanks. Two art dealers, Miss Bertha Schaefer and J. B. Neumann, generously supplied the archive with many photographs of paintings. The Sidney Janis Gallery is to be thanked for the photograph of the 1907 *Landscape* reproduced on page 79.

Recording, measuring and classifying the hundreds of paintings and drawings was carried on for the greater part by the author, with assistance from Miss Martha L. Dickinson of the Weyhe Gallery, Miss Diane Hunter and J. Frederic Lohman of the Bertha Schaefer Gallery, Miss Sandra Ellsworth of the American Art Research Council, and

Mrs. Julia Schneer, the last named of whom volunteered valuable time for recording. Miss Ruth M. Lindsay gave some weeks to classifying paintings in all mediums and to comparing them with Maurer's preliminary "dynamic symmetry" notes.

Interviews and correspondence comprised the second source of data. Information gathered from friends who knew Maurer in Paris and in this country has filled in many lacunae. Besides the reports from Mrs. Phillips and the late Mrs. Dana, the author has used data obtained by interviewing a number of persons and by corresponding with others. Not one but has been most eager to aid the study, and all deserve warm thanks. Among those who have helped with verbal and written data are: Mr. and Mrs. Harry N. Abrams, the late A. S. Baylinson, H. S. Bender, Charles Bittinger, Miss Myrtle B. Bjornson, Mr. and Mrs. Milton Bonn, Carle M. Boog, Holger Cahill, Miss Bartlett Cowdrey, the late Mrs. E. L. Dana, Pierre Daura, Mr. and Mrs. Jo Davidson, William C. Dove, Miss Mary Dugan, Miss Rose Dugan, Miss Roselle Fitzpatrick, Mrs. Eugenia M. Fuerstenberg, Mrs. Ernest Fuhr, Donald C. Gallup, Mrs. William J. Glackens, Robert Ulrich Godsoe, Arthur Granick, Mrs. Edith Gregor Halpert, Mr. and Mrs. John J. Hill, Bernard Karfiol, Sheldon Keck, Alfred L. Maurer, Mrs. Louis Meckes, Miss Dorothy C. Miller, Mrs. and Mrs. John L. Miller, Miss Georgia O'Keeffe, Mrs. J. H. Phillips, Mrs. Marie C. Sawyer, Phillip Ayer Sawyer, the late Mrs. F. W. Schramm, Sr., Mr. and Mrs. Fred W. Schramm, Jr., Mr. and Mrs. John Sloan, Edward Steichen, Maurice Sterne, Mrs. Abraham B. Susman, Thomas R. Thomson, Miss Alice B. Toklas, Eugene Paul Ullman, George Ullman, Robert Ullman, Mr. and Mrs. A. W. Venino, A. Walkowitz, William F. Waltemath, Mr. and Mrs. Richard W. Warnken, Max Weber, Mrs. Morris A. Weil, Mr. and Mrs. Harold Wengler, E. Weyhe, Mrs. Alice Woods, Mahonri M. Young, Carl Zigrosser, and Marguerite and William Zorach.

If old and close friends of Maurer were overlooked in this phase of the research, it was due either to lack of information in regard to them or the author's inability to make effective contact with them by correspondence or other means. Additional information of all kinds will be welcomed and added to the Maurer archive. For by the report of such witnesses we are able, slowly and laboriously, to recreate the lives of those artists who left little report of themselves except their work.

Bibliography

BIBLIOGRAPHY is a problem in projects like the Maurer study. Materials are often obscure, fugitive, and incomplete, or even lacking. The bibliographical apparatus recorded here does not profess, therefore, to include all materials printed about our subject. In the press of work, exhaustive searching of newspaper and magazine files could not be carried on in all areas, though the catalogues for the annual exhibitions of the National Academy of Design, the Carnegie Institute of Fine Arts, the Art Institute of Chicago, the Pennsylvania Academy of the Fine Arts, and the Society of Independent Artists have been searched, as have the files of the *Magazine of Art, The Arts,* and *International Studio,* all with little result. Newspaper comment is the source of information most often relied on, except for the verbal and written reports of old friends and acquaintances; and these entries are listed here along with book and magazine references, in chronological sequence. Since the bulk of critical coverage came from the New York press, the words "New York" have been omitted from newspaper names; all other cities are indicated in the title given.

1901. *Sun,* November 8. *Brush and Pencil,* December. *International Studio,* December.
1902. *Brush and Pencil,* September.
1905. *Gazette des Beaux-Arts,* October.

1906. *The Collector and Art Critic,* November.

1907. *Field and Stream,* April.

1908. *Times,* February 26. *Herald* (Paris edition), March 1. *Times,* April 11. *Burr-McIntosh Monthly,* November.

1909. *Sun,* February 24. *Evening Mail,* April 3. *Herald,* April 5. *Globe,* April 6. *Sun,* April 7. *Camera Work,* July.

1910. *Camera Work,* July.

1913. Catalogue, Folsom Galleries, January 15 to 29. Catalogue, *International Exhibition of Modern Art,* Association of American Painters and Sculptors, February 15 to March 15 (for the so-called "Armory Show.") *International Studio,* March. *Boston Transcript,* December 17.

1916. Catalogue, *Forum Exhibition of Modern American Painters,* March 13 to 25. *Arts and Decoration,* April.

1920. *World,* February 29.

1922. Catalogue, *Works of Art by Living American Painters of the Modern Schools,* February 23.

1924. *Herald,* January 20. *Evening Post,* January 26. *Herald,* January 27. *Times,* January 27. *Tribune,* January 27. *World,* January 27. *Christian Science Monitor,* February 2. *The Arts,* March. *Tribune,* March 6. *World,* March 8. *Sun,* November 15, *Times,* November 23.

1925. *Evening Post,* January 16.

1926. *New Yorker,* January 9. *Times,* January 10. *The Arts,* February. *Waterbury* (Conn.) *Republican,* February 21, 28. *Chicago Post,* March 30, June 22. *Toledo Topics,* October.

1927. *Herald-Tribune,* January 16. *Times,* January 16. *Chicago Post,* January 18. *New Yorker,* January 8, 22. *The Arts,* April. *Correct Eating,* May.

1928. *Herald-Tribune,* April 8. *Times,* April 8. *Chicago Post,* April 13. *Evening Post,* April 14. *The Arts,* May. *Times,* July 1.

1929. *Parnassus,* October.

1930. *Evening Post,* January 3. *Telegram,* March 7. *Sun,* March 8, April 4. *Evening Post,* April 30. *Times,* June 1. *Evening Post,* December 26.

1931. *Print Connoisseur,* January (article by Harry T. Peters on Louis Maurer). *Herald-Tribune,* January 18. *World,* January 18. *New Yorker,* January 24. *Herald-Tribune,* January 24. *World,* January 25. *Times,* January 25. *Herald-Tribune,* January 27. *Evening Post,* January 28. *Sun,* January 31. *New York Steuben Club Magazine,* February. *Herald-Tribune,* February 20. *Literary Digest,* February 21. *Brooklyn Eagle,* February 22. *Herald-Tribune,* March 1. *Caliper,* April.

1932. *Art Digest,* January 15 (for history of the Society of Independent Artists); February 1. *American,* February 1. *Times,* February 14. *Art Digest,* February 15. *Herald-Tribune, Evening Post,* February 19. *Sun,* February 20. *Times,* February 20. *Herald-Tribune,* February 21. *Times,* February 21. *Herald-Tribune,* February 22. *Times,* February 22. *Biebericher Tagespost,* March 11. *Evening Post,* March 29. *Metronome,* May. *New Yorker,* May. *Times,* July 12. *Herald-Tribune,* July 20. *Times,* July 20. *Art Digest,* August 1. *Herald-Tribune,* August 5. *Times,* August 5, 20. *Art Digest,* September 1. *Sun,* September 7. *Herald-Tribune,* September 11. *Times,* September 11. *Sun,* October 15. *New Republic,* November 30.

1933. Catalogue, seventeenth annual exhibition of the Society of Independent Artists. Catalogue, *Entering the Twentieth Century,* Art Institute of Chicago. *The Autobiography of Alice B. Toklas,* by Gertrude Stein.

1934. *America and Alfred Stieglitz* (*see* Chronology). Catalogue, *Memorial Exhibition: Works of the Late Alfred Maurer; Oils and Gouaches Covering Thirty-five Years,* Uptown Galleries, New York. *Art Digest,* November 1. *World-Telegram,* November 3. *Herald-Tribune,* November 4. *Times,* November 4. *Springfield* (Mass.) *Sunday Union and Republican,* November 11. *New Yorker,* November 17.

1935. Catalogue, *Abstract Painting in America,* Whitney Museum of American Art. *New Yorker,* March 2. *Springfield* (Mass.) *Sunday Union and Republican,* April 4.

1937. *Herald-Tribune,* May 30. *Times,* May 30, June 13, 27. *Evening Post,* November 27. *Sun,* November 27. *World-Telegram,* November 27. *Herald-Tribune,* November 28. *Times,* November 28. *Springfield* (Mass.) *Sunday Union and Republican,* November 28. *Parnassus,* December. *Art Digest,* December 1. *Art News,* December 4.

1938. *The Story of the Armory Show,* by Walt Kuhn.

1939. Catalogue, *Half a Century of American Art,* Art Institute of Chicago.

1942. Catalogue, *20th Century Portraits,* Museum of Modern Art. *The Emergence of an American Art,* by Jerome Mellquist.

1943. *Alfred H. Maurer: 1868–1932,* by Elizabeth McCausland. *Art News,* June-July. *World-Telegram,* June 5. *Herald-Tribune,* June 6. *Times,* June 6. *Springfield* (Mass.) *Sunday Union and Republican,* June 6.

1946. Catalogue, *Pioneers of Modern Art in America,* Whitney Museum of American Art. *World-Telegram,* October 12. *Herald-Tribune,* October 13. *Times,* October 13. *Sun,* October 18.

1949. *Art and Life in America,* by Oliver Larkin. Catalogue, *Juliana Force and American Art,* Whitney Museum of American Art. Catalogue, *A. H. Maurer: 1868–1932,* by Elizabeth McCausland, for Walker Art Center and Whitney Museum of American Art.

Extensive coverage of the 1949–1951 Maurer exhibition in the Minneapolis, New York, and national press succeeded the substantial completion of the Maurer biography and hence entries from this material are not included in this listing.

The quotations on pages 88, 89, and 122 are from Gertrude Stein's *Autobiography of Alice B. Toklas,* published by Harcourt, Brace and Company in 1933, and on page 107 from Jerome Mellquist's *Emergence of an American Art,* published by Charles Scribner's Sons in 1942.